NEW
ORLEANS
JAZZ

NEW ORLEANS JAZZ

A Family Album

AL ROSE

and

EDMOND SOUCHON

REVISED

LOUISIANA STATE UNIVERSITY PRESS

BATON ROUGE AND LONDON

LIBRARY OF CONGRESS CATALOGING IN PUBLICATION DATA

Rose, Al.
    New Orleans Jazz.

    Includes index.
    1. Jazz music—Louisiana—New Orleans. 2. Jazz
musicians—Louisiana—New Orleans—Biography. 3. Jazz
musicians—Louisiana—New Orleans—Portraits.
I. Souchon, Edmond, joint author. II. Title.
ML3561.J3R678   1977   785.4′2′0976335   77–24076
ISBN 0–8071–0374–8

CONTENTS

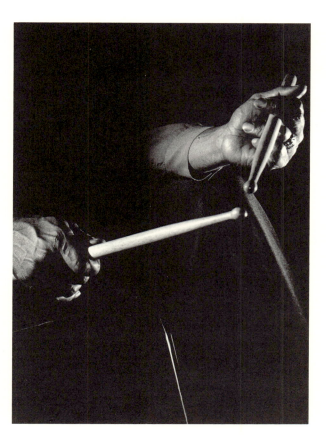

ABBREVIATIONS

acc accordion
ah alto horn
as alto saxophone
b string bass, tuba
bd bass drum
bh baritone horn
bjo banjo
c cornet
cl clarinet
d drums
eu euphonium
f flute
fh french horn
g guitar
har harmonica
l leader
mdl mandolin
mel mellophone
p piano
pc piccolo
s saxophone
sb string bass
sn snare drum
sou sousaphone
t trumpet
tar tarapatch
tb trombone
ts tenor saxophone
tu tuba
u ukelele
v violin
vo vocal
vt valve trombone
w washboard
x xylophone
z zither

PREFACE

The authors of this work do not intend that it should be a history of New Orleans jazz, though history pops from every page. Rather do we look upon it as a kind of deluxe family album of pictures of which it has been our good fortune to be the custodians. Many of the photographs herein, approximately four-fifths we estimate, have never before been published. Others have been offered to the public in volumes so poorly produced that most of their detail succumbed to cheap paper and slipshod press work.

Unfortunately, many of the photographs were taken in early times by people not in the photographic business. Mathew Brady, so far as is known, never turned his lens to the subject. Some of the shots are mere scraps luckily rescued either by design or accident. Some are scalloped by flame, others rent in anger, water-soaked or otherwise mutilated. For these we make no apology, but rather acknowledge our pride in being able to bring them to you at all.

In any work of this nature, selectivity is a factor, and the basis for our choices should be made clear without going into the theoretical aspects of jazz analysis. We do not scorn theory, but do feel that a picture book is not the place for it. Both of the authors have long since rejected the myth of the evolution of jazz from its so-called primitive or archaic form to what contemporary critics call modern or progressive. Hence, individuals like the late Lester Young (his experience in the King Oliver orchestra notwithstanding) and the ebullient Sam Butera, we consider, without discussing their musical merit, to be outside the scope of a book on New Orleans jazz, though both were born in the Crescent City. Likewise, the authors feel that such phenomena as rock-and-roll and what is called, in the commercial record field, rhythm and blues, while they have descended from jazz sources, at least in part, are so degenerate as to be of no interest to enthusiasts of legitimate jazz as an art form. Thus, data on many popular New Orleans personalities such as Fats Domino and the teenage idol Jimmy Clanton have no place between these covers.

Suffice it to say that the authors, disagreeing on many things between themselves, agree nevertheless that to be jazz, music must be (a) improvised, (b) played in 2/4 or 4/4 time, and (c) retain a clearly definable melodic line. All of the hundreds of musicians whose names and pictures appear in these pages have at one time or another played jazz music as we define it.

We are happy to observe that a great many of them are still among us and that a reasonable number of younger men are represented who are playing in the jazz idiom.

Foremost among our allies has been the indefatigable Bill Russell who has freely supplied rare photographs and detailed information. Such collectors as John Steiner of Chicago, Sinclair Traill of England, Hugues Panassie of France, Duncan P. Schiedt of Indianapolis, George Hoefer of New York, Myra Menville, Joe Mares, Danny Barker, Harry Souchon, and Barbara Glancey Reid of New Orleans all have contributed heavily. The magazine, *Eureka*, has supplied gems from its own files. Allen and Sandra Jaffe, besides providing many of the splendid portraits from their Preservation Hall publicity box, also gave us a headquarters in which to interview hundreds of musicians over a period of many months. Countless jazzmen helped identify the personnels of the group photographs, but special appreciation must be acknowledged for the aid given by Dave Winstein, president of local 174, American Federation of Musicians, Paul Barbarin, Creole George Guesnon, Papa John Joseph, Alvin Alcorn, Harry Shields, Louis Cottrell, Jr., president of Musicians Protective Union No. 496, Papa Jack Laine, Monk Hazel, Joe Capraro.

We are pleased to acknowledge the aid received from the Tulane University Jazz Archive and its research staff, especially Richard B. Allen and Paul Crawford.

vii

The work of many superb photographers is represented herein. Unfortunately, in many cases we don't know whose picture is whose, but for the record may we express our thanks to John Kuhlman, Ray Cresson, Jules L. Cahn, Carey J. Tate, Dan Leyrer, Mary Mitchell Rose, George Fletcher, Grauman Marks, Florence Mars, John Reid, and Ronnie Soderberg. The files of the New Orleans Jazz Museum are well represented here.

Important and unclassifiable help was rendered by Larry Borenstein, of New Orleans, and by Pancho Carner, of Philadelphia.

We will not attempt to establish finally who was the inventor of jazz. (Some of our best friends have claimed this distinction.) Nor will we assert that we know who were the first to play it. We feel that it was not invented at all, but that it came into being so gradually that any attempt to pin down a first time would be based on the most specious types of reasoning. Credit for the creation of jazz is due no individual man or race. If anything, it is a product, an inevitable product we think, of the avenues and alleys of an unique city, polyglot, multiracial, seething with love and conflict, a battleground of nations and cultures, a landscape of mire and magnolias.

The evidence of these photographs—their very existence—demonstrates the extent to which New Orleans was permeated with this music and, to a great extent, how it brought this music about.

Naturally, in an undertaking of this size, we have solicited the support of our talented friends who have generously helped to fill the gaps in our collections and scholarship. There are so many of these friends that we take for granted we must miss crediting some of them.

PREFACE TO THE REVISED EDITION

Not long after *A Family Album* was published in late 1967, it became apparent that a revision would be needed. My collaborator, the late Dr. Edmond Souchon, would have enjoyed sharing the task; but I am happy that he lived long enough to see the first edition in print and to sit with me on the dais when we received the Louisiana Library Association's Literary Award for that year.

In the original text, I have corrected errors, mostly dates and a few names. Several pictures have been replaced by better or more accurate ones. Unhappily, the most numerous additions have been the obituary dates of over a hundred jazzmen who have died since the original publication of *A Family Album*. Our celebrated brass bands have been playing "Oh, Didn't He Ramble" with distressing frequency since 1967.

New text and illustrations have been added in a supplement that opens on page 305. This includes biographical notes on some few musicians who should have been included in the first edition. Also, as a result of a general revival of interest in jazz, a substantial number of musicians who have been around for many years playing for the fun of it or devoting their careers to commercial music have latterly joined the ranks of serious jazzmen. In the period since 1967 they have established themselves in the forefront of New Orleans jazz.

We have been blessed with an invasion of young foreign musicians, intensely knowledgeable and thoroughly competent, who have become, or are in the process of becoming, American citizens in order to live in New Orleans permanently and play their music. They have filled many gaps in the depleting ranks, and they have an important place in this book.

Among additional material that turned up are some great photographs. I hope they add to the enjoyment of this book, and I believe they will add interest to the music on the LPs.

To the list of helpers I am pleased to add the names of Richard B. Allen, curator of the New Orleans Jazz Archives, Howard-Tilton Memorial Library, Tulane University, and his aides, Elizabeth S. Baur and Ralph Adamo; photographers Johnny Donnels and Justin D. Winston; Martha Bendich and Pat Wynn of the New Orleans Jazz Museum; Paul Lentz, proprietor of Heritage Hall; Lars Edegran and Orange Kellin, the Swedish jazzmen; Yoshio Toyama, the trumpet-playing archivist of Tokyo; also Joseph P. Mares and Tom Bethell of New Orleans.

AL ROSE

NEW
ORLEANS
JAZZ

WHO'S WHO IN
NEW ORLEANS JAZZ

How many jazzmen has New Orleans produced? The answer to this question depends on the point of view. Some will say, not without justification, that almost every family in the city could boast one or more between, say, 1900 and 1925.

But if we count those who have worked professionally to an appreciable extent, playing jazz at least part of the time, we find evidence for about a thousand—still a formidable number to work with. It has given the authors great satisfaction to be able to produce more than two hundred, generally unpublished, photographs with which to illustrate this list. Unfortunately, some of the greatest of the jazzmen never have been photographed. Others may have been, but our extensive efforts failed to uncover their pictures. Many musicians not shown individually in this section appear in photos of groups with whom they played (these are listed in the biographical notes), or in one or more of the informal shots to be found elsewhere in this volume.

Special attention of researchers is called to the fact that the details given here, especially the spellings of names, have been carefully checked and are, to the best of our knowledge, correct, though possibly unfamiliar. Such names as Roppolo, Duson, Coustaut, and Staulz have been so regularly misspelled in print that we welcome this opportunity to accord their owners the dignity of accurate orthography.

It should be noted that the amount of space allocated to each of the individuals represented is not related to any estimate by the authors of the relative importance of these people, but rather reflects requirements of book design and the photographic quality of the available pictures. Regrettably, it is a foregone conclusion that we will be guilty of omissions, because it seems that half the city has been involved in music. It is, however, no accident that the men of the apparently countless conventional dance bands of the city, many of superb quality, are not included. Such exceptional groups as the ones led by Al Streimann, Herb Leary, Leon Kellner, and Sidney Cates, and including the popular "Royal Dukes," should certainly be treated in a history of popular music in New Orleans, but not in a jazz book.

It will be noted that many musicians are merely listed, with perhaps little more information than their instruments and perhaps place of birth. To understand the reason for this, it is necessary to know, first, that there has always been a large pool of "job" musicians in New Orleans who never had any particular identification for a significant period with any group. These men got together—and still do—in infinite assortment for whatever occasion might arise. Among them are many of the finest Crescent City jazzmen.

Birth and death dates have been supplied wherever possible. It has been necessary to take into account the fact that many musicians simply don't know when they were born—perhaps not even the year. Others have given a variety of different dates in published interviews. Some merely left town without a trace and we have not been able to find out what happened to them. In some cases they may be presumed dead, but not too hastily. A spry Bill Johnson was last heard from in San Antonio at 92. Tom Albert has passed 90 in good health. At 83, bassist Eddie Dawson not only survives, but remains one of the finest active musicians in town.

As much as possible, the authors have avoided editorial comment or any attempt to evaluate the musicians, except to take note of existing universal opinion on such apparently non-controversial titans as Louis Armstrong, Baby Dodds, Leon Roppolo, Larry Shields, and a few others.

ABRAHAM, MARTIN, SR. (g, bjo, sb, tu). b. N.O., June 10, 1886. Known as Chink Martin. The grand master of jazz tuba. With Reliance Brass Band and Dance Band, Johnny Bayersdorffer, N.O. Rhythm Kings, Sharkey, Johnny Wiggs. In 1966 with Crawford-Ferguson Night Owls.

ABRAHAM, MARTIN, JR., "Little Chink" (sb). b. N.O., April 13, 1908. Family band in early 30's. With Sharkey during 40's and 50's. Also briefly with Dukes of Dixieland in 50's. Son of Chink Martin, nephew of Willie Abraham.

ABRAHAM, WILLIE (bjo, g, sb). b. N.O., about 1888. Played with most of the top dixielanders. Brother of Martin Abraham, Sr.

MARTIN ABRAHAM, SR.

MARTIN ABRAHAM, JR.

DON ALBERT

TOM ALBERT

ALVIN ALCORN

ADAMS, DOLLY (née Douroux) (p, b, d). b. N.O., 1904. Also plays all other instruments. Niece of Manuel Manetta. Mother of bass players Placide and Jerry Adams. Member of family band dating to last century.

ADAMS, JERRY (sb). b. N.O., April 22, 1927. Son of pianist Dolly Adams.

ADAMS, PLACIDE (sb). b. N.O., Aug. 30, 1929. Son of pianist Dolly Adams and grand-nephew of Manuel Manetta. Toured Japan with George Lewis.

ADDE, LEO (d). b. N.O., April 21, 1904; d. N.O., March, 1942. Famed rhythm star of the N.O. Rhythm Kings. Started playing a cigar box on the streets of N.O. with Raymond Burke on harmonica. In pre-1920 period was already popular. During 20's with Norman Brownlee, Halfway House Orchestra, Johnny Bayersdorffer, and the Christian brothers.

ALBERT, DON. See Dominique, Albert.

ALBERT, TOM (t). b. near Algiers, La., Dec. 23, 1877; d. N.O., Dec. 13, 1969. A true pioneer of jazz. One of the original members of the Eureka Brass Band. Led own band for 25 years from 1904.

ALCORN, ALVIN (t). b. N.O., Sept. 7, 1912. Sometimes seen in parades with Young Tuxedo Brass Band, and George Williams Brass Band. Worked in California with Kid Ory after Mutt Carey's death. Played on Bourbon St. under Octave Crosby, Papa Celestin through 40's, early 50's. Earlier with Sidney Desvigne, A. J. Piron, Clarence Desdunes, Don Albert. Widely recorded.

HENRY ALLEN, SR.

RICARD ALEXIS

GIUSEPPE ALLESANDRA
(Joe Alexander)

ALCORN, OLIVER (cl, s). b. N.O., Aug. 3, 1910. Late 20's, early 30's with Clarence Desdunes. Later in groups led by George McCullum, Jr. In Chicago was frequently to be seen with Lee Collins, Little Brother Montgomery. Brother of Alvin Alcorn.

ALEXANDER, ADOLPHE, SR. (c, bh). b. N.O., 1874; d. N.O., 1936. Golden Rule Orchestra, 1905; Superior and Imperial orchestras, 1909–12. Onward and Excelsior brass bands.

ALEXANDER, ADOLPHE, JR., "TATS" (s, cl, bh). b. N.O., July 15, 1898; d. Dec. 30, 1968. Began with Tuxedo Brass Band, 1921. With Sidney Desvigne, mainly on riverboats, 1922–33; WPA Brass Band during depression; Papa Celestin from mid-40's to 1954; Eureka Brass Band. Retired 1955.

ALEXANDER, JOE. See Allesandra, Giuseppe.

ALEXIS, RICARD (t, b). b. N.O., Oct. 16, 1896; d. N.O., March 15, 1960. With Bob Lyons' Dixie Jazz Band, 1918–25. Tuxedo Orchestra at Pelican Dance Hall under Bebé Ridgley, recorded with Papa Celestin, 1927. Jaw broken by hoodlums in mid-30's; switched to bass. From 1937 to death with Celestin, Paul Barbarin, Octave Crosby, Emma Barrett.

ALLEN, HENRY, SR. (c). b. Algiers, La., 1877; d. Algiers, La., Jan. 11, 1952. Leader of famous Allen Brass Band over 40 years. Father of trumpeter Red Allen.

ALLEN, HENRY, JR., "RED" (t, vo). b. Algiers, La., Jan. 7, 1908. Father's band, Excelsior, Eureka brass bands. Also during 20's with the Kid Rena, Chris Kelly, Sidney Desvigne dance bands. Joined King Oliver in New York, 1927. Riverboats with Fate Marable, Fats Pichon. Recorded with Luis Russell, Fletcher Henderson, Lucky Millinder, Louis Armstrong, Jelly Roll Morton. Led own band from 1940.

6

FRANK AMACKER

DUTCH ANDRUS

ALLESANDRA, GIUSEPPE (tu). b. Italy, Nov. 21, 1865; d. N.O., 1950. Also known as Joe Alexander. Played parades with Reliance Brass Band, 1904. Also in dance bands with Johnny Provenzano, Dominick and Joe Barocco.

ALMERICO, TONY (t). b. N.O., 1905; d. N.O., Dec. 5, 1961. Ran the Parisian Room on Royal St., 1948–60. With weekly coast-to-coast radio dixieland session. Noted disc jockey, TV host for jazz shows. Organized first band in 1936. During 40's played for dancing on Streckfus steamship line.

AMACKER, FRANK (p, g). b. N.O., March 22, 1890; d. N.O., 1976. One of Storyville's "professors." Veteran of brothels of red-light district.

ANDERSON, ANDY (t). b. N.O., Aug. 10, 1912. Well known in such marching bands as Young Tuxedo, George Williams. Sometimes plays dance jobs.

ANDRUS, MERWIN "DUTCH" (d, t). b. N.O., Feb. 25, 1912. Popular dance band leader. Usually on the S.S. *President*. Recorded in 50's for Southland, Sapphire.

ANGRUM, STEVE (cl). b. New Roads, La., July 4, 1895; d. N.O., Nov. 26, 1961. With Elton Theodore band, 1925. During 40's and 50's with George Williams and Young Tuxedo brass bands. Occasionally with Kid Howard, Kid Clayton. Frequently at Happy Landing in 50's with Charlie Love, Albert Jiles, Louis Keppard.

AQUILERA, BOB (p, tb, g). b. N.O., about 1895; d. N.O., Feb. 27, 1945. On a wooden leg, Aquilera marched with Fischer's Brass Band in 1907–10. Also played in Happy Schilling's brass band at ball park before World War I. After war toured southwestern U.S. as solo pianist. Was offered spot with Tom Brown's Band From Dixieland before this group went to Chicago.

7

ANDY ANDERSON

ALBERT ARTIGUES

LOUIS ARMSTRONG

ARCENAUX, WHITEY (bjo). b. N.O. With Young Superior Band, 20's.

ARMSTRONG, LOUIS (t, c). b. N.O., July 4, 1900. Most famous jazzman. Led own band from mid-20's. Protégé of King Oliver. Began in Waif's Home band in N.O. Most widely recorded of all jazz musicians. Was King Zulu in 1949 Mardi Gras. Was a top attraction and recording star.

WALTER ARNOLIA (d). b, N.O., about 1895. Played with Buddy Petit, Chris Kelly. Cousin of Sidney Brown.

ARODIN, SIDNEY (cl). b. N.O., March 29, 1901; d. Feb. 6, 1948. During 20's with Halfway House Orchestra, N.O. Rhythm Masters. Played under most top dixieland bandleaders. Composed "Up The Lazy River." On famed disc session Jones-Collins Astoria Hot Eight. With Louis Prima, Wingy Manone in 30's.

ARTIGUES, ALBERT (c, t). b. N.O., Aug. 23, 1907. Well known in the 20's, working with pickup bands that included many of his big-name contemporaries. His French Market Gang was one of the best informal groups in town.

ASSUNTO, FRANK (t). b. N.O., Jan 29, 1932; d. Feb. 25, 1974. Leader of world-famous Dukes of Dixieland.

ASSUNTO, FREDDIE (tb). b. N.O., Dec. 3, 1929; d. Las Vegas, Nev., Apr. 21, 1966. Entire musical career in Dukes of Dixieland. Married to singer Betty Owens. Brother of Frank, son of Jac.

ASSUNTO, JAC (tb, bjo). b. N.O., about 1902. Father of Frank and Freddie. Plays in Dukes of Dixieland. Was well-known New Orleans music teacher and high school bandmaster.

FRED AND FRANK ASSUNTO

JAC ASSUNTO

ATKINS, BOYD (v, s). b. N.O., about 1900. Left N.O. in 1922. With Fate Marable on the Streckfus steamship line. In 1923 formed band in Chicago. In 20's worked with Louis Armstrong, Carroll Dickerson, Clifford King. Composed "Heebie Jeebies."

ATKINS, EDDIE (tb, bh). b. N.O., 1887; d. Chicago, Ill., about 1926. Trombone with Olympia Orchestra, 1909. Played with Manuel Perez in Chicago, 1915–16. From late 1916–17 with Tuxedo Brass Band, Onward Brass Band. Also at Pete Lala's in Storyville with King Oliver. Drafted in 1917. Moved to Chicago permanently, 1919.

AUGUSTIN, GEORGE (b, bjo). b. N.O., about 1890. With Wooden Joe Nicholas, 1918. In pit band at Lyric Theater with John Robichaux in mid-20's. With Albert Snaer's Moonlight Serenaders, a co-op band, in 1926–28. Played on lake steamers with Fats Pichon, A. J. Piron.

AVERY, JOSEPH "KID" (tb). b. Waggeman, La., Oct. 3, 1892; d. Waggeman, La., Dec. 9, 1955. Pupil of Dave Perkins, 1912–15. With the Tulane Orchestra to 1922. On tour with Evan Thomas' Black Eagles. With Yelping Hounds of Crowley, La. Led own band from early 40's to mid-50's. Regular trombone with Young Tuxedo Brass Band. Recorded for Southland Records, 1954.

BACHMAN, JACK (t). b. N.O., May 21, 1917. With the Crawford-Ferguson Night Owls during the 1960's.

BADIE, PETE (cl). b. N.O., about 1900; d. N.O., about 1960. With Percy Humphrey's first band, 1925.

9

ACHILLE BAQUET

GEORGE BAQUET

BAILEY, DAVID (d). b. N.O., about 1898. During 20's with Chris Kelly. Dance jobs and parades, mainly with Gibson Brass Band until 1965.

BANKS, JOE (c). b. Thibodaux, La., about 1882; d. Thibodaux, La., about 1930. With Youka Brass Band, early 1900's. Led own dance orchestra in Thibodaux until mid-20's. Started many outstanding jazzmen from his home town.

BAPTISTE, ALBERT (v). b. N.O., about 1872; d. N.O., about 1931. Led the Silver Leaf Orchestra, 1896–1912.

BAPTISTE, QUENTIN (b, p). b. N.O. ——. Bass with Freddie Kohlman's band at Sid Davila's Mardi Gras Lounge on Bourbon St. during 50's.

BAPTISTE, RENE (g). b. N.O., about 1880; d. N.O., about 1933. Popular turn-of-the-century guitarist. Brother-in-law of Big Eye Louis Nelson. Played with Perez' Imperial Orchestra and with Edward Clem. Occasionally with the Buddy Bolden band.

BAPTISTE, "TINK" (p). b. N.O., 1897; d. Texas, 1960. Played with Foster Lewis Jazz Band in early 20's. Is on famous Columbia recording session with the Sam Morgan band, 1927.

BAQUET, ACHILLE (cl). b. N.O., Nov. 15, 1885; d. N.O., Nov. 20, 1955. Early clarinet great with Reliance Brass Band. Played with members of Original Dixieland Jazz Band in N.O. Played with N.O. Jazz Band in Coney Island, N.Y., 1915. Brother of famed clarinetist George Baquet and son of great teacher Theogene V. Baquet.

PAUL BARBARIN

LOUIS BARBARIN

DANNY BARKER   BLUE LU BARKER

BAQUET, GEORGE (cl). b. N.O., 1883; d. Philadelphia, Pa., Jan. 14, 1949. In 1900 with Onward Brass Band. Played with Buddy Bolden and with Imperial Orchestra. Toured, 1902–03, with P. T. Wright's Georgia Minstrels. With John Robichaux, 1903; between 1904–14 with Magnolia, Superior, Olympia orchestras. In 1914 joined Original Creole Orchestra in Los Angeles. Discs with Jelly Roll Morton in 1929. Through 40's worked in pit band at Earle Theater in Philadelphia.

BAQUET, THEOGENE V. (c). b. N.O., about 1858; d. N.O., about 1920. Great N.O. music teacher whose sons, George and Achille, made jazz history. Leader of Excelsior Brass Band, about 1882–1904.

BARBARIN, ISIDORE (mel, ah, eu, tu). b. N.O., Sept. 24, 1872; d. N.O., 1960. With Onward Brass Band, 1889–98, 1899–1927; occasionally filled in with other brass bands. Recorded with Zenith Brass Band (Circle) and with Bunk's Brass Band in 40's. Father of Paul and Louis.

BARBARIN, LOUIS (d). b. N.O., Oct. 24, 1902. In 30's worked on Pontchartrain steamships with Eddie Pierson, Harold Dejan. Later identified with Papa Celestin's band, late 40's, early 50's. After Papa's death remained with remnants of band under Albert French.

BARBARIN, PAUL (d). b. N.O., May 5, 1901; d. N.O., Feb. 17, 1969. Great New Orleans drummer. Played with King Oliver, Louis Armstrong, A. J. Piron, Walter Pichon. For 20 years led own band. Composed "Come Back Sweet Papa," "Bourbon Street Parade," "The Second Line," etc. Widely recorded.

BARKER, LOUISE "BLUE LU" (vo). b. N.O., about 1914. Much-recorded, blues-singing wife of Danny Barker. Strong influence on Billie Holiday, Eartha Kitt.

11

EMILE BARNES

JOE BAROCCO

BARKER, DANNY (g, bjo, vo). b. N.O., Jan. 13, 1909. Studied clarinet with Barney Bigard; drums with his uncle, Paul Barbarin; guitar with Bernard Addison. One of best known of N.O. rhythm men. Close student of Creole songs and dialects. Author of widely quoted, as yet unfinished, autobiography. During 30's and 40's with big bands such as Cab Calloway, Benny Carter. Much recorded as accompanist to great blues singers including his wife Blue Lu Barker. Played for a long time at Jimmy Ryan's (DeParis Bros.), New York City. Assistant curator, N.O. Jazz Museum, 1966.

BARNES, EMILE (cl). b. N.O., Feb. 18, 1892; d. N.O., March 2, 1970. With Chris Kelly, 1919–27. Active career from 1908 to occasional appearances in 1966, one of longest in jazz history. During 50's frequently at Mama Lou's and Happy Landing. Seen in 1961 at Preservation Hall.

BARNES, HARRISON (tb, mel, bh, c). b. Magnolia Plantation, La., Jan. 13, 1889; d. N.O., 1960. Pupil of Professor Jim Humphrey. Eclipse Brass Band, 1906; Henry Allen Brass Band, 1907; to 1918 with Chris Kelly; NOLA Band, 1923. Pit band at Lyric Theater with John Robichaux, 1924. Excelsior Brass Band. Recorded with Zenith Brass Band, 1946; Kid Thomas, 1951.

BARNES, PAUL "POLO" (cl, s). b. N.O., Nov. 22, 1902. Brother of Emile Barnes. Debut with Young Tuxedo Orchestra, 1920. Joined Original Tuxedo Orchestra under Celestin and Ridgley, 1921; with Celestin until 1927. Toured with King Oliver until 1935; his diary of these years is an important jazz document. Worked with Kid Howard at Lavida Ballroom. In Navy during World War II, played in Algiers Naval Station band. Settled in New York. Worked with John St. Cyr at Disneyland in 60's. Now in New Orleans.

PAUL BARNES

EMMA BARRETT

BARRETT, EMMA (p, vo, l). b. N.O., March 25, 1898. Popular leader known as "Sweet Emma the Bell Gal." Started in 1923 with Papa Celestin and worked with city's top "reading" bands, Robichaux, Desvigne, Piron—but can't read music. Much recorded in recent years.

BAROCCO, DOMINICK (t, mdl, g, bjo, l). b. N.O., Oct. 5, 1893; d. N.O., Jan. 28, 1970. Studied trumpet with Frank Christian. With brother Joe started own band in 1912. Their Susquehanna Band played on the lake steamer of the same name, 1923–24. Dominick was still leading a band and playing in 1966. In his early days he played with Johnny Provenzano, Nick La Rocca, Clem Camp, and Larry Shields.

BAROCCO, JOE (sb, tu). b. N.O., Oct. 16, 1891; d. N.O., 1947. Brother of Dominick and co-leader of the Susquehanna Band. Also played with Reliance Brass Band and Johnny Fischer's Brass Band.

BAROCCO, VINCENT (ah). b. N.O., about 1878. An early member of the Reliance Brass Band. Not related to other Baroccos.

BART, WILHELMINA (p). b. N.O., about 1900. During 20's, played with Willie Pajeaud at the Alamo Dance Hall and with Amos White's orchestra, the N.O. Creole Jazz Band, at Spanish Fort. At one time played with Jimmie Noone.

BARTH, GEORGE (t, mel, s). b. N.O., about 1895. Talented, versatile jazzman with Norman Brownlee's orchestra, Fischer's Brass Band, and other leading dixieland groups of the World War I era.

BAUDUC, JULES (bjo). b. N.O., about 1904. Bandleader active in early 20's. Brother of famous drummer Ray Bauduc.

BAUDUC, RAY (d). b. N.O., June 18, 1909. Participated in first live broadcast of jazz from N.O. Left home in 1926 to join Joe Venuti in New York after playing in N.O. with Johnny Bayersdorffer and other top local

13

DOMINICK BAROCCO

JULES BAUDUC

RAY BAUDUC

bands. Was with Dorsey Brothers in Scranton Sirens orchestra; with Ben Pollack, Freddy Rich, Red Nichols through 20's. Recorded in 1926 with Memphis Five. Was with Bob Crosby, 1935–42, and gained national fame. Led own band and recorded for Capitol in 40's. With Jimmy Dorsey, 1947–50. In early 50's, toured with Jack Teagarden.

BAYERSDORFFER, JOHNNY (t). b. N.O., Sept. 4, 1899. Most popular dixieland bandleader of the 20's; employed top performers. Recorded on Okeh, March, 1924. Played for many years at Tokyo Gardens in Spanish Fort. Also played in bands of Happy Schilling, Tony Parenti, and in Triangle Jazz Band with Irwin Leclere.

BEAULIEU, PAUL (p, cl, clo). b. N.O., Oct. 20, 1888; d. N.O., 1967. Melrose Brass Band with Joe Oliver, 1907. With John Robichaux, 1915. More active as symphonic musician.

BEAULIEU, RUDOLPH "BIG RUDOLPH" (d). b. N.O., 1900; d. March 9, 1972. Discontinued his carrer as an active performer and operated a popular drum shop.

BECHET, DR. LEONARD V. (tb). b. N.O., April 25, 1877; d. N.O., Sept. 17, 1952. Dentist. With Young Superior Brass Band during 20's. In 1903 led own Silver Bells Band until World War I. Brother of Sidney.

14

SIDNEY BECHET   LEONARD BECHET

BECHET, SIDNEY (cl, ss). b. N.O., May 14, 1897; d. Paris, France, May 14, 1959. Brother's Silver Bells Band, 1911; Eagle Band, 1914. With King Oliver at Lala's in Storyville. To Texas, 1915–17, with Clarence Williams; 1917 to Chicago with Fred Keppard. Europe with Will Marion Cook, 1919–21; Russia with "Black Revue," 1930. With Noble Sissle Band in 30's. Emigrated permanently to France in 50's. Autobiography *Treat It Gentle*.

BEHRENSON, "DOC" (c). b. N.O., about 1893. Pre-World War I dixielander. Worked with Johnny Stein in Chicago, 1916.

BEHRENSON, SIDNEY (tb). b. N.O., about 1895. Pre-World War I dixielander.

BELASCO, MANUEL (bh). b. N.O. Charter member of Reliance Brass Band frequently mistaken for leader Jack Laine, because of close physical resemblance.

BELL, JOHN (sb, tu). b. N.O., about 1910; d. N.O., July 28, 1946. With Melon Pickers in 20's. Recorded on Keynote with George Hartman in 40's.

BELLIS, HENRY (t). b. N.O., about 1915. Leader of small dance bands through late 20's and 30's. Frequently played with Candy Candido in 30's.

BEN, PAUL (tb). b. N.O., about 1895. With Bob Lyons' Dixie Jazz Band from World War I through early 20's. Also, same period, in Lawrence Marrero's Young Tuxedo Orchestra and in band led by Bush Hall.

BENARBY, JIM (tb). b. N.O., about 1904; d. about 1926. Member of Nat Towles' Creole Harmony Kings for the band's engagement in Yucatan, Mexico, 1924–25. Uncle of trombonist Ernest Kelly.

BENINATE, JOHNNY (cl). b. N.O. Pre-World War I with Johnny Bayersdorffer's band.

BENINATE, NICK (t). b. N.O., about 1910. Active dixielander, frequently seen with Jeff Riddick.

15

HAMILTON BENSON

BARNEY BIGARD

BENOIT, JOHN (d). b. Pass Christian, Miss. An active musician in the bands of Storyville between 1908–13. With Lawrence Duhé, Peter Bocage, Fred Keppard.

BENSON, HAMILTON "HAMP" (tb). b. N.O., 1885. In 1901 with trio in district along with Andrew Kimball, till 1905. In 1906 with mandolinist Tom Brown at Tom Anderson's. Led own band later that year. Left N.O. in 1915. Played with Sidney Bechet in Springfield, Ill., in 40's.

BENTON, TOM (bjo, vo). b. N.O., about 1890; d. N.O., about 1945. Crescent Band, 1914. With Papa Celestin, 1915; Jimmie Noone, 1915. Considered best singer of pop tunes in town. Left N.O. in 1926.

BERRY, MEL (tb). b. N.O., about 1897; d. Los Angeles about 1929. Virtuoso musician. Worked in theater pit bands, and in early 20's with Johnny DeDroit.

BERTRAND, BUDDY (p). b. 1897; d. N.O., March 23, 1956. Solo performer in brothels of Storyville.

BIGARD, ALBANY LEON "BARNEY" (cl). b. N.O., March 3, 1906. Taught by Luis and Lorenzo Tio, Jr. With Oak Gaspard, 1921; Albert Nicholas, 1922. Joined King Oliver on tour in 1925. Then in Chicago with Charles Elgar, Luis Russell, Albert Wynn before 14-year stint with Duke Ellington. Settled in California. Led own trio and worked with Freddie Slack in early 40's. Late 40's and 50's on tour with the Louis Armstrong All-Stars. Much recorded.

BIGARD, ALEC (d). b. N.O., Sept. 25, 1898. A. J. Piron's Orchestra, 1917. At Tom Anderson's and the Humming Bird Lounge with quartet; with Excelsior Brass Band, 1918. Maple Leaf Orchestra, 1919–20; Sidney Desvigne, 1925; John Robichaux, 1927; Kid Rena, 1944. Brother of famous clarinetist Barney.

BIGARD, EMILE (v). b. N.O., about 1890; d. N.O., about 1935. During World War I was with the Magnolia Orchestra and also worked with King Oliver and Kid Ory. In 1919 joined Maple Leaf Orchestra. Retired from music in 1924. Brother of Alec, Barney.

16

ESTHER BIGEOU

BIGEOU, CLIFFORD "BOY" (p, bjo). b. N.O. ——.
Through the depression with Crescent City Serenaders. Brother of singer Esther Bigeou.

BIGEOU, ESTHER (vo). b. N.O., about 1895; d. about 1936. "The Creole Songbird," sang and recorded with A. J. Piron Orchestra in 30's. Was with Peter Bocage; toured Theater Owners' Booking Association vaudeville circuit. Cousin of Paul Barbarin.

BISSO, LOUIS (p). b. N.O., about 1905. Early 20's played piano in silent movie theaters. Was head of N.O. City Planning Board in 50's. Appeared frequently at NOJC.

BLAISE, ED "KID TOTTS" (d). b. N.O., about 1895; d. N.O., about 1944. Totts worked with the Jack Laine, Frank Christian, and Bill Gallaty bands in the pre-World War I era.

"BLIND" GILBERT (c, g). b. N.O., about 1900. A partially blind beggar who worked the streets of the district and the French Quarter, made unissued recordings for Columbia in the 20's and claims to be the true composer of "Angry" and "Where the Morning Glories Grow." Last heard from in Los Angeles, Calif. Legal name, Gilbert Meistier.

BLOUNT, JACK (v). b. N.O. —— With Liberty Bell Orchestra, 1919–33.

BLUNT, CARROLL (tb). Gibson Brass Band.

BOCAGE, CHARLES (bjo, g, vo). b. N.O., about 1895; d. N.O., Nov. 4, 1963. With A. J. Piron after World War I. Recorded with this band for Victor, Columbia in 1923. Later mainly in bands led by brother, Peter. Continued active until mid-50's.

BOCAGE, HENRY (tu, sb, t). b. N.O., about 1893. 1918–19 with A. J. Piron Orchestra. Recorded with the group at the Victor and Columbia sessions in 1923. Cousin of Peter and Charles.

PETER BOCAGE

STIRLING BOSE

BOCAGE, PETER (t, tb, v). b. Algiers, La., Aug. 4, 1887; d. Algiers, Dec. 3, 1967. Began career in 1906. Original Superior Orchestra, 1909; Original Tuxedo Orchestra, 1910–13; Onward Brass Band with Joe Oliver at Lala's. With Fate Marable S.S. *Capitol* Orchestra, 1916. After 1918 with A. J. Piron Orchestra. Wrote "Mama's Gone Good Bye"; introduced "Shimmy Like My Sister Kate." Creole Serenaders recorded in 60's by Riverside.

BODOYER, RUDOLPH (d). b. N.O., about 1902. Played with Young Morgan Band under Isaiah Morgan, 1922–26. With Sam Morgan, 1926; in 30's with Kid Rena. Seen often in early 40's with Alphonse Picou.

BOLMAN, "RED" (c, t, l). b. N.O., about 1899. Led own band in 20's and 30's. Toured with N.O. Rhythm Masters in early 20's.

BOLDEN, CHARLES "BUDDY" (c). b. Sept. 6, 1877; d. Jackson, La., Nov. 4, 1931. Sometimes called the first jazz band leader. Undoubtedly one of the

greatest N.O. horn men. Mainly led own band until incapacitated by mental illness in 1907.

BOLTON, "HAPPY," "RED HAPPY" (d). b. N.O., about 1885; d. N.O., 1928. Bolton was the mainstay of the King Oliver band in N.O. from 1912 to 1916. He remained in N.O. when Oliver went to Chicago and after World War I worked with John Robichaux at the Lyric Theater. In the early 20's he was in a Canal St. cabaret-dance hall with Peter Lacaze's band.

BONANO, JOSEPH "SHARKEY" (t). b. N.O., April 9, 1904; d. N.O., March 27, 1972. Dixieland band leader from 1922. On tour with Jean Goldkette, 1927. Trademarks: brown derby, high-pitched vocals, and impromptu "cootchie" dances. He employed top N.O. dixieland stars and toured with them in Europe, Asia, South America. Once for a short time, he replaced Bix Beiderbecke in Wolverines orchestra. He also replaced Nick La Rocca in Original Dixieland Jazz Band.

18

LESTER BOUCHON

SHARKEY BONANO

BONANSINGA, FRANK (p, l). b. Jacksonville, Ill., April 8, 1900. With campus bands at University of Illinois, 1923. Fronted own band in 1924. Longtime N.O. resident. Headed N.O.J.C. in 1956 and played piano with top musicians at club functions through the 50's and early 60's.

BONTEMPS, WILLIE (bjo, g). b. N.O., about 1893; d. N.O., in 1958. Tuxedo Orchestra under Bebé Ridgley in 1917; Maple Leaf Orchestra, 1920–21. Worked with Willie Pajeaud at Thom's Road House, 1923. Did specialty comedy-music act at Lyric Theater during 20's but was not member of the Robichaux pit band. Best known as singer and comic.

BOSE, STIRLING (c, t). b. Florence, Ala., Feb. 23, 1906; d. St. Petersburg, Fla., June, 1958. With Norman Brownlee in late 20's and later with Crescent City Jazzers centered in Mobile, Ala. Usually considered a "New Orleans musician," but mainly worked with swing bands until he died.

BOUCHON, LESTER (cl, s, l). b. N.O., Sept. 29, 1906; d. N.O., April 13, 1962. 1920's with Domino Orchestra, Bayersdorffer's Red Devils. Toured in name bands through swing era. During 40's and 50's with Sharkey, Johnny Wiggs, Santo Pecora.

BOURGEAU, JOSEPH "FAN" (p. bjo). b. N.O., July 29, 1891; d. N.O., 1970. Frequent performer at Luthjen's in late 40's and 50's.

BOURGEOIS, WILFRED S. "BILL" (cl, s). b. N.O., April 14, 1907. Mainly associated with Sharkey.

BOYD, GEORGE "GEORGIA BOY" (cl). b. N.O., about 1904; d. about 1931. Wild, untrained musician with Jack Carey's Crescent Orchestra, 1916; and Kid Lindsey's Jazz Band, 1917. Joined Punch Miller, 1920, and Chris Kelly when Punch left N.O. 1922–25 with Kid Rena Dixie Jazz Band.

19

WELLMAN BRAUD

STEVE BROWN

TOM BROWN

BRAUD, WELLMAN (sb, v). b. St. James Parish, La., Jan. 25, 1891; d. June 6, 1967. In string bass trio in the district, 1908–13, at Tom Anderson's and at the Terminal Saloon. Switched to string bass in Chicago, 1917, with Sugar John Smith, Lawrence Duhe. Charles Elgar Orchestra, 1920–23; Wilbur Sweatman, 1923. Toured in burlesque. With Duke Ellington, 1926–36.

BRAUN, BILLY (p, mel). b. N.O., 1892; d. N.O., April, 1974. Norman Brownlee, Johnny Fischer, Johnny Bayersdorffer.

BRAZLEE, HARRISON (tb). b. N.O., Oct. 25, 1888; d. N.O., Nov., 1954. Began with Excelsior (Mobile, Ala.) Brass Band. Toured with carnival and minstrel bands and with Ringling Brothers and other circuses. Joined Evan Thomas' band in mid-20's. Settled in N.O. and at time of his death was a regular performer at Luthjen's.

BREAUX, MC NEAL (sb, tu). b. N.O., 1916. Started on tuba in Henry Allen, Sr.'s, brass band. Played string bass with Isaiah Morgan's orchestra in early 30's. In 30's and 40's was active in Moonlight Serenaders and the Dixie Syncopators. Briefly in U.S. Navy. Through late 40's and 50's mainly with groups led by Papa Celestin and Paul Barbarin.

BROOKS, JOE (bjo, g). Member of Alcide Frank's Golden Rule Orchestra, working at Fewclothes Cabaret in Storyville in 1905.

BROUSSARD, THEO (sb). First bass player in Papa Celestin's Original Tuxedo Orchestra that opened in Storyville in 1912.

BROWN, JAMES (sb). b. N.O., about 1880; d. N.O., about 1922. Played in the Golden Rule Orchestra under Alcide Frank at Fewclothes Cabaret in 1905. Also with Manuel Perez' Imperial Orch., 1907.

TOM BROWN

STEVE BRUE

BROWN, JOHNNY (cl). b. N.O., about 1880; d. about 1935. Played "vaudeville" style clarinet. Used horn mainly for comic effects, but led bands of fine musicians, beginning about 1910. In early 20's worked with Wooden Joe Nicholas and later with Dan Moody's dance group from Bogalusa, La.

BROWN, RAY (tb). b. N.O., about 1892; d. about 1940. Clarence Desdunes' Joyland Revelers in early 20's. With Fats Pichon, 1927. Joined Sidney Desvigne in 1928.

BROWN, SIDNEY (b, tu, v). b. Deer Range, La., July 19, 1894; d. N.O., 1968. Also known as Jim Little. Played violin in Golden Leaf Band, 1919, after service discharge. Young Morgan Band, 1922; with his uncle, Jim Robinson, recorded on Sam Morgan discs until depression years. In 30's played tuba with Tuxedo Brass Band and from early 40's to 1954 was with Papa Celestin.

BROWN, STEVE (tu, sb). b. N.O., about 1890; d. Sept. 15, 1965. Original bass man with N.O. Rhythm Kings in early 20's. Played in N.O. earlier under leadership of his brother, Tom Brown. Worked in Chicago with Husk O'Hare organization.

BROWN, TOM (g, mdl). b. N.O., about 1878; d. N.O., about 1918. Popular string trio musician of early Storyville days, 1898–1906. Played at Tom Anderson's. Brother-in-law of Willie and Papa John Joseph.

BROWN, TOM (tb, sb, l). b. N.O., June 3, 1888; d. N.O., March 25, 1958. Led first dixieland group to go north, 1915. This was the first band advertised as a "jass" band. Toured and recorded with Ray Miller, Yerkes band during 20's. In later years heard frequently in N.O. with Johnny Wiggs-led groups. Late records on GHB, Southland.

BROWN, WILLIAM (tu., sou). b. N.O., July 31, 1918; d. N.O., Oct. 25, 1975. Popular sousaphone player with George Williams' Brass Band for many years. In 1966 played with Eureka Brass Band.

MERRITT BRUNIES   GEORGE BRUNIES   ALBERT BRUNIES   RICHARD BRUNIES

BROWNLEE, NORMAN (p, sb). b. Algiers, La., Feb. 7, 1896; d. Pensacola, Fla., April 10, 1967. His orchestra played in New Orleans from 1920 until 1930. Recorded on Okeh in January, 1925. Moved to Pensacola in 1932, where he became secretary-treasurer of the musicians' union.

BRUE, STEVE. b. Feb. 10, 1904; d. Netherlands, Oct. 11, 1944. Princeton Revellers, Owls, Triangle Band.

BRUNDY, WALTER (d). b. N.O., about 1883; d. Natchez, Miss., 1941. One of the truly great drummers of all time. Teacher and inspiration to Baby Dodds and Ernest Rogers, among others. Original Superior Orchestra, 1905–14; John Robichaux orchestra, 1912. Led own band in Baton Rouge during World War I. Killed in auto crash.

BRUNIES, ALBERT "ABBIE" (c). b. N.O., Jan. 19, 1900. In his early years, 1917–18, he led Jack Laine units at Bucktown and Milneburg lakefront resorts. 1919–26 led famous Halfway House Orchestra. Had best nightclub jobs in town until he went into war industry in late 30's. Moved to Biloxi, Miss., in 1945 and was still leading a band there in 1960.

BRUNIES, ALBERT "LITTLE ABBIE" (d). b. N.O., 1914; d. New York, N.Y., Feb. 12, 1955. An outstanding dixieland drummer and member of a famed jazz clan; nephew of brothers Albert, George, Henry, Merritt, Richard. He died on the bandstand of Child's Paramount in New York on an engagement with Sharkey's band just as he'd begun to receive recognition.

BRUNIES, GEORGE (tb). b. N.O., Feb. 6, 1902; d. Chicago, Nov. 19, 1974. Best known of the many Brunies jazzmen. Original member of the N.O. Rhythm Kings. At age 8 was member of Papa Laine's junior band and played in family bands all his early life. Worked regularly from 1923 to 1925 in the Ted Lewis orchestra. Was identified with the Condon group in New York for 20 years. In 1964 was leading his own group in Cincinnati.

BRUNIES, HENRY "HENNY" (tb). b. N.O., about 1882; d. N.O. Reliance Brass Band; Fischer's Brass Band; recorded with Merritt Brunies orchestra in 20's.

BRUNIES, MERRITT (t, tb). b. N.O., Dec. 25, 1895; d. Biloxi, Miss., Feb. 4, 1973. His was the band that replaced the N.O. Rhythm Kings at Friars Inn in Chicago. The seven records he cut for Okeh and Autograph are among the rarest and most prized of collectors' items. Recorded for American Music in the 50's.

22

JOSEPH BUTLER

ALBERT BURBANK

RAYMOND BURKE

BRUNIOUS, JOHN "PICKETT" (p, t). b. N.O., Oct. 17, 1920; d. May 7, 1976. A nephew of Paul Barbarin, Brunious played and recorded on trumpet in his uncle's band. During late 40's as pianist he drifted into modern movement, but returned in early 50's to legitimate N.O. jazz. In 60's he helped revive the Onward Brass Band.

BURBANK, ALBERT (cl). b. N.O., March 25, 1902; d. Aug. 15, 1976. Studied with Lorenzo Tio, Jr., 1916. Played in the city and at lakefront through 20's. During depression worked with Kid Milton's band. After Navy duty worked with Herb Morand and Albert Jiles, mainly at Little Woods. Through 50's worked at the Paddock, mainly with Octave Crosby, Paul Barbarin. Played with Eureka and Young Tuxedo brass bands.

BURKE, RAYMOND (cl). b. N.O., June 6, 1904. One of the greatest creative artists jazz has produced; completely self-taught. Has worked sporadically with all top dixieland stars and is widely recorded, but is disinclined to commit himself to steady employment. Nephew of early jazzmen Jules and Leo Cassard and drummer Harold Peterson. Burke keeps an antique and curiosity shop on Bourbon St. Legal name is Barrois.

BURRELLA, TONY (d). b. N.O. ——. With Dixola Band in late 20's and early 30's.

BUTLER, JOSEPH (sb). b. Algiers, La., Dec. 25, 1907. Kid Thomas' band for many years. First job with Robert Clark's band. His more familiar nickname, unfortunately, is unprintable.

BRUNIES, RICHARD "RICHIE" (c). b. N.O., Nov. 29, 1889; d. N.O., 1960. Powerful cornetist whose tone was said to rival Buddy Bolden's. Leader of one of Papa Laine's Reliance brass bands in pre-World War I era. Played with Fischer's Brass Band in 1907–08.

23

CAGNOLATTI, ERNIE (t). b. Madisonville, La., April 2, 1911. Worked with Celestin, Paul Barbarin and the Young Tuxedo Brass Band. Played during the 30's with Herb Leary's large swing band. Frequently seen at Preservation Hall.

CALIER, MANUEL (t). b. N.O. ——. Leader of the Bulls Club Brass Band in 1921.

CAMP, CLEM (cl). b. N.O. about 1898; d. N.O., 1968. Early dixieland musician played with Brunies brothers, Jack Laine, Nick La Rocca, all prior to 1914.

CAMPBELL, ARTHUR (p). b. N.O., about 1890; d. Chicago, Ill. ——. Mainly a "professor" in the brothels of the red-light district between 1908 and 1917, he sometimes worked with bands, too. With Joe Oliver, 1915; at Pete Lala's cafe; with A. J. Piron at Old Spanish Fort, 1918. Recorded with Fred Keppard.

CANDIDO, "CANDY" (sb, vo). b. N.O., about 1913. During 30's played with bands of Louis Prima and Leon Prima. Became nationally known, along with Otto "Coco" Himel, as comedy-accompanist to popular singer, Gene Austin, appearing both on records and in the movies. Joined Ted Fiorito band and later became a stand-up comic in night clubs.

CAPRARO, ANGELO (g, l). b. N.O., March 22, 1910; d. Las Vegas, Nev., Dec. 1963. Brother of Joe Capraro. Played w. Leon Prima, Louis Prima, Sharkey bands in 30's. Led own band on tour under show name, Jimmy Capra. Worked in brother's band at Cotton Club.

CAPRARO, JOE (g, l). b. N.O., June 26, 1903. Played w. Sharkey, New Orleans Rhythm Masters band with Sidney Arodin, Leo Adde, Martin Abraham. Led own band on WSMB in 20's. Also at Cotton Club. Extensively recorded on Southland.

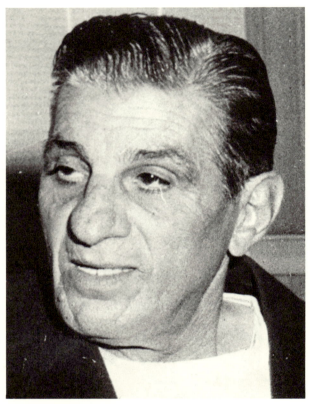

JOE CAPRARO

MUTT CAREY

JOHN CASIMIR

PAPA CELESTIN

CAREY, JACK (tb). b. Hahnville, La., about 1889; d. N.O., about 1935. May have been first to play in tailgate style. From 1908 was among first to use French melodies for jazz. His Crescent Jazz Band was one of the great early bands. The celebrated tune "Tiger Rag" was previously called "Jack Carey."

CAREY, THOMAS "PAPA MUTT" (c). b. Hahnville, La., 1891; d. San Francisco, Calif., Sept. 3, 1948. In brother Jack's Crescent Orchestra, 1910–14. Worked in district until 1916, mainly with Kid Ory. In 1917 went to Chicago with Johnny Dodds, replaced King Oliver orchestra at Dreamland. Back in N.O. in 1918 with Wade Whaley. Rejoined Ory in Calif., 1919. In 1944 made weekly network broadcasts with Ory for Orson Welles. Played in New York during late 40's, mainly with Edmond Hall.

CARR, SON (b). A member of Little Joe Lindsey's band at Rice's Cafe in the district during 1916–17.

CARROLL, ALBERT (p, tb). b. N.O., about 1880; d. ——. Played piano in the brothels of Basin St. until Storyville closed in 1917, then worked best band jobs in town, notably at the Lyric Theater until 1927. He sometimes played trombone in parades.

CARTER, BUDDY (p). b. N.O., about 1870; d. ——. A Storyville piano player to about 1910 who is generally spoken of by his contemporaries as "King of the Blues."

CASEY, BOB (p). Regular with The Last Straws.

CASIMIR, JOE (d). b. N.O., about 1902. Brother of John Casimir. Worked with him in Young Eagles Band, 1919. Kid Milton's band in early 20's.

CASIMIR, JOHN (cl). b. N.O., Oct. 16, 1898; d. N.O., Jan. 3, 1963. For many years manager and clarinetist for the Young Tuxedo Brass Band until his death; recorded on Atlantic with this group. Started career in 1919 with Young Eagles Band of Lee Collins.

CASSARD, JULES (sb, tb). b. N.O., about 1890. Early dixieland musician. Played with members of Original Dixieland Jazz Band before they left for fame in New York. Composer of jazz standard, "Angry." Uncle of Raymond Burke. Lives in Miami, Fla.

CASSARD, LEO (bjo, cl). b. N.O., about 1892; d. N.O., Oct. 16, 1972. Early dixieland musician. Played many jobs at lakefront resorts. Uncle of Raymond Burke; brother of Jules Cassard.

CASTAIGN, JOHNNY (d). b. N.O., 1912; d. N.O., Oct. 30, 1972. Dixielander associated primarily with Sharkey, Tony Almerico, Earl Danton orchestra.

CASTIGLIOLA, ANGELO J. "BUBBY" (tb). b. N.O., Aug. 28, 1924. Only jazzman from a noted concert-trained family. Toured with Jack Teagarden's dance band. Worked with Irving Fazola, Tony Almerico, and in WWL studio band, the Dawnbusters.

CATES, SIDNEY (bjo, g). b. N.O., about 1900; d. N.O., Sept. 6, 1968. Active musician from 20's. Started with Leo Dejan's Moonlight Serenaders. During mid-30's worked in WPA music program. Was executive of musicians' union.

CATO, ADAM (p). Active dance band piano man during late 20's and early depression years.

"CATO" (d). b. N.O., about 1875; d. ——. Full name not known. Very popular drummer with Frank Duson's Eagle Band, 1907, after latter took over Bolden group. Also with Herb Lindsay's Primrose Orchestra, 1912; and Amos Riley's Tulane Orchestra, 1915.

"CATO, BIG" (bjo). b. N.O., about 1869; d.——. Correct full name not known. Member of Amos Riley's Tulane Orchestra in 1915. Uncle of Cato the drummer. May have introduced "Careless Love."

CELESTIN, OSCAR "PAPA" (t, c). b. Napoleonville, La., Jan. 1, 1884; d. N.O., Dec. 15, 1954. Played with Algiers Brass Band in early 1900's. Founded Original Tuxedo Orchestra, 1910; founded Tuxedo Brass Band, 1911. Popular bandleader in N.O. for 44 years. Recorded for Okeh in 1925, Columbia in 1926–28, and many other firms in his last years.

CENTOBIE, LEONARD "BOOJIE" (cl). b. N.O., Oct. 14, 1915. Dixielander who made reputation with Sharkey, Wingy Manone, Johnny Wiggs beginning in mid-30's.

CHAMBERS, TIG (c). b. N.O., about 1880; d. Chicago, Ill., 1950. In 1907, joined Eagle Band under Frank Duson. In 1910, formed the Magnolia Sweets. Played at Fewclothes Cabaret, Pete Lala's, Abadie's. Left N.O. permanently in 1915.

CHANDLER, DEDE "DEE DEE" (d). b. N.O., about 1866; d. N.O., 1925. Drummer for John Robichaux before Spanish-American War. First drummer to play jazz style in dance band. Often credited with inventing foot pedal. Excellent showman and comic. Played with grace of a professional juggler.

CHARLES, HIPPOLYTE (c). b. St. Martinville, La., April 18, 1891. With Manuel Perez, 1909; Silver Leaf Orchestra, 1911; played with Tuxedo Brass Band before World War I. Joined Maple Leaf Orchestra, 1919, then started own band. Active until illness forced retirement from music in 1925.

CHARLES, JESSE (cl, s). b. N.O., June 25, 1900; d. N.O., Aug. 4, 1975. Parade musician for many years in George Williams' Brass Band. In 40's with Abby Williams' Happy Pals Brass Band.

CHASE, SAMUEL (bjo).

CHERIE, EDDIE (s, cl). b. N.O., 1889; d. Chicago, Ill., 1941. Played with Sidney Desvigne on the S.S. *Island Queen* (1927). Also with Manuel Perez.

CHEVEZ, JULIUS (p). b. N.O., Aug. 16, 1908. Very popular dixieland rhythm man, much favored by Johnny Wiggs, Julian Laine, Irving Fazola, the Melon Pickers.

BOOJIE CENTOBIE

JULIUS CHEVEZ

EMILE CHRISTIAN

CHRISTIAN, CHARLES (tb). b. N.O., July 25, 1886; d. N.O., July 11, 1964. Brother of Frank and Emile. Played in the Dominos Orchestra.

CHRISTIAN, EMILE (tb, sb, t). b. N.O., April 20, 1895; d. N.O., Dec. 31, 1973. Played in the Reliance Brass Band, later replaced Eddie Edwards in Original Dixieland Jazz Band when the band went to England, 1919–21. With Morgan's Euphonic Band, 1910. Trombone and string bass for top N.O. dixieland groups like Sharkey's, Santo Pecora's, 1966.

CHRISTIAN, FRANK (t, cl, v, tu). b. N.O., Sept. 3, 1887; d. N.O., Nov. 27, 1973. Ragtime bandleader, 1910–18 in N.O. Then led N.O. Jazz Band in Chicago and New York, with Jimmy Durante on piano. Started in N.O. about 1908 with Jack Laine's Reliance Band and worked with Fischer's Brass Band, and in groups including his brothers Emile and Charles. Featured in vaudeville in early 20's with Gilda Gray. Last jobs in N.O. were with Durfee's. Band.

CHRISTIAN, NARCISSE J. "BUDDY" (p, bjo, g). b. N.O., about 1895; d. late 40's. Another of the legendary Storyville "professors," Christian also played in bands with Peter Bocage at the Tuxedo, 1912–13, and with Joe Oliver at Lala's Cafe, 1915–16. During the 20's recorded extensively on piano with bands led by Clarence Williams and on banjo and guitar in smaller groups.

CINQUEMANO, PAUL (tb). N.O., about 1893. With Johnny Bayersdorffer in pre-World War I era.

CLARK, AARON WARREN (bh). b. Louisville, Ky., 1858; d. N.O., Sept. 4, 1894. With Excelsior Brass Band, 1882–90; and Onward Brass Band, 1890–94. Father of Red Clark.

RED CLARK

KID SHEIK COLAR

KID CLAYTON

CLARK, JOSEPH "RED" (tb, tu). b. N.O., Feb. 12, 1894; d. N.O., Nov. 30, 1960. Studied brass with Dave Perkins and with his father Aaron Clark. Joined the Tonic Triad Band in 1928. With the Masonic Brass Band in the 30's. Beloved manager and musician of the Eureka Brass Band, 1947–60. A diligent collector and preserver of the music of the earlier N.O. marching bands.

CLAYTON, JAMES "KID" (t). b. Jasper County, Miss., March 2, 1902; d. N.O., Dec. 17, 1963. An untutored musician, Clayton was limited to blues. Played with Jack Carey's band in the 20's. Worked many jobs with saxophonist John Handy. Mainly a rhythm and blue type musician.

CLEM, EDWARD (c). b. St. Joseph, La., before Civil War; d. N.O., in early 20's. An almost blind, one-

28

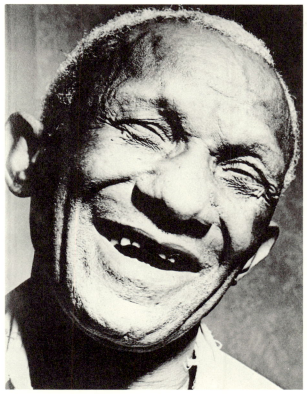

WALLACE COLLINS

same year. In 20's worked in New York, Chicago with Luis Russell, Dave Peyton, Zutty Singleton, Mezz Mezzrow orchestras. Cut famed 1929 discs of Jones-Collins Astoria Hot Eight in N.O. Settled and worked in Chicago. Went to France in 1951 on tour with Mezzrow. Played for a while in 1954 on Bourbon St. at the Paddock with his close friend, Ricard Alexis.

COLLINS, WALLACE (tu, bh). b. N.O., 1858; d. about 1944. Led own group as early as 1888. Member of Charlie Galloway orchestra in 1894. Played with Buddy Bolden.

eyed musician, but a fast "reader." Before Spanish-American War played with Charlie Galloway's orchestra and group led by Wallace Collins. Replaced Bolden when Frank Duson took control of Buddy's band. Led own band from 1907–12. Ended musical career in Johnny Brown's band, about 1920. Marched sometimes with Onward and Excelsior brass bands.

COLAR, GEORGE "KID SHEIK" (t). b. N.O., Sept. 15, 1908. Protégé of Wooden Joe Nicholas. Has led small dance groups for many years. During mid-30's was in Kid Rena's marching band. Since 1952, with Eureka Brass Band.

COLLINS, LEE (t). b. N.O., Oct. 17, 1901; d. Chicago, Ill., July 3, 1960. At age 15 was filling in with Original Tuxedo Orchestra and marching with Tuxedo Brass Band. In 1919 worked parade with Buddy Petit, Chris Kelly. Pupil of Professor Jim Humphrey. In 1920 with Young Eagles and Golden Leaf Band. In 1924 replaced Armstrong in King Oliver's orchestra in Chicago. Recorded with Jelly Roll Morton,

LEE COLLINS

ANN COOK

BOB COQUILLE

CÓMES, COUNT (p). b. N.O. ———. Played with the Dixola Jazz Band in the 20's.

COOK, ANN (vo). b. Franzenville, La., about 1888; d. N.O., Sept. 29, 1962. A popular blues singer who recorded in 1927 accompanied by Louis Dumaine's Jazzola Eight.

COOPER, HAROLD (cl, ts). b. N.O., July 21, 1924. In 50's with George Girard, Al Hirt, Dukes of Dixieland. In 1966 with Alamo Jazz Band, San Antonio.

COPLAND, THOMAS (sb, tu). b. N.O.; d. N.O., about 1945. With Magnolia Orchestra, 1910. Early member of the Sam Morgan band, 1918–19. From 1927 was in

the second Olympia Orchestra formed by Arnold Depass. Sometimes played with Dee Dee Pierce.

COQUILLE, ROBERT (sb). b. N.O., Sept. 15, 1911. Regular with George Girard's N.O. Five. Played with Al Hirt, Pete Fountain groups.

CORDILLA, CHARLES JOSEPH (cl, s). b. Baton Rouge, La., May 25, 1899. Early dixielander much associated with the Brunies groups, Leon Roppolo, Emmett Hardy, Jack Laine. Worked five years at Halfway House in 20's. Also with Stalebread Lacoume and the Shields brothers. Was with Leon Prima, Sharkey on the S.S. *Greater New Orleans.*

CORNISH, WILLIE (vt). b. N.O., Aug. 1, 1875; d. N.O., Jan. 12, 1942. An early jazz pioneer. With Buddy

LOUIS COTTRELL, SR.

LOUIS COTTRELL, JR.

WILLIE CORNISH

Bolden. Veteran of Spanish-American War. From 1903 played almost exclusively in brass bands. Joined Eureka Brass Band soon after it was founded.

COSTA, ANTHONY J. "TONY" (cl, s). b. Feb. 9, 1910. Associated with Tony Almerico and Phil Zito, Dukes of Dixieland, Sharkey.

COSTA, MICHAEL A. (cl, s). b. N.O., May 4, 1915.

COTTRELL, LOUIS, SR. (d). b. N.O., about 1875; d. N.O., 1927. One of the greatest of N.O. drummers. Prominent with A. J. Piron Orchestra from 1918 until his death. Worked in district, 1909–13. In 1915

was with Manuel Perez in Chicago. Made the record sessions with Piron in early 20's.

COTTRELL, LOUIS, JR. (cl, s). b. N.O., March 7, 1911. Studied with Lorenzo Tio, Jr. and Barney Bigard. Joined Young Tuxedo Orchestra, 1927. In 1928, worked with Golden Rule Orchestra, Bebé Ridgley, Sidney Desvigne, and Chris Kelly. Toured with Don Albert Orchestra from 1929–39. With A. J. Piron on riverboats. Returned to Desvigne in 1942. Marched with Young Tuxedo Brass Band. Plays frequently with Paul Barbarin. President of local 496, AFM.

COUSIN JOE. See Joseph, Pleasant.

COUSTAUT, MANUEL (c). b. N.O. before Civil War; d. N.O.———. Early dance band leader, 1888–93.

COUSTAUT, SYLVESTER (c). b. N.O., before Civil War; d. N.O., about 1910. Founding member of the Onward Brass Band, 1886. Played in dance band led jointly by his brother, Manuel, and Daniel Desdoumes, 1890.

31

OCTAVE CROSBY

PAUL CRAWFORD

COYCAULT, ERNEST "NENNY" (c). b. Violet, La., about 1890. Left N.O. in 1914, but between 1908 and that time worked with Peerless Orchestra under Bab Frank, with Superior Orchestra, and with Gaspard brothers. Brother of Pill Coycault.

COYCAULT, JEROME "PILL" (cl). b. Violet, La., about 1895; d. Cleveland, Ohio, Oct. 4, 1928. Crippled; often worked with Buddy Petit. Had jobs with N.O. Creole Jazz Band under Amos White and with Peter Lacaze for dance hall work. Actually played in N.O. for only three years, 1919–21.

COZZENS, JIMMY (d). b. N.O., about 1898. Dixielander active in 20's and 30's, especially with Alfred Laine.

CRAIS, WILLIAM J. "BILL" (tb). b. N.O., June 20, 1927. Attorney, now living in Rochester, N.Y. Popular dixielander of the 50's and early 60's with Al Hirt, Pete Fountain, Sharkey. Operated Vieux Carre Record Shop, Bourbon and St. Peter sts.

CRAWFORD, PAUL (tb, sb, tu, l, arr). b. Atmore, Ala., Feb. 16, 1925. Co-leader of Crawford-Ferguson

Night Owls. Began jazz career in the '50's. Made first recording session in 1957 with Lakefront Loungers on GHB. Periodically seen with Punch Miller at Preservation Hall. Works in the jazz archive at Tulane University and frequently makes musical arrangements for out-of-town bands. Mainly known as trombonist.

CREGER, BILL (cl, s). b. N.O., about 1900; d. N.O., July 26, 1927. Dixielander worked with Johnny Bayersdorffer in post-World War I era.

CROMBIE, ALONZO (d, tb). b. N.O., about 1895. Dixieland-style drummer active in N.O. in post-World War I years. Mainly identified with Norman Brownlee Orchestra and with Emmett Hardy.

CROSBY, OCTAVE (p). b. N.O., June 10, 1898. From 1953 to 1962 a fixture at the Paddock on Bourbon St. as bandleader. Began his career with Herb Morand about 1922. Soon organized own combination.

JOE DARENSBOURG

PERCY DARENSBURG

CRUMB, EARL (d, l). b. N.O., April 30, 1899. Invincibles String Band, Six and 7/8 String Band. Leader of famous N.O. Owls, 1920–28.

CRUMP, FRANK (s). b. N.O., about 1903; d. N.O., 1957. Worked with Chris Kelly in mid-20's. During depression years was in Crescent City Serenaders Orchestra led by Albert Walters. Was in ERA Orchestra in 1935.

CUNY, FRANK (p). b. N.O., Dec. 14, 1890; d. N.O., 1966. Played with Tony Parenti, Johnny DeDroit, 1917–28.

DALMADO, TONY (t). b. N.O., Oct. 25, 1918. Trumpet player on outstanding Keynote session with Irving Fazola.

DARENSBOURG, JOE (cl, ts). b. Baton Rouge, La., July 9, 1906. Career began in 1924 with Martel's family band of Opelousas. He then went to work traveling with a medicine show playing to attract attention to the "medicine man's" pitch. In the late 20's with Fate Marable and worked for a while on the riverboats. Through the 40's and 50's he was identified with the Kid Ory band in California. Under his own name made the record of "Yellow Dog Blues" which became the nation's overnight juke-box favorite.

DARENSBURG, CAFFREY (bjo, g). b. N.O., about 1880; d. Texas, late 20's. Virtuoso soloist. Sometimes with A. J. Piron, Manuel Perez.

DARENSBURG, PERCY (bjo, g, mdl). b. N.O., about 1882. Played banjo on 1928 discs under name of Frenchy's String Band, a quartet (Johnny St. Cyr, Tommy Ladnier, Lonnie Johnson).

DARENSBURG, WILLIE (t, c, v). b. N.O., about 1885.

SID DAVILLA

DAVE, JOHNNY (bjo). b. N.O., about 1898; d. N.O., about 1943. Banjo player on the historic Sam Morgan disc sessions of 1927. During depression with Kid Milton and in nickel-a-dance palaces with Alphonse Picou.

DAVILLA, SID (cl, s). b. N.O., Sept. 9, 1915. For many years musician-owner of the Mardi Gras Lounge on Bourbon St. Veteran of swing band era.

DAVIS, GEORGE (d). b. Algiers, La., about 1875. Bass drummer with the Pacific Brass Band from 1900 to beginning of World War I. Sometimes played with Allen Brass Band.

DAVIS, HOWARD (s). b. N.O., about 1900. Played in dance groups during 20's; sometimes marched with Louis Dumaine's Brass Band. Was in ERA Orchestra in 1935 and WPA Brass Band in 1936, both under Dumaine direction. In 1962 was still playing parades sponsored by NOJC of Southern California.

DAVIS, SAMMY (p). b. N.O., about 1881. Reputed to be one of the fastest hot piano players in history. Played in the district's brothels from 1897 to 1915. Was still going strong in mid-50's in upstate New York night clubs.

DAVIS, STUART (sb). b. N.O., about 1927. Played with Celestin band.

HAROLD DEJAN

DAWSON, EDDIE (sb). b. N.O., July 24, 1884; d. Memphis, Tenn., Aug. 12, 1972. A favorite of King Oliver, he played with him in pre-World War I years in Storyville. Jobbed around town all his life. Frequently seen in the 50's playing at Mama Lou's in Little Woods with Peter Bocage.

BUGLIN' SAM DEKEMEL

LOUIS NELSON DELISLE
(Big Eye Louis Nelson)

JACK DELANEY

DECOU, WALTER (p). b. N.O., about 1890; d. N.O., Dec. 12, 1966. Band piano player in N.O. during Storyville days. Led own group during 20's at cabarets. He is on the Sam Morgan records of 1927. Recorded with Bunk Johnson.

DEDROIT, JOHNNY (t). b. N.O., Dec. 4, 1892. Leader of a popular dance band for nearly forty years.

DEDROIT, PAUL (d, x). b. N.O., Dec. 24, 1894; d. Los Angeles, Calif., Jan. 2, 1963. Mainly in theater pit

bands, with Emile Tosso, and in brother Johnny's band.

DEICHMANN, BENNY (tb). b. N.O., 1893, d. N.O. Jan. 13, 1939. Dixieland pioneer worked with Jack Laine bands and with the Barocco brothers. In 20's was on the lake steamer, *Susquehanna*.

DEICHMANN, CHARLES (v, c, l). b. N.O., Oct. 12, 1894; d. N.O. Oct. 3, 1927. A major bandleader before W W I. Held many carnival ball contracts, and his Moonlight Serenaders were the house band at the Tudor. He was a concert-trained musician, but pioneered with a dixieland band in New York almost simultaneously with the ODJB. Brother of Benny.

DEJAN, HAROLD (s). b. N.O., Feb. 4, 1909. Usually a leader of small rhythm and blues type groups. Played in his brother Leo's Moonlight Serenaders as a teenager, about 1918. In 30's was leading a band on the lake steamers. During 50's was frequently in the Young Tuxedo Brass Band. Leads brass band of his own, the Young Olympia.

DEJAN, LEO (t). b. N.O., May 4, 1911. At 15 led his own band, the Moonlight Serenaders. Later in the 20's led a group he called the Black Diamond Orchestra.

DEKEMEL, MATTHEW ANTOINE DESIRE (bugle, vo). b. N.O., about 1900; d. Jan. 6, 1967. Known at "Buglin Sam, the Waffle Man." Dekemel's bizarre specialty was playing jazz tunes on a regulation army bugle. He was featured for years in Tony Almerico's Parisian Room broadcasts and has been adequately recorded.

DE LA HOUSSAYE, FRANK (p). b. N.O. ——. The Last Straws.

DELANDRY, FRANK (g). b. N.O., about 1888. A virtuoso who worked in the brothels of Storyville where music was desired but no piano was available, about 1900.

DELANEY, JACK (tb). b. N.O., Aug. 27, 1930; d. N.O., 1976. With Tony Almerico and Sharkey in 50's. Played with Leon Kellner's Orchestra in the Roosevelt Hotel during 60's.

DELAY, MIKE (t). b. N.O., Sept. 29, 1909. Dance band leader of 30's. The Hollywood Orchestra of N.O. Member of Johnny St. Cyr's band, Disneyland, 1966.

DELISLE, BAPTISTE (tb). b. N.O., about 1868; d. N.O. about 1920. Joined Onward Brass Band about 1890; John Robichaux in 1894. Delisle and entire unit of members of Onward Brass Band enlisted for Spanish-American War. Rejoined Robichaux in 1905 after long illness.

DELISLE, LOUIS NELSON "BIG EYE LOUIS" (cl, sb, bjo, acc). b. N.O., Jan. 28, 1885; d. N.O., Aug. 20, 1949. Known as Big Eye Louis Nelson. One of all-time great jazzmen. Studied with the Tios. Worked in Storyville from age 15. Led own Ninth Ward Band. Joined Imperial Orchestra, 1907; Superior Orchestra, 1910. In 1916 replaced George Baquet to tour U.S. with Original Creole Orchestra. Recorded well past his prime, 1940 and 1949. Played spot jobs and "jitney" joints through 30's and 40's.

DELROSE, HAROLD (s). b. N.O. ——. Played in Pop Hamilton's orchestra in the early depression years.

DELROSE, HENRY (cl).

DENT, LAWRENCE (cl). b. N.O. ——. With Gibson Brass Band. Nephew of Johnny and Baby Dodds.

DEPASS, ARNOLD (d). b. N.O., about 1900; d. N.O., about 1945. Led small combinations in the district during pre-World War I years. After coming out of service, played with Jack Carey, Chris Kelly, Buddy Petit, and Kid Rena. Mainly played with Punch Miller, 1920–27. Until depression days, led own group, the Olympia Orchestra, 1927–32. Gave up music about 1934.

DEPASS, DAVE (cl). b. N.O., about 1888. Older brother of Arnold Depass, the drummer. Played in Magnolia Orchestra in 1910.

DERBIGNY, ARTHUR (t, s). b. N.O., about 1906; d. N.O., Oct. 20, 1962. With Young Superior Orchestra, mid-20's, on trumpet; and with Bebé Ridgley's Original Tuxedo Orchestra on saxophone, 1925.

DESDUNES, CLARENCE (v. bjo, l). b. N.O., 1896; d. Arizona, about 1934. Concert-trained bandleader. With help of A. J. Piron, formed The Joyland Revelers, a successful big band employing many prominent jazzmen during 20's mainly touring the South. Active during late 20's, early 30's. Well known throughout midwest, especially in Omaha, Nebraska.

DESVIGNE, SIDNEY (t). b. N.O., Sept. 11, 1893; d. Los Angeles, Calif., Dec. 2, 1959. Although leader of a large swing orchestra of the 30's, Desvigne was an excellent jazz musician. Began at Rice Cafe and 101 Ranch in the district, 1917; later with Maple Leaf Orchestra and Excelsior Brass Band. With Fate Marable on S.S. Capitol, 1922. Through most of 20's, led own band on the Island Queen, New Orleans–Cincinnati. Moved to California in 1946.

DIAZ, HORACE (p). b. N.O., about 1906. Played with Leon Prima, Jules Bauduc.

DIENTRANS, PETE (t). b. N.O., about 1882. Pre-WW I dixieland musician. Worked with Jack Laine, Frank Christian, Bill Gallaty, Sr.

DIMES, BILL (cl). b. N.O., about 1895. Played for and managed the Liberty Bell Orchestra, 1919–20.

DINKEL, WILBUR (p). b. N.O., about 1880; d. April 8, 1940. Early dixielander with Tony Parenti. Also in pit band at Dauphine Theater.

DODDS, JOHNNY (cl). b. N.O., April 12, 1892; d. Chicago, Ill., Aug. 8, 1940. Widely considered the greatest of N.O. clarinets. Pupil of Lorenzo Tio, Jr. Began

HORACE DIAZ

JOHNNY DODDS

BABY DODDS

NATTY DOMINIQUE

professional career about 1910 with Frank Duson's Eagle Band. Worked with Ory. Left N.O. in 1918 with Billy Mack vaudeville troupe. Joined King Oliver in Chicago. Led own group, 1924–30. Member of Louis Armstrong's Hot Five recording group. Accurate biography of Dodds in "Kings of Jazz" paperback series, A. S. Barnes & Co.

DODDS, WARREN "BABY" (d). b. N.O., Dec. 24, 1896; d. Chicago, Ill., Feb. 14, 1959. King of N.O. drummers. Brother of Johnny. Musically trained by Walter Brundy, Dave Perkins, Manuel Manetta. From 1913 to 1918 worked with Celestin, Jack Carey, Willie Hightower, Louis Delisle. On steamers *Sidney*, *St. Paul* and *Capitol* under Fate Marable. Joined Oliver on tour in California, 1921, and jobbed around Chicago for next 15 years. Widely recorded, mainly with Jelly Roll Morton, Louis Armstrong. Joined Bunk Johnson band in 1944. Worked in New York through 1949, mainly at Jimmy Ryan's, with weekend concerts at Stuyvesant Casino, the Central Plaza, and at the Philadelphia Academy of Music, in Al Rose's "Journeys Into Jazz." Made series of dem-

onstration drum recordings for students. Excellent autobiography, Contemporary Press, Los Angeles.

DOLLIOLE, MILFORD (d). b. N.O., Oct. 23, 1903. Member of the Young Tuxedo Orchestra in the early 20's. Retired from music about 1950 after having played for many years in lakefront resorts.

DOMINGUEZ, PAUL, JR. (v, g). b. N.O., about 1887. Concert musician, but played jazz in the Storyville cabarets. Was with Armstrong in 1923 at Anderson's on Rampart St. In California in 1965.

DOMINGUEZ, PAUL, SR. (sb). b. N.O., about 1865; d. ——. A classical musician who frequently played jobs with jazzmen. Did not pluck, but bowed the string bass. Frequently seen with John Robichaux in early 1900's.

DOMINIQUE, ALBERT (t). b. N.O., 1909. Nephew of Natty Dominique. Known as Don Albert. Trained by Lorenzo Tio, Jr., and Milford Piron. Led swing band based in San Antonio, Texas, during 30's. Southland Records with Louis Cottrell, Jr., Paul Barbarin. Lives in Texas. Recorded with Alamo City Jazz Band in San Antonio, 1962.

DOMINIQUE, ANATIE "NATTY" (t). b. N.O., Aug. 2, 1896. Career mainly tied to the Dodds brothers in

Chicago. Played little in N.O. before his family moved north. In 1925 was with J. Dodds at Kelly's Stables. Played a concert in 1965. Uncle of Don Albert.

DON, WESLEY (t). N.O., about 1892; d. Baton Rouge, La., 1934. Leader of the Liberty Bell Orchestra, 1919–20. Excellent trumpet man whose career was cut short by an auto accident.

DORIA, AL, SR. (d). b. N.O., Dec. 24, 1899; d. May 26, 1977. Dixieland drummer who worked with most of top musicians in this field of jazz from 1920. Worked in band instrument department at Werlein's music store in N.O.

DOUROUX FAMILY. A large family of musicians which has been supplying jazz, dance and concert music in the New Orleans area for a century. Its distinguished membership includes Dolly Adams and her sons Placide and Jerry. The Manettas, too, are part of this clan.

DUCONGE, ALBERT (t). b. N.O., about 1895. Member of great early jazz family. Played with Fate Marable on S.S. *Capitol*, 1925, and briefly with Sidney Desvigne on the *Island Queen*.

DUCONGE, OSCAR (c). b. Napoleonville, La., about 1870; d. about 1924. Early member of the Onward Brass Band, 1890. Entire band enlisted at time of Spanish-American War. Later led dance band in which Alphonse Picou played.

DUCONGE, PETE (cl). b. N.O., about 1900. Played on Streckfus steamers in early 20's.

DUCIE, "RED" (p). With N.O. Creole Jazz Band under Amos White in mid-20's, playing at Spanish Fort.

DUHÉ, LAWRENCE (cl). b. LaPlace, La., April 30, 1887; d. Lafayette, La., 1959. Made jazz debut in N.O. in 1913, coming from hometown with friend, Kid Ory. Became leader same year at 101 Ranch and studied with Lorenzo Tio, Jr. Left N.O. for Chicago in 1917, led band at Deluxe Cafe, 1917–19. After brief tour in vaudeville returned to Louisiana. Played in small towns with Evan Thomas' band. Retired from music in 1944.

LAWRENCE DUHÉ

LOUIS DUMAINE

FRANKIE DUSON

MAURICE DURAND

SAM DUTREY, JR.

DUKE, CHARLIE (d). b. N.O., Aug. 23, 1913; d. N.O., Nov. 4, 1973. Dixielander usually associated with Basin Street Six, George Girard in 50's.

DUMAINE, LOUIS (c, t). b. N.O., about 1890; d. N.O., about 1949. From 1922 to his death usually worked as a leader. Played in Tuxedo Brass Band in early and mid-20's. Also had own marching band. Led WPA Band in 1935, ERA Orchestra in 1936, and during depression years was partner of Fats Houston in a dance band. His Jazzola Eight made some early jazz discs.

DUPONT, CHARLES (t, sb). b. N.O., Oct. 20, 1907. Active dixielander; was business agent of AFM local 174 during 50's. Played Fairhope, Ala., with Von Gammon, 1965.

DURAND, MAURICE (t). b. N.O., July 4, 1893; d. Calif., Nov. 23, 1961. Played in Onward and Tuxedo brass bands in 20's. Also led own dance band through this period. Known to have been an exceptional technician. Resided in California.

DUSON, FRANK (vt). b. Algiers, La., 1881; d. N.O., April 1, 1936. Early 1900's with Buddy Bolden. Took over Bolden band in 1907 when Bolden was committed to mental institution. Active musically until the mid-30's. On S.S. *Capitol* and with own band at cabarets and Thom's Road House. In mid-depression was in the ERA Orchestra. Worked irregularly with Louis Dumaine.

DUTREY, HONORE (tb). b. N.O., 1894; d. Chicago, Ill., July 21, 1937. Started with Melrose Brass Band at 17. Worked with brother, Sam, in Silver Leaf Orchestra; with Noone-Petit Orchestra, 1913. Lungs injured in accident during World War I. Joined King Oliver in Chicago from 1919–24. Also worked through late 20's with Carroll Dickerson, Johnny Dodds, and in 1927 for Louis Armstrong.

DUTREY, SAM, SR. (cl, s). b. N.O., 1888; d. N.O., 1941. Silver Leaf Orchestra, 1907; Tulane Orchestra, 1915; Papa Celestin, 1916; S.S. *Capitol* orchestra, 1920. With Eddie Jackson's dance band in early 20's and with John Robichaux at the Lyric Theater in 1925. Brother of Honore.

DUTREY, SAM, JR. (cl). b. N.O., about 1915; d. N.O., Aug. 26, 1971. Occasionally played parade jobs and dances. Recorded on Southland records. Worked with Joe Robichaux in 30's.

40

DADDY EDWARDS

CHARLES ELGAR

EARLY, TOM (sb). b. N.O., about 1880; d. N.O., Sept. 8, 1958. Dixieland man, worked irregularly. Led Harmony Band.

EASTWOOD, BILL (bjo, g, s). b. N.O. Aug. 31, 1899; d. N.O., about 1960. With Norman Brownlee in early 20's. Also in 20's with Halfway House Orchestra. In later years was business agent for the American Guild of Variety Artists.

EDWARDS, EDDIE "DADDY" (v, tb). b. N.O., May 22, 1891; d. New York, N.Y., April 9, 1963. About 1910 was playing violin for silent movie theaters. Began trombone in 1914 in parades. With Ernest Giardina Orchestra, 1914. Played in Reliance Brass Band with Nick La Rocca. The two founded the Original Dixieland Jazz Band, 1916. Edwards quit music about 1925 but played with this group when it was revived in the 30's. Recorded with his own band for Commodore in the 40's.

EDWARDS, PAUL (d). b. N.O., Aug. 6, 1916. Dixieland rhythm man with George Girard, Sharkey, Santo through 50's. With Pete Fountain group.

EDWARDS, WILLY (c). d. ——. With A. J. Piron Orchestra in 1920.

EIERMANN, EDWARD "LEFTY" (sb, tu). b. N.O., about 1894; d. N.O., May 27, 1971. Worked with Happy Schilling from 1915 through World War I and remained active until the early 40's.

ELGAR, CHARLES (v). b. N.O., June 13, 1879. Classically trained musician who played only occasionally with jazzmen. Worked at the Tuxedo Dance Hall in pre-World War I days and emigrated to Chicago in 1913. Began to book bands and later became active in the union movement.

ELLERBUSCH, JOE (tb). b. N.O. ——. Pre-World War I dixielander.

ESPOSITO, ALEX (g, mdl). b. N.O., about 1880; d. N.O., about 1951. Played in Regal ragtime band in 1904.

41

ALEX ESPOSITO

HOMER EUGENE

EUGENE, HOMER (tb, bjo, s). b. N.O., June 16, 1914. Brother of Wendell. Frequently seen in bands led by Peter Bocage and has paraded with the Young Tuxedo Brass Band.

EUGENE, WENDELL (tb). b. N.O., Oct. 12, 1923. Nephew of Albert Burbank and Paul Barbarin. First job with Kid Howard, 1938. With Celestin, George Lewis. Toured with the Lucky Millinder and Buddy Johnson orchestras.

EVANS, ROY (d). b. Lafayette, La., about 1890; d. about 1943. Played drums on famed second session of Sam Morgan band in fall of 1927. With Earl Humphrey, 1920; Buddy Petit, 1920; Red Allen, 1927.

FAZOLA, IRVING "FAZ" (cl). b. N.O., Dec. 10, 1912; d. N.O., Feb. 20, 1949. Legally named Irving Prestopnik. In 20's at Fern Cafe No. 2. With Armand Hug, Julian Laine; played in N.O. with Louis Prima, Candy Candido. Later toured with Ben Pollack, Gus Arnheim, Glenn Miller, Bob Crosby, Muggsy Spanier, Tiny Thornhill. Recorded with Sharkey, Billie Holiday, and under own name. Well known for records with the Bobcats.

FEDERICO, FRANK (g, vo). b. N.O., about 1908. With many top dixieland stars during professional life. Especially identified with Leon Prima, 20's; Louis Prima, 30's; and through the 50's with Tony Almerico. Also worked with regular dance bands.

FERGUSON, LEONARD (d, l). b. Harriman, Tenn., May 2, 1923. Co-leader of the Crawford-Ferguson Night Owls, a band which has the widest repertoire of jazz classics in New Orleans. In '65–'66 on steamer *President*, Saturday nights.

FERRER, EDWARD HARRY "MOSE" (p, v). b. Biloxi, Miss., Feb. 12, 1894. One of the Invincibles. Founding member of N.O. Owls. Left N.O., 1915, to join Tom Brown's band in Chicago. Musical career only from 1914 to 1925.

FERRER, FRANK WILLIAM (p, g, v, uk). b. N.O., July 17, 1896. Veteran of Invincibles and N.O. Owls. Active only from 1919 to 1923. Now successful Lake Charles, La. banker. Brother of Mose Ferrer.

FIELDS, FRANK (sb, tu). b. Plaquemine, La., May 2, 1914. Began with Claiborne Williams band in Donaldsonville, La. Worked with Papa Celestin and in Navy band. In 1965 was with Albert French's band.

FIELDS, MERCEDES GARMAN (p). b. N.O., d. N.O., Nov. 14, 1967. With Celestin in 30's and 40's.

FILHE, GEORGE (tb). b. N.O., Nov. 13, 1872; d. Chicago, Ill., 1954. Started with Coustaut-Desdoumes Orchestra, 1892. Played 18 years with Onward Brass Band, 1893–1911. Peerless Orchestra, about 1903–04; Imperial Orchestra, 1905. Went to Chicago in 1913 after several years in Storyville. During early 20's worked with Oliver, Perez, Sidney Bechet, Lawrence Duhé. In late 20's worked in pit at Grand Theater in

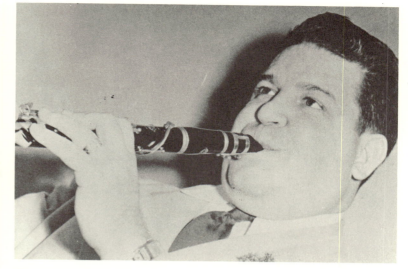

IRVING FAZOLA

LEONARD FERGUSON

Chicago. Dave Peyton's Orchestra. Retired from music at beginning of depression.

FISCHER, JOHNNY. See Phillips, John Henry, Sr.

FORD, HENRY (sb). b. N.O., about 1878; d. N.O. about 1919. String band musician of turn-of-century era. Louis Nelson Delisle started with Ford's group in 1903. Ford played in a dance band with Alphonse Picou and Bouboul Valentin in the early 1900's. Later led own band on Delacroix Island, La., 1908–12.

FOSTER, ABBEY "CHINEE" (d, vo). b. N.O., 1900; d. N.O., Sept. 8, 1962. Chinee is ranked with the all-time great Crescent City drummers. Started career in Storyville, playing for Bebe Ridgley's Tuxedo Orchestra. Associated with Buddy Petit from 1915 in Eagle Band through 1931. Recorded with Celestin, 1927. He was reactivated by Allen and Sandra Jaffe and had reached a new success at Preservation Hall at the time of his death.

FOSTER, "DUDE" (t). b. N.O., about 1890; d. N.O., about 1958. Foster Lewis Jazz Band, 1922; Young Tuxedo Orchestra, 1916; Kid Avery Orchestra, 1946.

FOSTER, EARL (d). b. N.O., about 1902. Busy jazz band leader of the 20's. Played in groups led by

GEORGE FILHE

Percy and Willie Humphrey during depression.

FOSTER, GEORGE "POPS" (sb, tu). b. McCall, La., May 19, 1892; d. San Francisco, Oct. 29, 1969. Joined stringed trio in 1906; Magnolia Orchestra in 1908. Till World War I worked in Olympia Brass Band, the Eagle Band, and with Kid Ory. In 1919 joined Fate Marable on S.S. *Capitol.* With Charlie Creath, 1921.

POPS FOSTER

ABBEY FOSTER

With Ory in California, 1920's. Worked with big bands through late 20's and 30's, especially with Louis Armstrong's. During 40's was featured on Mutual Radio Network in "This Is Jazz." Probably most recorded of all bass players. In 40's and early 50's played many concerts in New York and at Al Rose's "Journeys Into Jazz" concerts at the Philadelphia Academy of Music. About 1953 moved to California to play in Earl Hines-led jazz band. In 1966 toured Europe.

FOSTER, WILLIE (bjo, v, g). b. McCall, La., Dec. 27, 1888. Brother of the famed bass player Pops Foster. Willie frequently worked with his brother in N.O.; during 1910–13 they were in the cabarets of the district with King Oliver. During the 20's he worked the riverboats under both Sidney Desvigne and Fate Marable, recording with the latter's band for Okeh in 1924.

FOUCHÉ, EARL (s, cl). b. N.O., Feb. 5, 1903. With Young Morgan Band, 1925; Sam Morgan Band, 1926. With Ridgley's Tuxedo Orchestra during early depression years. With Don Albert's big band, 1937,

1938. Migrated to California after World War I. Nephew of Willie and Papa John Joseph.

FOUGERAT, TONY (c, t). b. N.O., April 25, 1900. A popular dixieland bandleader from the early 20's to 1966.

FOUNTAIN, PETE (cl, s). b. N.O., July 3, 1930. Once a member of the Dukes of Dixieland and star of the Basin Street Six during the 50's. Fountain became world renowned through the success deriving from his appearances on the Lawrence Welk TV show, during the late 50's.

FRANCIS, ALBERT (d). b. N.O., March 24, 1894. Active musician from early 20's, he once played with Louis Armstrong at Anderson's on Rampart St. In later years he was seen at Mama Lou's or the Happy Landing, and as late as the 60's made appearances in Preservation Hall.

FRANCIS, EDNA. See Mitchell, Edna.

FRANK, ALCIDE (v). b. N.O., about 1875; d. 1942. Leader of the Golden Rule Orchestra in 1905 at

44

PETE FOUNTAIN

JOSIAH "CIÉ" FRAZIER

WILLIE FOSTER

Fewclothes Cabaret in the district. Brother of piccolo player, Bab Frank.

FRANK, GILBERT "BAB" (pc, f). b. N.O., about 1870; d. St. Louis, Mo., June, 1933. Leader of the Peerless Orchestra in early 1900's. Made solo appearances with John Robichaux. Migrated to Chicago in 1919 and worked briefly at the Deluxe Cafe with Lawrence Duhé.

FRANKLIN, HENRY "CAREFUL" (cl). b. N.O., 1903; d. N.O., Aug. 12, 1969. A part-time musician of excellent ability. Late teens with King Oliver, Louis Armstrong. Played in early 20's with Yank Johnson. With Gibson Brass Band in early 60's.

FRANKS, "BUNNY" (sb). b. N.O., Sept. 17, 1914. Manager and bass player for the Basin Street Six during the 50's.

FRANZELLA, SAL (cl). b. N.O., Apr. 25, 1915; d. N.O., Nov. 8, 1968. First professional job in Saenger Theater pit band, 1930. Spent six years working with local dance bands, then on tour with Benny Meroff, 1936; Isham Jones, 1937; Paul Whiteman, 1938. Later was involved with concert and studio work, mainly in Hollywood.

45

ALBERT FRENCH

FRAZIER, JOSIAH "CIÉ" (d). b. N.O. Feb. 23, 1904. Veteran of the best-known dance bands of the city. Played with A. J. Piron, Sidney Desvigne, John Robichaux, Papa Celestin. Made his first records with Celestin in 1927. Started professionally about 1921 with Lawrence Marrero. Was in the Young Tuxedo band in 1923. Worked in the ERA and WPA bands in the mid-30's and with all the leading brass bands of his time. In recent years associated with Emma Barrett, the Humphrey brothers, and Billie and Dee Dee Pierce with whom he has made frequent tours.

FRENCH, ALBERT (bjo). b. N.O., Nov. 16, 1910. Outstanding banjo rhythm man always identified with Celestin groups during his career.

FRENCH, BEHRMAN (bjo). b. N.O. about 1900. With Brownlee's band in early 20's. Played with Emmett Hardy.

FRENCH, MAURICE (tb). b. LaPlace, La., about 1890. One of the great pre-World War I virtuosi, played with Kid Rena in the early 20's. Lyons Brass Band, 1928–30.

FRISCO, JOHNNY (d). b. N.O., June 23, 1895; d. N.O., July 15, 1969. Played in school with Larry Shields, Clem Camp. By 1915 was Schilling's regular drummer and assistant manager of the band. Associated with Schilling for 30 years.

FROEBA, FRANK, JR. (p). b. N.O., about 1904. Son of a "legitimate" musician, Froeba was a boy wonder of the keyboard much in demand for theater work. He played some jobs in the 20's with Johnny Wiggs's and John Tobin's band, but hit the road to re-emerge as pianist with the big Benny Goodman band of 1935. Has worked in recent years at the Gold Coast night club in Hollywood Beach, Fla., and is widely recorded as a soloist. Also played with Johnny De-Droit.

GABRIEL, ALBERT (cl). b. Algiers, La., about 1875; d. ——. Trained musician. With Tom Albert, 1910; Pacific Brass Band, 1910–12. Worked with some ragtime bands to 1912. Last jobs in band led by Manuel Manetta.

GABRIEL, CLARENCE (g, bjo, p). b. N.O., June 3, 1905; d. N.O., 1973. With Louis Dumaine in late 20's. Toured with Sam Morgan. With Mike Delay at Lavida. Spent depression days working in nickel-a-dance places.

BILL GALLATY, SR.

46

LOUIS GALLAUD

VON GAMMON

GABRIEL, MANNY (cl). b. N.O., about 1897.

GAGLIARDI, NICK (tb). b. New York, June 22, 1921. Regular with the Last Straws.

GALLATY, BILL, SR., (vt). b. N.O., Nov. 9, 1880; d. N.O., Sept. 29, 1943. Standout star of Reliance Brass Band. Said by Papa Laine to have been greatest of all trombone players. Led own band before World War I.

GALLATY, BILL, JR. (t). b. N.O., Oct. 23, 1910. Son of Papa Laine's legendary trombonist. Became active dixielander, notably with Santo Pecora. Worked in swing bands of the 30's, with Charley Bourgeois, Joe Petrie.

GALLAUD, LOUIS (p). N.O., Feb. 27, 1897. Frequently at Milneburg in 20's. Luthjen's with Big Eye Louis in 40's. Often with Kid Howard, Albert Burbank.

GALLE, JULES (cl). b. N.O., about 1903. With Brunies brothers band in Biloxi-Gulfport area during the 50's.

GALLOWAY, CHARLIE "SWEET LOVIN" (g). b. N.O., during Civil War; d. N.O., about 1916. Polio-paralyzed Galloway was playing on the street for tips in the mid-80's. Became extraordinarily skilled instrumentalist. Led ragtime band in the 90's. Played frequently with Buddy Bolden.

GAMMON, WILLIAM A. "VON" (d, vib). b. N.O., July 12, 1905; d. Fairhope, Ala., March 25, 1974. Johnny Wiggs, Sharkey, Santo Pecora, Hal Jordy bands. Was with combo, Grand Hotel, Fairhope.

GARLAND, ED "MONTUDIE" (sb, tu, bd). b. N.O., Jan. 9, 1895. Already an active parade drummer at 13. Worked with Frankie Duson's Eagle Band, 1910, on bass drum; and with Excelsior Brass Band on tuba. In 1911 was with Perez' Imperial Orchestra on string bass. Also played regularly in the same year in Joseph Petit's Security Brass Band. Left town in 1913 and worked with Lawrence Duhé at the Deluxe Cafe, then with Freddie Keppard, Manuel Perez. Joined Oliver in 1916 for a five-year hitch which took him to California. During the early de-

47

ED GARLAND

RENE GELPI

GEORGE GIRARD

pression years, he led a band of his own, The One-Eleven Jazz Band. In the early forties participated in the Kid Ory-led revival. Living in Los Angeles, 1966.

GASPARD, ED (d). b. N.O., about 1877; d. ——. Sometimes played bass drum for Onward Brass Band and Excelsior Brass Band prior to Spanish-American War. Best known to early musicians as a teacher. Younger brother of Oak and Vic Gaspard.

GASPARD, NELSON OCTAVE "OAK" (sb). b. N.O., about 1870; d. Dallas, Texas ——. Mainly a concert musician. Played with Peerless Orchestra, 1903–13. Earlier was in Piron-Gaspard Orchestra led by his father and A. J. Piron's father. Between 1913 and 1917 with John Robichaux. In 1920, with brother, Vic, organized Maple Leaf Orchestra which operated until Oak emigrated to Texas early in the depression.

GASPARD, VIC (tb, bh). b. N.O., April 14, 1875; d. N.O., Aug. 27, 1957. Worked in Onward Brass Band, to 1910, and in the Peerless Orchestra. Sometimes marched with Excelsior Brass Band with John Robi-

chaux, 1913–17, 1926–30. From 1917 to 1926 worked with his brother, Oak, as co-leader of the Maple Leaf Orchestra. Retired from music at start of depression.

GELPI, RENE (g, bjo [5-str.]). b. N.O., March 18, 1904. First with Invincibles String Band; later with N.O. Owls. Became prominent architect.

GERBRECHT, "PINKY" (t, l). b. N.O., 1901; d. Nov. 29, 1963. Pioneer dixielander. Recorded early with Naylor's Seven Aces. Participated in first live music broadcast from N.O. in 1923.

GEROSA, JOE (g). b. N.O. ——. Pre-World War I dixielander.

GIARDINA, ERNEST (v, vo). b. N.O., about 1870. Leader of early ragtime band. Played in Frank Christian's ragtime band.

GIARDINA, TONY (cl). b. N.O., 1897; d. N.O., about 1956. Jazz pioneer played with Reliance Brass Band before World War I. Frequently played in groups led by the Brunies brothers and with members of the Original Dixieland Jazz Band. Also with Frank Christian's ragtime band.

GIBSON, JIM (bjo).

GILBERT, VERNON (t). b. N.O. ——. Member of Young Tuxedo Brass Band in 40's.

48

TONY GIARDINA

BOOKER T. GLASS

GILLEN, BILL (t). b. N.O., about 1903. With N.O. Swing Kings in 20's; 30's with Arodin, Cordilla, Joe Capraro.

GILLIN, MIKE (d). b. N.O., about 1868; d. ——. Founding member of Onward Brass Band and its first bass drummer, 1889.

GILMORE, EDDIE (sb). b. N.O., about 1897. With the Liberty Bell Band, 1920; with N.O. Creole Jazz Band under Amos White, 1923. Played briefly with John Robichaux.

GIRARD, GEORGE (t). b. Jefferson Parish, La., Oct. 7, 1930; d. N.O., Jan. 18, 1957. Pupil of Johnny Wiggs. Toured with Jimmy Archer Orchestra, 1946, at age 16. Featured along with Pete Fountain in Basin Street Six, 1950–54. Organized own band for Famous Door, 1954. His N.O. Five played opposite the Dukes of Dixieland. Had weekly CBS broadcast. Recorded with Phil Zito, Basin Street Six, and own band. Was featured at Los Angeles Jazz Jubilee, 1955, with Raymond Burke, Johnny St. Cyr.

GLAPION, RAYMOND (g). b. N.O., about 1895. A "reading" musician usually employed during World War I at the lakefront resorts, mainly with the Gaspards

or with Paul and Emile Barnes. Was in Polo Barnes's big traveling dance orchestra in 1932.

GLASS, BOOKER T. (d). b. N.O., Aug. 10, 1888. One of the great brass band bass drummers. Pupil of Ed Gaspard. Began with Holcamp's touring carnival in 1908. With Camelia Brass Band, 1918; Wooden Joe Nicholas, 1918–19; Johnny Predonce's dance orchestra, 1920. With Eureka Brass Band, 60's.

GLASS, NOWELL (d). b. N.O., May 18, 1927. Played with George Williams, Theo Riley brass bands. Eureka Brass Band, 1966. Son of Booker T. Glass.

GLENNY, ALBERT (acc, bd, tu, sb). b. N.O., March 25, 1870; d. N.O., June 11, 1958. For 75 years an active jazzman. Played bass drum in Bolden's marching band in 1901. Played with virtually all the great names of N.O. jazz. During the depression was with WPA and ERA bands. Considered by musicians among the greatest of all bass players.

GOLDSTON, CHRISTOPHER "BLACK HAPPY" (d). b. N.O., Nov. 27, 1894; d. March 17, 1968. Started before World War I in Tulane Orchestra; with Crescent Orchestra, 1917; with Golden Leaf Band, 1920–21;

ALBERT GLENNY

HAPPY GOLDSTON

Onward Brass Band, 1922; WPA Brass Band in mid-30's. With Papa Celestin after World War II. Later, to 1955, at the Paddock with Bill Matthews and Octave Crosby.

GONSOULIN, TOMMY (t). b. Opelousas, La., Feb. 12, 1910. Worked mainly in traveling swing bands.

GOODSON, SADIE (p). b. Pensacola, Fla., about 1900. Well known in 20's as pianist for Buddy Petit's band, especially during its run on the S.S. *Madison*. Also in the band was her husband Chinee Foster. Played cabaret jobs during 30's with Kid Rena. Also for dances with Alec Bigard. Sister of Billie Pierce.

GORDET, ALLEN "HUNTER" (ts). b. N.O., about 1905; d. N.O., 1954 Played trumpet with Joe Gable during mid 20's. Reeds with ERA Orchestra during depression days. Brother-in-law of Wilbert Tillman.

GORMAN, ISRAEL (cl). b. Oakville, La., March 4, 1895; d. Sept. 21, 1965. Worked in district before 1917—with Henry Peyton, 1913; Tom Brown's trio at Anderson's, 1914; Camelia Orchestra and Brass Band, 1917–22. During mid-20's with Chris Kelly, Louis Dumaine, Buddy Petit, Lee Collins, Kid Rena. During depression worked with Dumaine-Houston Orchestra and WPA Brass Band and ERA

Orchestra. During 50's own band played in Little Woods resorts and on other dance jobs. Recorded with Kid Howard.

GOUDIE, FRANK "BIG BOY" (cl, c). b. Royville, La., 1898; d. California, about 1964. Pupil of Bunk Johnson, 1915. Played with Magnolia Orchestra; in 1920 played with Yank Johnson. Left N.O. in 1924, toured Mexico, Central America; lived and worked in Europe from 1925 to World War II then went to Brazil. During early 30's switched to clarinet. Became very popular in South America. After war recorded in Europe with Sidney Bechet, Bill Coleman, Django Reinhardt. Returned to U.S., 1957. Played concert in San Francisco with Amos White in 1960.

GREENE, JERRY (sb, tu). b. N.O., June 23, 1910. Primarily a dance musician with such bands as William Houston's; in jazz bands, 50's, 60's with Sweet Emma Barrett. Tuba with brass bands.

GREGSON, HARRY. b. N.O., about 1885; d. N.O., Feb. 19, 1963. A member of Stalebread's spasm band before 1900, playing homemade instruments and singing. During WW I years was police captain of Storyville district.

ISRAEL GORMAN

EMILE GUERIN

CREOLE GEORGE GUESNON

GUARINO, FELIX (d). b. N.O. about 1898. Drummer in Crescent City Jazzers and Arcadian Serenaders during the 20's.

GUERIN, EMILE (p). b. N.O., Jan. 3, 1911. Dixieland musician often with Julian Laine, Sharkey, Leon Prima. Worked on steamer "J.S." in 1930 with Earl Danton orchestra.

GUESNON, GEORGE "CREOLE GEORGE" (bjo, g). b. N.O., May 25, 1907; d. May 5, 1968. Outstanding musician and musicologist; began to work in cabarets just before the depression. Was on the road with Sam Morgan in early 30's; later recorded for Decca in New York. Returned to N.O. in 1946. Worked with George Lewis in mid-50's. Exceptional student of jazz history; preserved gombo French dialect songs.

GUIFFRE, JOE (g). b. N.O. ———. Pre-World War I dixielander.

GUIFFRE, JOHN (sb, tu). b. N.O. ———. Pre-World War I dixielander.

GUITAR, WILLIE (sb). b. N.O., about 1894; d. N.O., about 1945. Early dixielander dating back to Papa Laine bands. Later with Tony Fougerat. In early days was in Bill Gallaty's band, about 1912; and with Frank Christian until after World War I.

GUMA, PAUL (cl, g). b. N.O., June 30, 1919. Dixielander.

RAM HALL

EDMOND HALL

HALL, CLARENCE (cl, s). b. Reserve, La., about 1900. Worked with Papa Celestin's Original Tuxedo Orchestra, from about 1924–31, recording with the group in 1927. Brother of Edmond, Herb, and Robert. Started in Reserve in 1915 in band composed of his own family, with Kid Thomas, the only outsider.

HALL, EDMOND (cl). b. N.O., May 15, 1901; d. Feb. 11, 1967. One of most famous N.O. jazzmen. Began in Kid Thomas' orchestra in Reserve, La. in 1915. With Buddy Petit, 1920, and briefly with Bud Roussel, Lee Collins, Jack Carey, and Chris Kelly. Went to Pensacola in early 20's. Played with Mack Thomas' Orchestra. In big bands of New York during 30's, Claude Hopkins, Lucky Millinder. During late 40's and 50's with Louis Armstrong's All-Stars. Played mainly New York in 60's.

HALL, EDWARD (c). b. Reserve, La., about 1875. Father of the family of great reed musicians. Played cornet in the Onward Brass Band in Reserve during the early 1900's.

HALL, FRED "TUBBY" (d). b. Sellers, La., Oct. 12, 1895; d. Chicago, Ill., May 13, 1946. At 18, played in Jack Carey's Crescent Orchestra. Joined Eagle Band, 1915; Silver Leaf Orchestra, 1916. Left for Chicago in 1917 to join other N.O. exiles, Lawrence Duhé, Sugar Johnny Smith. In 20's was with Oliver at Lincoln Gardens and with Armstrong at Sunset Cafe. Worked with Jimmie Noone, Carroll Dickerson, Boyd Atkins during mid-20's. Through the depression, mostly with Louis Armstrong, Half-pint Jaxon, Johnny Dodds.

HALL, HERB (cl, s). b. Reserve, La., about 1904. Member of the family from Reserve, La. Active in New York in 60's.

HALL, MINOR "RAM" (d). b. Sellers, La., March 2, 1897; d. Los Angeles, Calif., 1963. Started in 1914 substituting on jobs for brother Tubby Hall. To Chicago in 1916. Went to California with Oliver in 1921. Joined Kid Ory in 1922; was in the successful Ory revival band of the mid-40's.

HALL, RENE (bjo, g). b. N.O., about 1905. One of city's most dexterous technicians and fastest "readers." Played with Jones-Collins Astoria Ballroom Orchestra, 1929, and worked with Sidney Desvigne's big band in the 30's.

HALL, ROBERT (cl, s). b. Reserve, La., about 1912. Another member of the famous Reserve clan. Played with Hippolyte Charles orchestra from 1920–25 and afterwards was associated with the Original Tuxedo Orchestra under Bebe Ridgley leadership in 1926. Recorded in the spring, 1927, session of the Original Tuxedo Orchestra under Papa Celestin.

HALL, SAM "BUSH" (t). b. N.O., about 1904; d. N.O., about 1934. With Marrero's Young Tuxedo Orchestra in 1920; through 20's and 30's led a small band of his own with constantly shifting personnel on minor jobs.

HAMILTON, BILL (g). Led a band in the mid-20's called the Oriental Orchestra.

HAMILTON, CHARLIE (p, bjo). b. Ama, La., April 28, 1904. First jobs with Evan Thomas Black Eagles band (1927). Played mainly with big dance bands, such as Herb Leary's in 20's and 30's. During 60's reverted to traditional jazz. Toured Orient with George Lewis. Frequently at Preservation Hall.

HAMILTON, GEORGE "POP" (t, b, ah). b. New Iberia, La. Oct. 9, 1888. Led the Lyons Brass Band in 1928; this group stayed together only four months. Organized his own dance orchestra in 1930, which lasted almost a year before being killed off by the depression. In 1919 he was with Chris Kelly and played frequently with Sam Morgan in the 20's. Also was in early bands with Bunk Johnson, Lawrence Duhé, Evan Thomas and worked in Gus Fortinet's Banner Band about 1909.

HAMILTON, LUMAS (t, c, fh). b. N.O., Feb. 12, 1912. With Lyons Brass Band under his father's leadership, 1928. With Pop Hamilton's orchestra, 1930.

HANDY, JOHN "CAPTAIN JOHN" (as, cl). b. Pass Christian, Miss., June 24, 1900; d. N.O., Jan. 12, 1971. Started a band called the Louisiana Shakers in 1930.

HANDY, SYLVESTER (sb). b. Pass Christian, Miss.; June 24, 1900; d. N.O., Oct. 12, 1972. Brother of John Handy. Worked riverboats in the 30's.

HARDIN, HENRY (cl, t, l). b. N.O., about 1905; d. N.O., about 1955. With the Joe Robichaux, John Handy, and Kid Rena bands. Led own dance group during the depression days and worked in the ERA Orchestra.

HARDY, EMMETT (c). b. Gretna, La., June 12, 1903; d. Gretna, La., June 16, 1925. Hardy, boy prodigy of the dixieland world who died at 22, had already toured the Orpheum circuit with Tony Catalano's band, played in Chicago with the N.O. Rhythm Kings and in Carlisle Evans' band in Davenport, Iowa, where he is said to have influenced the young Bix Beiderbecke. In N.O. he played mainly in the Norman Brownlee orchestra and was replaced by Johnny Wiggs.

HARRIS, DENNIS (s). Golden Rule Orchestra, 1920.

HARRIS, JOE (tb). Bandleader of 20's. Joe Harris dixieland band.

HARRIS, KID (t). b. N.O., about 1906; d. N.O. about 1951. Active in 20's and 30's. Was in ERA Orchestra.

HARRIS, TIM (sn). b. N.O., about 1882. Drummer for Papa Laine's Reliance Brass Band in early 1900's.

HARRIS, TOM (sb, sou, tu). Played with the Kid Avery jazz band in the post-World War I period.

HARTMAN, GEORGE (t, sb). b. N.O. 1910; d. N.O., Feb. 13, 1966. Played for many years with trio at Pete Herman's cabaret in the Vieux Carre. Made Keynote recording session in 40's.

HARTMANN, CHARLES (tb). b. N.O., July 1, 1898. With Johnny Bayersdorffer, Parenti's Liberty Syncopators, and Johnny Hyman's Bayou Stompers. Was secretary of local 174 for many years. Was prominent jazzman for over thirty years.

HARVEY, CHARLES "BUZZ" (sb). b. N.O. La. about 1885. Played with Alex "King" Watzke orchestra and on jobs with members of the Shields family.

CHARLIE HARTMANN

GEORGE HARTMAN

MONK HAZEL

HAYS, "BLIND CHARLIE" (g, bjo, v, vo). b. N.O. about 1885; d. N.O., Feb. 1949. Played with Bunk Johnson and with Louis Dumaine. In 1948 was in Peter Bocage's band.

HAZEL, ARTHUR "MONK" (d, c, mel). b. Harvey, La., Aug. 15, 1903; d. N.O., Mar. 5, 1968. Kingpin of Dixieland style drummers. Began career with Emmett Hardy in 1919. Played in N.O. through 20's with Happy Schilling, Bill Creger, Jules Bauduc, and with Abbie Brunies at the Halfway House. He recorded first in 1927 with Johnny Hyman's Bayou Stompers; in 20's too, with N.O. Rhythm Kings, Tony Parenti's orchestra and Jack Pettis' Pets. Was on network radio in 1934 behind singer Gene Austin. Widely recorded. From 40's through late 60's was associated closely with Sharkey's Kings of Dixieland, plus short intervals of work with Santo Pecora and George Girard.

HENDERSON, GEORGE (d). b. N.O., Sept. 17, 1900. Led Black Diamonds, 1919–22. Entire career in pickup jobs. Worked at Luthjen's in 50's. Recorded with Kid Thomas in 1951.

HENDERSON, TOMMY (d). b. Gretna, La., about 1905. Played with Elton Theodore band in early 20's. Mainly in Algiers, La.

HENRY, CHARLES "SUNNY" (tb). b. Magnolia Plantation, Nov. 17, 1885; d. N.O., Jan. 7, 1960. Began at age 17 with Eclipse Brass Band under Jim Hum-

CHARLES HENRY

CHICKEN HENRY

phrey, 1902. Began in N.O. in 1913; to 1920 played in Excelsior Brass Band and with Hippolyte Charles dance orchestra. Worked with Amos White during the early 20's, and with John Robichaux at the Lyric Theater to 1927. For years worked in a taxi dance hall at Carondelet and Canal Sts. Henry was lead trombone under Louis Dumaine in the WPA Band during the 30's. Into the 40's he worked with the Young Tuxedo Brass Band until 1947, then switched to the Eureka Brass Band for which he played until his death.

HENRY, OSCAR "CHICKEN" (tb, p). b. N.O., June 8, 1888. Began his career as a bordello "professor," playing piano at Hattie Rogers' sporting house in 1906. Studied music at Straight University. His hand was severely burned in an accident and in 1931 he switched to trombone because of this. During the depression he worked in the WPA Brass Band, in the ERA Orchestra, and sometimes in a group led by Kid Howard. Became a fixture in the Eureka Brass Band about 1959.

AL HIRT

FATS HOUSTON

KID HOWARD

56

HENRY, SON (d).

HENRY, "TRIGGER SAM" (p). b. N.O., about 1875. One of the best of the Storyville piano players. Much admired by Jelly Roll Morton. Played in the district from 1898 to 1914.

HESSEMER, AL (b, bjo, g, v). b. Jackson, Mich., Jan. 21, 1909. Mainly with leading dance bands in 30's. Charlie Bourgois, Joe Petrie. Frequently heard on riverboats S.S. *President, Capitol* with best dixieland leaders. At times with Crawford-Ferguson Night Owls. One of busiest musicians in town in 1965.

HIGHTOWER, WILLIE (c, t). b. Nashville, Tenn., Oct. 1889; d. Chicago, Ill. Leader of American Stars orchestra. Played dance jobs in St. Katherine's Hall in 1913. By 1917 the group was more or less regularly at the Cadillac. Moved to Chicago in 1921, worked in Lottie Hightower's band and in other big bands until 1927, when he again became a leader. Band lasted until the depression. Made one recording under his name in 1924.

HIMEL, OTTO "COCO" (g). b. N.O. about 1904. Dixieland rhythm man associated, in his New Orleans days, with Frank Clancy groups in Jefferson parish. Played jobs with Raymond Burke in the late 20's and early 30's. Later, joined singer Gene Austin as comedy-accompanist, where he worked with fellow Orleanian, Candy Candido. Monk Hazel also was in this group, but after Candy had left.

HIRT, AL (t). b. N.O., Nov. 7, 1922. Internationally famous. Symphonically trained, has little traditional jazz background. Physically powerful, energetic, he has captured popular fancy. His success is based mainly on extraordinary virtuosity.

HIRT, GERALD "SLICK" (tb). b. N.O. ——. Trombone-playing brother of trumpeter Al Hirt. Long active in the N.O. police department band. In 60's with brother's combo.

HOLLOWAY, "KILDEE" (t, arr). b. N.O.; d. N.O., 1953. Kildee worked for Papa Celestin through the depression and with Joe Robichaux in late 30's. Though he was an excellent trumpet player, he was best known for his easy-to-play arrangements for the Celestin band.

HOOKER, GEORGE (c, bh). b. Algiers, La., 1882. A brass band musician, almost exclusively with Pacific Brass Band, about 1900; Tuxedo Brass Band in mid-20's. Until the depression worked regularly with Allen Brass Band of Algiers, La. and occasionally with Excelsior Brass Band during this period.

HOUSTON, MATTHEW "FATS" (d). b. N.O., July 22, 1910. Well known as the Grand Marshal of the Eureka Brass Band, Houston shared leadership of a dance band with Louis Dumaine during the depression days.

HOWARD, AVERY "KID" (c, t, d). b. N.O., April 22, 1908; d. N.O., March 28, 1966. During the depression became prominent on cornet. Played drums with Chris Kelly and Isaiah Morgan. Sometimes played with Young Tuxedo Brass Band, but mainly led a brass band of his own, and organized small combinations for dances. During the 50's played in the George Lewis band as regular trumpet. Has been widely recorded in the 50's and 60's.

ARMAND HUG

57

PERCY HUMPHREY

WILLIE HUMPHREY (younger)

HOWARD, JOE (c, tu). b. Waggeman, La., about 1870; d. N.O., 1946. Started in N.O. during the Storyville days. With Celestin in the Original Tuxedo Orchestra after having played in brass bands at home and in Algiers, Allen Brass Band, 1909–11. During World War I, he led his own group both in the district and at the lake resorts; later worked on riverboats. In 1920 with Louis Dumaine's Jazzola Eight. Made the celebrated discs in 1927. Through the 20's and 30's was a mainstay of the Tuxedo Brass Band. Recorded with the Zenith Brass Band, 1946.

HUG, ARMAND (p). b. N.O., Dec. 6, 1910; d. N.O., Mar. 19, 1977. Considered finest piano soloist in N.O. First professional job, 1926, in Fern Cafe at 15. Self-taught; played with all the dixieland stars; was world-renowned for his records. For years was cocktail lounge performer, but played an enormous repertoire in wide variety of styles, from Joplin rags to low-down blues and pop tunes. Was avid student of jazz history.

HUMPHREY, EARL (tb, sb). b. N.O., 1902; d. N.O., June 26, 1971. Learned trumpet from celebrated grandfather, Jim Humphrey. At age 15 was working

jobs at lakefront resorts. At 17 toured with dad for Al G. Barnes Circus. Spent more time on road than most N.O. musicians, but appeared irregularly in town to play with his brothers or Buddy Petit, Chris Kelly, or Louis Dumaine. Moved to Charlottesville, Va., but returned to N.O. in 1960's.

HUMPHREY, JIM (t). b. N.O., about 1861; d. N.O., 1937. One of the greatest of the music teachers, Humphrey taught the Eclipse Brass Band of the Magnolia plantation. Among his protégés are his own son and daughters and grandchildren, one of the most celebrated families in jazz. Also Sam, Isaiah, Albert, and Andrew Morgan, Chris Kelly, Harrison Barnes, and Sunny Henry.

HUMPHREY, PERCY (t, d). b. N.O., Jan. 13, 1905. Leader, since 1947, of Eureka Brass Band. Youngest of the Humphrey brothers and a protégé of his grandfather, Jim Humphrey. No stranger to dance hall and nightclub work, he is most widely known for his role as a brass band musician. During the late 40's played with the George Lewis band, but in recent years usually is a leader himself, or works with Emma Barrett.

HUMPHREY, WILLIE ELI (cl). b. N.O., about May 24, 1880; d. N.O., Jan. 8, 1964. Father of the famed Humphrey brothers. He, too, learned from Jim Humphrey, his father, and played in the Magnolia plantation's Eclipse Brass Band, 1900–10. He was in the Crescent Orchestra in 1913 and was frequently seen with Tig Chambers.

HUMPHREY, WILLIE JAMES (cl). b. N.O., Dec. 29, 1900. Oldest of the Humphrey brothers. Began professionally with George McCullum in the Excelsior Brass Band, 1919. Made short trip to St. Louis and Chicago to play with George Filhe. Veteran of the riverboats. Played with Jelly Roll Morton. Worked at Anderson's restaurant on Rampart St.; led band of his own with Maurice Durand; with Lee Collins at Spanish Fort. Seen in the 40's in Young Tuxedo and Eureka brass bands. Frequently plays in brother Percy's band, with Paul Barbarin or Emma Barrett. Much recorded.

HUMPHRIES, BILL (bjo, g). b. Allendale, S. C., March 19, 1927. With Crawford-Ferguson Night Owls in 60's.

HUNTINGTON, BILLY (g, b, s, bjo). b. N.O., Oct. 2, 1937. As a youth was closely associated with members of the George Lewis band, especially Lawrence Marrero, and was jobbing around in his teens with such old masters as Charlie Love, Steve Angrum, Emile Barnes, and Albert Jiles. At age 15, recorded with British bandleader Ken Colyer on banjo. Gave up traditional jazz in mid-50's.

HYMAN, JOHN WIGGINTON. b. N.O., July 25, 1899. Known as Johnny Wiggs and Johnny Hyman. Worked in early 20's with Happy Schilling's band, Tony Parenti, Norman Brownlee. Recorded for Victor in 1927 with own Bayou Stompers band. In early 30's was with Ellis Stratakos. The revival of jazz in this era, from 1946 on, is due largely to his efforts. He founded the NOJC, brought many a great jazzman out of involuntary retirement. As a teacher he turned out distinguished pupils for a new jazz generation, including George Girard, Pete Fountain. Widely recorded in the 50's when his power and creativeness were at their peak. Retired from music about 1960 for personal reasons, but remains the idol of "purists" around the world. Began to make appearances at Preservation Hall, 1965.

ICE, BOB (sb, l). b. Fairmont, W. Va., Jan. 3, 1931. Leader of the popular Last Straws dixieland band of the 60's.

ICE, BOB (bjo). b. N.O. about 1914. Not related to Bob Ice of the Last Straws. Regular with the Crawford-Ferguson Night Owls.

JACKSON, ALBERT "LOOCHIE" (tb). b. N.O., March 13, 1898. Began his musical career in 1918 with the Elton Theodore Orchestra of Algiers, La. Sometimes played in the Tuxedo Brass Band in 1920 and was with the Young Tuxedo Brass Band from 1932 until his retirement from music in the early fifties.

PRESTON JACKSON

59

TONY JACKSON

JACKSON, EDDIE (tu, sb). b. N.O., about 1867; d. N.O., 1938. For 40 years among the finest N.O. bassists. Began with Edward Clem about 1907. Was a veteran of the advertising wagons and the "jitney" dance halls. With the Onward Brass Band in 1910–12. During late 20's led his own dance band and played with Tuxedo Brass Band. During the late 30's played in the Young Tuxedo Brass Band.

JACKSON, FRANK (c, tu, bd). b. N.O., about 1866; d. N.O., about 1912. Played with Onward, Oriental, and Excelsior brass bands, from 1899 to 1912. Sometimes played bass drum with Buddy Bolden's marching band about 1900.

JACKSON, "PICKLES" (d). d. N.O., 1972.

JACKSON, PRESTON (tb). b. N.O., 1903. Never played in New Orleans but gained considerable fame playing in Crescent City tradition. Family moved to Chicago in 1917. During 20's worked with big bands, Dave Peyton, Erskine Tate, Carroll Dickerson; also with the Dodds brothers, Jimmie Noone, Natty Dominique. Recorded with Richard M. Jones, Punch Miller, Noone and others.

JACKSON, SKEETER (g, sb). b. N.O. Played with Tom Albert's orchestra in 1910, later with Sam Ross.

JACKSON, TONY (p). b. N.O., June 5, 1876; d. Chicago, Ill., April 20, 1921. Unrivaled king of Storyville "professors"; a rare musical genius. Jackson worked the brothels, from the age of 15 to 1904. In N.O. he played mainly at Gipsy Shafer's, Hilma Burt's, Lulu White's, and Countess Willie Piazza's. He returned to N.O. 1911–12 and worked in (Frank) Early's. Composed hundreds of popular songs and sold them for five or ten dollars each. Somehow retained copyright ownership of some numbers, including "Some Sweet Day," "Pretty Baby."

JACKSON, "NEW ORLEANS WILLIE" (vo). b. N.O. about 1895. A popular entertainer of the 20's whose fourteen recorded sides had distinguished accompaniments, specifically, Steve Lewis, Clarence Williams, Buddy Christian. Drew big crowds to Brown's Ice Cream Parlor.

JAEGER, ALFRED L. (d). b. N.O., 1869; d. N.O., Jan. 6, 1953. Veteran of early vaudeville, circus bands. Left N.O. in 80's. Worked in original Paul Whiteman groups. Was with Jefferson marching bands in N.O. area under Frank Clancy. Was last seen in early 50's in a Tony Almerico Parisian Room jam session.

JAFFE, ALLAN (tu). b. Pottsville, Pa., April 24, 1935. Young proprietor of Preservation Hall. Sometimes sits in with the bands there. Played in the Zulu parade, 1965 Mardi Gras, with The Young Olympia Brass Band. Regular in this group in 1966.

JAMES, JOE (p). b. Algiers, La., 1901; d. N.O., 1964. Long-time, until his death, piano player for the Kid Thomas orchestra.

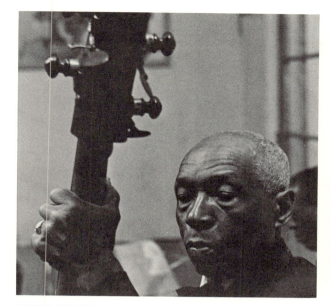

LOUIS JAMES

ANDREW JEFFERSON

JAMES, KID (d). b. N.O. about 1907. Played some jobs with Bunk Johnson, but chiefly known as member of the Louis Keppard-Wooden Joe Nicholas band.

JAMES, LOUIS (cl, s, sb), b. Thibodaux, La., April 9, 1890; d. N.O., Oct. 26, 1967. In 1905 played in family band in hometown. Came to N.O. in 1917, worked with Jack Carey, Frank Duson, the Tulane Orchestra with Joe Howard at Villa Cabaret. Played again at home with family. Recorded with Dumaine on famed Jazzola Eight session, 1927; with Dumaine on and off until 1949. In 50's played bass for Percy Humphrey; was seen occasionally at Preservation Hall in 1965.

JEAN, NELSON (t). b. N.O., Dec. 28, 1902. Polished musician, related to the Joseph family. He worked on riverboats on lake steamers through the 30's.

JEAN, ULYSSES (t). b. N.O. about 1905. A nephew of Nelson Jean and John Joseph, he was on the road in the early 30's with Paul Barnes, and during the 40's sometimes had jobs with George Lewis, Lawrence Marrero, Eddie Summers.

JEFFERSON, ANDREW (d, vo). b. N.O., Nov. 24, 1912. Older brother of popular trumpet player Thomas Jefferson; he played for a long time at the lake resorts, mainly with Peter Bocage at Mama Lou's in the 50's. Frequently marches with Young Tuxedo Brass Band.

JEFFERSON, THOMAS (t, vo). b. N.O., about 1923. Oriented to Louis Armstrong style. Worked in Lafon Brass Band in late 30's. Seen mainly at the Paddock during the late 40's and through the 50's under Octave Crosby. Frequently marched with Young Tuxedo Brass Band.

JILES, ALBERT, SR. b. Thibodaux, La., about 1878; d. N.O,. about 1922. Son of a Civil War drummer boy, Jiles played in turn-of-the-century brass bands; Youka Brass Band, 1904.

JILES, ALBERT (d). b. Thibodaux, La., Nov. 7, 1905; d. N.O., Sept. 3, 1964. Nephew of great bass drummer Clay Jiles. First job in 1922 with Chris Kelly. In 1923 began long run with Lawrence Toca. Worked during the depression with Kid Howard's band and with Isaiah Morgan's Young Morgan Band. Early 40's with Papa Celestin or Kid Clayton. Recorded with Wooden Joe Nicholas for American Music in 1949. Worked in 50's at Happy Landing.

JILES, CLAY (d). b. Thibodaux, La., about 1880; d. June 15, 1927. Played in Excelsior Brass Band in early 1900's; sometimes worked with Onward or Allen brass bands.

JOHNSON, ALPHONSE (ah). b. N.O., about 1900. Founding member of the Eureka Brass Band, 1920.

JOHNSON, "BUDDY" (tb). b. Algiers, La., about 1870; d. N.O., 1927. Allen Brass Band; Pacific Brass Band, about 1900; Onward Brass Band, about 1910. Imperial Orchestra under Manuel Perez, about 1905; Superior Orchestra with Bunk Johnson, Big Eye Louis Nelson, 1910. During mid-20's with Perez' dance orchestra. Older brother of Yank Johnson.

JOHNSON, "CHICK" (s, cl). b. N.O. ———. Dixielander of the 20's, 30's with Dixola Jazz Band. His only record date, Goofus Tin Roofers, with Blind Gilbert, Ray Burke, 1927, was never released by Columbia. In 60's with Dominick Barocco.

JOHNSON, DAVE ERNEST (d). b. N.O., about 1890; d. about 1932. With Chris Kelly band, 1919–25.

JOHNSON, "DINK" (cl, p, vo, d). b. Biloxi, Miss., Oct. 28, 1892; d. Portland, Ore., Nov. 29, 1954. With Original Creole Orchestra in California as drummer. Also with Freddie Keppard, George Baquet, Jelly Roll Morton. Later was nightclub entertainer in California, playing piano and singing blues. Recorded for American Music. Dink was a brother-in-law of Jelly Roll Morton.

JOHNSON, "DUCK ERNEST" (b). b. N.O., about 1888; d. about 1931. With Chris Kelly band, 1919–25. Led own band at Beverly Gardens in mid-20's.

DINK JOHNSON

JOHNSON, JIMMY (sb, tu). b. N.O., about 1876; d. about 1937. Buddy Bolden band. Played in Silver Leaf Orchestra, 1911. Toured with Don Albert's orchestra out of San Antonio, Texas in late 20's, early 30's.

JOHNSON, JOE (c). b. N.O. about 1890; d. N.O. about 1928. Played in district with Herb Lindsay's Primrose Orchestra, 1912, and in Eagle Band.

JOHNSON, LONNIE (g). b. N.O., Feb. 8, 1889; d. Philadelphia, Pa., June 18, 1970. Played solo guitar in Storyville bordellos in 1910–17. Went to London with a show, 1917, as intermission entertainer. Played on riverboat S.S. *St. Paul* with Charlie Creath and on S.S. *Capitol* with Fate Marable. One of the most recorded of jazzmen, he made

NOON JOHNSON

ROGER JOHNSTON

63

BUNK JOHNSON

PAPA JOHN JOSEPH

his first cuts with Creath in 1927. Never returned to N.O., but spent whole life on tour. Was in Philadelphia, 1966.

JOHNSON, NOON (tu, bazooka, g). b. N.O., Aug. 24, 1903; d. N.O., Sept. 18, 1969. Led "skiffle" trio. Paraded with Young Tuxedo Brass Band. As youth, played in streets of Storyville for coins.

JOHNSON, STEVE (vt). b. N.O., about 1865. In 1889 a founding member of the Onward Brass Band.

JOHNSON, WILLIAM MANUEL "BILL" (sb, g, ah, tu, bjo). b. N.O., Aug. 10, 1872; d. Mexico, 1975. Began career playing guitar in district bagnios in 1890. Played bass with a trio in Tom Anderson's Basin St. Cafe, 1900–1909. During the days, he

worked with the Excelsior, Uptown, Eagle, Peerless brass bands. Organized Original Creole Orchestra and toured the U.S. on the Orpheum circuit until 1918. Johnson originally got the job at the Royal Garden and invited King Oliver to front the band, bringing world fame to Oliver. Johnson stayed busy with the best jazz and dance bands for another 20 years, to build the longest active musical career of any major jazzman.

JOHNSON, WILLIE "BUNK" (c, t). b. N.O., Dec. 27, 1879; d. New Iberia, La., July 7, 1949. A giant of N.O. jazz from his first job in 1894 with Adam Olivier's orchestra through 20 busy years. From 1914 on, he played outside of N.O., mainly in Mandeville and Baton Rouge, La., and in the western part of the state. Toured with tent shows in the early 20's. Was rediscovered mainly through the efforts of Bill Russell, and went on to several years of concerts and extensive recording. Was largely responsible for the jazz revival of the 40's.

RICHARD M. JONES

Original Tuxedo Orchestra in 1918 and 1919. Joined King Oliver up north in 1924; then worked in Milwaukee with Art Sim's orchestra and Bernie Young's orchestra. Back in Chicago in 30's, with Charlie Elgar and worked steadily thereafter. He appeared at a Chicago concert with Bunk Johnson in 1946.

JONES, DAVID (d, mel, s). b. Lutcher, La., about 1888; d. Los Angeles, 1953. In 1910 began career in local band, Holmes Brass Band of Lutcher. Worked jobs in the district, then joined Fate Marable in 1918 for three years on S.S. *Capitol.* Joined King Oliver in Chicago in 1921. In mid-20's was leader at Pelican Dance Hall; worked for a short while with Bebe Ridgley's Tuxedo Orchestra. In 1929, with Lee Collins, he cut four recorded sides under the name of the Jones-Collins-Astoria Hot Eight that made jazz history.

JOHNSON, "YANK" (tb). b. N.O., about 1878; d. N.O., 1938. Younger brother of Buddy Johnson. Worked with Imperial Orchestra, 1906; later with Superior Orchestra, 1910. In 1920 was in a band with Big Boy Goudie and Chinee Foster. Mostly after World War I worked with Sam Morgan band to 1925, then for a while with Chris Kelly, and in the Magnolia Orchestra under Willie Pajeaud. Worked with Pajeaud and others in dance halls till about 1938.

JOHNSTON, ROGER (d). b. N.O., March 12, 1918; d. N.O., Oct. 9, 1958. Began professional dixieland career at age 13. Worked with Santo Pecora, Leon Prima, Sharkey, Rob Liberto, Dukes of Dixieland. Many years at Famous Door.

JONES, BRIS (cl). b. N.O., July 12, 1926. Regular with The Last Straws.

JONES, CHESTER (d). b. N.O., March 3, 1913. Worked with George Lewis, Eureka Brass Band, and many dance groups. Still active in 1966.

JONES, CLIFFORD "SNAGS" (d). b. N.O., about 1900; d. Chicago, Ill., Jan. 31, 1947. In his teens worked with high-school buddy, Lee Collins; Jack Carey; Buddy Petit. Sometimes substituted in Celestin's

JONES, RICHARD MYKNEE (p). b. Donaldsonville, La., June 13, 1889; d. Chicago, Ill., Dec. 9, 1945. Primarily a solo pianist, Jones worked the higher class Basin Street bordellos before he was 20 years old. From a musical family; knew many instruments. At 13 was playing alto horn in a brass band. Led own groups at Abadie's, the Poodle Dog, and Fewclothes in the district in 1910–12. Oliver worked regularly in his band. In 1919 he joined the Clarence Williams Publishing Co. in an administrative capacity. In 1925 became Chicago "race" recording director for Okeh. During the late 30's he worked for Decca. From about 1940 was mainly active as an arranger. His composition credits include "Trouble in Mind," "Riverside Blues," and "Jazzin' Babies Blues."

JOSEPH, EDGAR "SAMBO" (t). b. N.O., Nov. 6, 1906; d. N.O., Feb. 27, 1977. Mainly a brass band musician. With Young Tuxedo Brass Band till late 50's.

JOSEPH, JOHN "PAPA JOHN" (sb, cl, g, s). b. St. James Parish, La., Nov. 27, 1877; d. N.O., Jan. 22, 1965. Came to N.O. in 1906. Led his own group in the district until 1917. Played brass band jobs with Claiborne Williams band in East Baton Rouge Parish. Sometimes worked with Original Tuxedo Orchestra. Retired to follow his profession of barbering in the

WILLIE JOSEPH

KAHN, MARCUS (p, tb, bh). b. N.O., about 1890; d. N.O. about 1946. Early dixieland pianist who played frequently with members of Original Dixieland Jazz Band, Ernest Giardina's band, and with the Brunies', Fischer's bands.

KAY, ARMIN (t). Dixielander with Santo Pecora.

KEELIN, FRANK (t). Eagle Band.

KELLY, CHRIS (c). b. Deer Range, La., 1891; d. April 19, 1929. Joined the Eclipse Brass Band in 1916. A protégé of Jim Humphrey. Drafted in 1917. Joined the Magnolia Orchestra, replacing retiring Edward Clem in 1919. During the 20's led his own band, and was considered by many to be the best cornet man in the city. The band frequently traveled to Biloxi and Mobile, and was challenged for popularity only by Buddy Petit. Never recorded.

20's, but played frequently in the 60's in Preservation Hall. Joseph toured the Orient as late as 1963 with the George Lewis band. Brother of Willie Joseph.

JOSEPH, PLEASANT (g, p, vo). b. Wallace, La., Dec. 21, 1907. Popular entertainer made several successful records, notably on Decca, under the pseudonym "Cousin Joe," during the 40's. In New Orleans he is known as "Smilin' Joe."

JOSEPH, WALDREN "FROG" (tb). b. N.O. about 1918. A popular N.O. trombone player with exceptional facility. Was in Joe Robichaux's band in 30's. Played with most of the Bourbon St. bands, including Octave Crosby's and Papa Celestin's. Worked in 60's in bands led by Albert French, Paul Barbarin.

JOSEPH, WILLIE "KAISER" (cl). b. St. James Parish, about 1892; d. N.O., 1951. Jobbed around in the district until it closed, 1917, frequently in Ridgley's segment of the Tuxedo Orchestra. He is on the recordings of the Louis Dumaine Jazzola Eight. During the depression he was frequently with Willie Pajeaud. Younger brother of Papa John Joseph.

JOYCE, JOHN "J.J." (d). b. N.O., April 17, 1939. Regular with The Last Straws.

MARCUS KAHN

KELLY, ERNEST (tb). b. N.O. about 1886; d. N.O. about 1927. Trombonist of the pre-1920 era. Was in Tig Chambers' Magnolia Sweets, 1910, and with Bob Lyons' Dixie Jazz Band in 1918. Played many jobs with Chinee Foster. Played in first band organized by George Lewis, 1923.

KELLY, GUY (t). b. Scotland, La., Nov. 22, 1906; d. Chicago, Ill., Feb. 24, 1940. Began playing in Baton Rouge with Toots Johnson. Moved to Houston in 1927 and came to N.O. late same year. Worked at the Humming Bird Lounge with John Handy, then joined Celestin, with whom he recorded. Went to Chicago, 1929. Worked with Dave Peyton and with Orleanians Jimmie Noone, Louis Armstrong, Boyd Atkins.

GUY KELLY

FREDDIE KEPPARD

67

JEANNETTE KIMBALL

NARVIN KIMBALL

KEPPARD, FREDDIE (c, v, mdl). b. N.O., Feb. 15, 1889; d. Chicago, Ill., July 15, 1933. First job at Spanish Fort with Johnny Brown's band, 1901. Pupil of Adolphe Alexander, Sr. Organized first Olympia Orchestra, 1906, with Alphonse Picou on clarinet. Sometimes played with Eagle Brass Band about 1910. Played at Lala's, Groshell's Dance Hall in the district, 1910–12. Toured with Original Creole Orchestra on Orpheum circuit, 1913–18. Worked in Chicago with Doc Cooke's Dreamland Orchestra, John Wycliffe's orchestra; with Erskine Tate, Jimmie Noone, and Lil's Hot Shots. Used many "hokum" effects and was known to be very powerful. A prime favorite of Jelly Roll Morton.

KEPPARD, LOUIS (g, tu, ah). b. N.O., Feb. 2, 1888. Began playing professionally about 1906, mainly as a guitarist, and was in the Magnolia Orchestra with the Depass boys, Joe Oliver, and Frank Goudie. He also worked at times with his brother Freddie's Olympia Orchestra, mainly in the district. He some-

times played in the lake resorts in the 40's and 50's and was still seen in street parades with the Gibson Brass Band in the 60's.

KIMBALL, ANDREW (c). b. N.O., about 1880; d. Pascagoula, Miss., about 1929. With Peerless Orchestra, 1905–12, under both Bab Frank and A. J. Piron. Worked with John Robichaux from 1913 until 1925; in the interim played daytime jobs with the Onward Brass Band.

KIMBALL, HENRY (sb). b. N.O., 1878; d. N.O., 1931. With John Robichaux, 1894–1919. During the early 20's, toured in Jelly Roll Morton Band and worked with Manuel Perez. Played in N.O. in late 20's with Walter Pichon, occasionally in Papa Celestin's band. Frequently on riverboats.

KIMBALL, JEANNETTE (née Salvant) (p). b. N.O., Dec. 18, 1908. Virtually all her musical life has been with the Papa Celestin organization. She

BILL KLEPPINGER

played with Celestin's band on his 1926 disc session and on the Southland recordings of 1954. Was still working with Celestin musicians under Albert French's direction in 1965.

KIMBALL, MARGARET (p). b. N.O., about 1896. Wife of Andrew Kimball, she, too, played with the John Robichaux Lyric Theater pit band of the early 1920's.

KIMBALL, NARVIN (bjo, sb). b. N.O., March 2, 1909. Identified with the Papa Celestin Original Tuxedo Orchestra from late 20's, when he recorded with the band, through the depression. On Bourbon St. frequently as a bandleader in Dixieland Hall in the 60's. Son of Henry Kimball; often incorrectly listed as Henry Kimball, Jr.

KING, FREDDIE (d). b. Springfield, Conn., 1917. Active in N.O. during the 50's, he was an early president of the NOJC. Frequently a member of the Johnny Wiggs band, with whom he recorded. Also made discs with Santo Pecora on Capitol.

KING, WILEY "PEP" (sb, tu). b. N.O., about 1885. Played in the Crescent Orchestra in 1913, and marched in parades with the Jack Carey band.

KIRSCH, CHARLIE (tb). b. N.O. ——. Pre-World War I dixielander.

KIRSCH, MARTIN (cl). b. N.O., about 1889. Member of the Reliance Brass Band.

KLEIN, BUSTER (d). b. N.O., about 1895; d. N.O. about 1946. A dixieland drummer who played in the early Johnny Bayersdorffer bands.

KLEPPINGER, BILL (mdl). b. N.O., about 1897. A mainstay of the Six and 7/8 String Band and the Invincibles, dating back to 1912. Still appears with the former group, capping a jazz career of more than a half century. Brother-in-law of the late Paul Mares, leader of the N.O. Rhythm Kings.

KMEN, HENRY "HANK" (cl, s, vo). b. Saratoga Springs, N. Y., Nov. 3, 1915. Now a professor at Tulane University, but had wide experience in both jazz and big band work before coming to New Orleans. During 60's has been with Crawford-Ferguson Night Owls.

KNECHT, HENRY (c, tb). b. N.O., 1898; d. N.O., July 21, 1968. Noted brass virtuoso said to be fastest "reader" in the city. Worked with dance bands; marched with Schilling's brass band; worked with him in Heineman's ball park ragtime band.

KNOX, EMILE (bd). b. N.O., May 2, 1902; d. N.O., Aug. 20, 1976. Long-time parade drummer, with Young Tuxedo Brass Band in 50's.

KOHLMAN, FREDDIE (d). b. N.O., Aug. 25, 1915. With Joe Robichaux in 30's. Bandleader at Sid Davilla's Mardi Gras lounge during 50's. Frequently played snare drums with the Young Tuxedo Brass Band. Regular drummer at Jazz Ltd., Chicago in mid-60's.

KUHL, CHARLIE (p). b. N.O. about 1897; d. N.O. about 1947. With the Alfred Laine Orchestra.

LACEY, "LI'L MACK" (d). b. N.O. ——. Crescent Orchestra, pre-World War I. With Kid Punch Miller in the 20's.

LACAZE, PETER (t). b. St. Bernard Parish, July 14, 1893. Popular dance hall musician of the 20's. In late 20's organized his popular NOLA Band.

EMILE LACOUME

TOMMY LADNIER

OGDEN LAFAYE

LACOUME, EMILE "STALEBREAD" (z, g, p, bjo, vo, l). b. N.O., 1885; d. N.O., 1946. Led Razzy Dazzy Spasm Band in Storyville streets as early as 1897, playing homemade instruments, considered by many to be the first jazz band. In early 1900's, though blind, performed actively at lakefront resorts. Member of Halfway House Orchestra. Later, 20's and early 30's, at Lavida Ballroom in Charlie Fishbein orchestra.

LADA, ANTON (d, x). b. N.O., about 1893. Played around N.O. in his early teens. Led small group called Five Southern Jazzers. Went north almost simultaneously with the Original Dixieland Jazz Band and made Columbia records in the same era competing with the La Rocca group under the name of the Louisiana Five. This group included Yellow Nunez.

LADNIER, TOMMY (c, t). b. Florenceville, La., May 28, 1900; d. New York City, June 4, 1939. At 14 Ladnier was under tutelage of Bunk Johnson, and he played for several years in bands that Bunk organized. Never actually played in N.O., but much influenced by Johnson and by Buddy Petit. He was in

PAPA JACK LAINE

JULIAN LAINE

Chicago in 1920; and in 1922 to 1927 worked with Jimmie Noone, King Oliver, Fletcher Henderson, and recorded with Lovie Austin. A year before his death he made records with Sidney Bechet and with Mezz Mezzrow.

LAFAYE, OGDEN (p). b. N.O. about 1896. Popular pianist, much associated with Irving Fazola's N.O. career. Recorded and broadcast daily with Faz over WTPS. Now in landscape business.

LAINE, ALFRED "BABY," "PANTSY" (c, ah, d). b. N.O., July 12, 1895; d. N.O., March 1, 1957. Son of Papa Laine. Started playing with Papa's Reliance Brass Band in 1908 and worked mainly with Reliance groups or led his own dance band until early depression years.

LAINE, JACK "PAPA" (d, ah, l). b. N.O., Sept. 21, 1873; d. June 1, 1966. Earliest dixieland bandleader. His seven dance groups all were named Reliance and worked simultaneously in N.O. His brass band was celebrated throughout the Gulf Coast. Withdrew from music at start of World War I before Original Dixieland Jazz Band won its success. Never appeared on records, but made tapes at Tulane University under Johnny Wiggs's leadership in early 60's.

LAINE, JULIAN "DIGGER" (tb). b. N.O., 1907; d. N.O., Sept. 10, 1957. Began career at old Fern Cafe No. 2, a dime-a-dance place. Through most of his career was mainly identified with Johnny Wiggs, Irving Fazola, Sharkey. Worked for a while in Chicago with Muggsy Spanier's band. Not related to Papa Laine.

71

MIKE LALA

NAPPY LAMARE

LALA, JOE (c). b. N.O. ——. Pre-World War I dixie-lander.

LALA, JOHN (c). b. N.O. 1893. Pre-World War I dixielander. With Happy Schilling, Reliance, Johnny Fischer.

LALA, MIKE (t). b. N.O., Oct. 24, 1908; d. N.O., Oct. 8, 1976. A leading dixieland and dance band-leader for forty years. Featured through two dec-ades in such leading French Quarter locations as La Lune, Famous Door. Earlier played in bands led by Joe Capraro, Oscar Marcour, Jules Bauduc.

LAMAR, "SLIM" (sb, l). b. N.O. about 1900. Leader of Argentine Dons, big vaudeville and recording band which featured many well-known dixieland stars.

LAMARE, HILTON NAPOLEON "NAPPY" (bjo, g, vo). b. N.O., June 14, 1907. Nappy got his first banjo while a student at Warren Easton High School, in N.O., and was a professional by 1925, working in bands led by Johnny Wiggs, Bill Lustig, Johnny Bayersdorffer, Sharkey, and Monk Hazel. He made his recording debut with Johnny Hyman's Bayou Stompers in 1927. His fame, however, is based on his success with the public achieved while working with the Bob Crosby Bob Cats in the middle 30's to the early 40's. Now a permanent resident of North Hollywood, Calif. Led band, jointly with drummer Ray Bauduc, The Riverboat Dandies, touring the nation's best night spots in 60's.

BILLY LAMBERT

NICK LA ROCCA

LAMBERT, ADAM (p, b, vt). b. N.O., about 1886. Versatile early jazzman first played valve trombone, then string bass for the Silver Leaf Orchestra; and in 1932 was touring with Paul Barnes's dance orchestra as regular pianist.

LAMBERT, BILLY (d). b. N.O., about 1893; d. N.O., April 30, 1969. Early dixielander; as member of original Tom Brown's Band from Dixieland, made historic trip to Chicago's Lamb's Cafe in 1915.

LANDRY, ALCIDE (t). b. N.O., about 1880; d. N.O., 1949. During the 20's played with Tuxedo Brass Band, Lyons Brass Band. Leader of the Eureka Brass Band during the 30's. He played in the WPA Brass Band during the mid-30's; and in the 40's worked at Luthjen's, sometimes at Happy Landing, and with the Tulane Brass Band.

LANDRY, TOM (vt, tu, sb). b. N.O., about 1870; Occasionally marched with the Onward Brass Band in the pre-Spanish-American War period. Before 1900 was playing in bands led by Oscar Duconge, along with Alphonse Picou, and Edward Clem. As early as 1894, he was in Charlie Galloway's dance band.

LANGLOIS, ISIDORE (g). b. N.O., about 1910. Left U.S. in early 30's. Recorded with Big Boy Goudie in 1939.

LANOIX, AUGUST (tu, sb). b. N.O., Aug. 13, 1902. First job with Martin Gabriel. Early jobs with Leo Dejan.

LAPORTE, JOHN (d, l). b. N.O. ———. Dance band leader, 20's & 30's.

LA ROCCA, DOMINICK J. "NICK" (c, l). b. N.O., April 11, 1889; d. N.O., Feb. 22, 1961. Leader of Original Dixieland Jazz Band. Made first jazz disc. Credited as composer of many standard tunes. Authorized biography in *The Story of the Original Dixieland Jazz Band.*

LAUDEMAN, PETE (p). b. 1908; d. May 13, 1963. Dixielander with most of top bands.

LEBLANC, DAN (sb, tu). b. N.O., 1902; d. N.O., April 9, 1962. Princeton Revellers, the Little Owls, Mike Lala's band, Murphy Campo's outfit, Saenger Theater pit orchestra, Sharkey, the Big Owls, Grunewald Hotel.

LECLERE, IRWIN (p, vo). b. N.O., about 1893. Well known as composer and house pianist at the Triangle Theater up to World War I. Traveled with popular vaudeville act The Fuzzy Wuzzy Twins. Tunes include "Triangle Jazz Blues," "Cookie."

LEE, BILL (ss, cl). b. N.O., Dec. 19, 1926. Regular member of The Last Straws.

LEGLISE, VIC (d), b. N.O., about 1900. Dixieland drummer with Princeton Revellers about 1920. With Bill Padron, Pinky Vidacovich.

LEGNON, ALBERT "RED" (s). b. N.O. about 1898. In the 20's worked with Alfred Laine's band.

LEGNON, ROSCOE (sb). b. N.O., about 1895; d. N.O., about 1963. With Bayersdorffer's Jazzola Six in pre-WW I period. In later years often with Barocco brothers.

LENARES, ZEB (cl). b. N.O., about 1885; d. N.O. about 1928. Fine clarinetist who played in many of the district combinations between 1909–17. With the Magnolia Sweets in 1910. During the early 20's was heard with the Foster Lewis Jazz Band and with Kid Rena.

LEWIS, "DANDY" (d, sb). b. N.O., about 1888; d. about 1932. Played string bass and managed Eagle Band from 1911–16. During same period was regular bass drummer with the Onward Brass Band.

LEWIS, FOSTER (d). Bandleader of the early 20's.

IRWIN LECLERE

LEWIS, FRANK (cl). b. N.O., about 1870; d. Bogalusa, La., 1924. Charter member of the Buddy Bolden band. Left N.O. in 1917 to play in Louisiana country towns. Played with Dan Moody orchestra until 1924.

LEWIS, GEORGE (cl). b. N.O., July 13, 1900; d. N.O., Dec. 31, 1968. Most celebrated of the pure traditionalists. Played his first jobs in Mandeville, La., with Black Eagle Band, 1917. During 20's marched with Chris Kelly's band, Eureka Brass Band, Buddy Petit, Kid Rena's brass band. With Bunk Johnson, 1945 and 1946. Had a band on tour in Japan in 1963, 1964, and 1965. A biography of Lewis by Jay Alison Stuart has been published in England.

LEWIS, ROBERT "SON FEWCLOTHES" (bd). b. N.O., March 10, 1900; d. N.O., June 24, 1965. One of the great bass drummers of N.O. marching bands. Started with Tulane Brass Band in 1925, played with Chris Kelly for parades in the mid-20's, and

GEORGE LEWIS

SON FEWCLOTHES LEWIS

STEVE LEWIS

with Kid Rena in the 30's. From 1939 to 1963 was the backbone of the Eureka Brass Band. Incapacitated by a stroke in 1963.

LEWIS, STEVE (p). b. N.O., March 19, 1896; d. N.O., 1939. Just established as a top Basin St. "professor" when the district closed down. Left for vaudeville tour with Billy Mack's troupe, along with Johnny Dodds, Mutt Carey. In 1918 joined A. J. Piron at Tranchina's, Spanish Fort; played with Piron on S.S. *Capitol* and operated the boat's calliope. Composed many great tunes including A. J. Piron's theme, "Purple Rose of Cairo," "Kiss Me, Sweet," and "Sud Bustin' Blues." Recorded with the Piron orchestra, and made a piano roll of "Mama's Gone Goodbye." Also backed New Orleans Willie Jackson on Columbia Records in 1926.

LIBERTO, ROY (t, l). b. N.O. March 11, 1928. Leader of novelty dixieland band similar in style to Dukes of Dixieland. Usually on tour.

JOHN LINDSAY

RAY LOPEZ

LINDSAY, JOHN (sb, tu, tb). b. Algiers, La., Aug. 23, 1894; d. Chicago, Ill., July 3, 1950. One of the true N.O. giants of jazz. Started in the red-light district in 1910. Through 20's worked with John Robichaux, A. J. Piron, Papa Celestin. Left in 1924; played in Chicago with King Oliver, Willie Hightower, Carroll Dickerson. Recorded on bass or trombone with A. J. Piron, Jelly Roll Morton, Jimmie Noone, Richard M. Jones. Toured with Louis Armstrong.

LINDSEY, JOSEPH "LITTLE JOE," "SEEFUS" (d). b. N.O., Sept. 7, 1899; d. N.O. First bandleader to employ Louis Armstrong, 1916. After World War I played with Dixie Jazz Band, Bob Lyons, and on pickup jobs with Kid Rena through the 20's. Worked occasionally in dance halls.

LITTLE, JIM. See Brown, Sidney.

LIZANA, FLORIN J. "CURLY" (cl.). b. N.O., July 31, 1895; d. July 31, 1967. Early dixielander, much admired by Larry Shields.

LLAMBIAS, JOE (bjo). With Leon Prima.

LINDSAY, HERB (v). b. N.O., about 1888; d. ——. Played in the district from about 1909. Was at Hanan's saloon, Liberty and Iberville, in a band that included Freddie Keppard, 1910–11. In 1912, he was with the Primrose Orchestra. Left for Chicago in 1917 where he sometimes played in the Lawrence Duhé band.

CHARLIE LOVE

ARNOLD LOYACANO

LONG, GLYNN LEA "RED" (p). b. Houston, Tex., 1895; d. Oct. 13, 1945. Rhythm man of Halfway House Orchestra.

LOPEZ, RAY (c). b. N.O., Nov. 28, 1889, d. Los Angeles, 1976. Member of Tom Brown's Band From Dixieland that went to Chicago in 1915. Toured vaudeville with The Five Rubes. Became movie musician.

LOPOSER, AVERY (tb). b. Mobile, Ala., about 1898. Member of Crescent City Jazzers, Arcadian Serenaders recording groups.

LOVE, CHARLIE (c). b. Plaquemines Parish, La., 1885; d. N.O., Aug. 7, 1963. Love did not play regularly in N.O. until 1925 when he went into the Lyric Theater pit band led by John Robichaux. Since about 1900, however, he'd been in and out of N.O., working mainly in his hometown, and with the Caddo Jazz Band in Shreveport. Worked in dance halls through the depression. In the late 40's and in the 50's he was often at the Happy Landing. He recorded for American Music in 1949. Toward the end of his life he was busy preserving the Robichaux band's book of rags, and rehearsing a ragtime band which was recorded on Riverside in 1960. Throughout his lifetime, he took time to play in the marching bands of the city and was frequently seen in the Tuxedo Brass Band.

LOVETT, "BABY" (d). b. Alexandria, La., about 1900. Long-time resident of Kansas City where he played at one time with Bunk Johnson at the Yellow Front Cafe.

LOYACANO, ARNOLD "DEACON" (p, sb, tu, g, d). b. N.O., 1889; d. N.O., Oct. 5, 1962. Child prodigy played at Milneburg and the French Opera House at age 11. Also with Jack Laine's Reliance Brass Band and Dance Orchestra as early as 1900. Went to Chicago with Tom Brown's band in 1915. Was with N.O. Rhythm Kings, the Original New Orleans Jazz Band, led by Jimmy Durante, and Sig Meyer's Druids Orchestra. Joined the music staff of NBC in early years of radio. In N.O. in later years played with

JOE LOYACANO

BUD LOYACANO

Johnny Wiggs, Sharkey, Leon Prima, George Hartman, the Dukes of Dixieland, George Girard, and Tony Almerico.

LOYACANO, FREDDIE (g, bjo). b. N.O. about 1905. Dixieland man frequently seen with the Sharkey, Leon Prima, Fazola groups; also with Ellis Stratakos. Brother of Steve.

LOYACANO, JOE "HOOK" (tb. sb, tu). b. N.O., 1893; d. N.O., Nov. 30, 1967. Recorded saxophone Halfway House Orchestra. Worked with leading N.O. dixielanders, steadily with Tony Almerico in the 50's. Brother of Arnold, John.

LOYACANO, JOE, b. 1906; d. N.O., March 19, 1969. Played in Halfway House Orchestra, Brother of Steve, Freddie; not related to Joe "Hook" Loyacano.

LOYACANO, JOHN "BUD" (sb, tu). b. N.O., Nov. 15, 1879; d. N.O., Feb. 25, 1960. Dixieland rhythm man with Dan Hughes, Reliance Brass Band and Dance Orchestra, Sal Margiotta. Played with left hand a bass strung for right-handed musician. Brother of Arnold, Joe.

LOYACANO, STEVE (g, bjo, v). b. N.O., Dec. 19, 1903. Started in band led by Pinky Gerbrecht. Went to Johnny Bayersdorffer in time for celebrated record date in 20's. In 1925 worked with N.O. edition of N.O. Rhythm Kings. Led band at Saenger Theater and had his own club, the Chez Paree, in 1935. Brother of Freddie.

LYONS, BOB (sb, tu, g, bjo). b. N.O., about 1868; d. N.O., about 1949. Started playing for pay about 1885

BOB LYONS

RED MACKIE

KID SHOTS MADISON

in "skiffle" bands, working the streets for coins. With Charlie Galloway in mid-90's and at the turn of the century played in the Oscar Duconge band. In 1901 and 1902 he sometimes played with Buddy Bolden; between 1907–10 with Frankie Duson. Was with Kid Ory in 1914. Organized his Dixie Jazz Band in 1918.

MACKIE, RICHARD H. "DICK" (c). b. N.O., Nov. 26, 1906. One of founders of N.O. Owls. Later led own band. Went on tour with big commercial bands, Hal Kemp, Kay Kayser. Sometimes plays informally, and coaches young musicians. Brother of Red.

MACKIE, FRANK "RED" (sb, tu, g, bjo, p); b. N.O., April 16, 1904; d. N.O., 1969. Began playing at about

79

MANUEL MANETTA

age 12. One of original Invincibles and N.O. Owls. Played and appeared with the Six and 7/8 String Band. Made all the discs with this group. Was brother of Dick Mackie.

MAC MURRAY, JOHN (d). b. N.O., about 1878; d. N.O., about 1920. A great N.O. drummer who exerted much influence on the music of the big names that blossomed later in the field. During the early 1900's he was often with Buddy Bolden, and was picked by Manuel Perez for the Imperial Orchestra. Ernest Rogers, Baby Dodds, and Louis Cottrell all showed signs of his style. He built his own drums, and mainly used homemade equipment through his professional career.

MAC NEIL, JAMES (c, p). b. N.O., about 1870; d. Chicago, 1945. Charter member of the John Robichaux orchestra in 1894, he also played in the Onward Brass Band and enlisted in the army with that group for the Spanish-American War. Up to depression times he was a popular music teacher in N.O. Moved to Chicago in 1938. Brother of Wendell.

MAC NEIL, WENDELL (v). b. N.O., about 1872. Was a member of the John Robichaux orchestra from its inception in 1894 to the leader's death in 1939, at which time MacNeil moved to Detroit. He is a brother of the late James MacNeil.

MADISON, LOUIS "KID SHOTS" (t). b. N.O., Feb. 19, 1899; d. N.O., Sept., 1948. Fellow inmate, with Louis Armstrong and Kid Rena, of the Waif's Home in N.O. Studied with David Jones, Joe Howard and Louis Dumaine. Played with Papa Celestin at Beverly Gardens and worked with Frankie Duson—all before World War I. Recorded with the Original Tuxedo Orchestra in 1925. Veteran of the Eureka Brass Band, the Young Tuxedo Brass Band and the WPA Brass Band. He played out his last days at the P & L Club on Lake Pontchartrain. Recorded with George Lewis and Bunk Johnson (American Music).

MAESTRI, "KATZ" (d). b. N.O., about 1906. Frequently with Albert Artigues. Earlier, about 1925, with Norman Brownlee. Toured in 30's with Fortmeier band.

MAHIER, LOUIS (d). b. N.O., about 1902. Member of Nat Towles's Creole Harmony Kings in early 20's.

MANADAY, BUDDY (bjo). Played with Buddy Petit band in early 20's.

MANETTA, MANUEL (all instruments). b. Algiers, La., Oct. 3, 1889; d. Algiers, Oct. 10, 1969. Began 1906 with Tom Albert. Member of notable musical family, Manetta spent more than 50 years as music teacher. Played with Buddy Bolden, Frankie Duson, Edward Clem before 1910. Solo pianist with Willie Piazza's Basin St. brothel about 1908. Was with Tom Albert and the Original Tuxedo Orchestra until 1913, when he tried his luck in Chicago, but soon returned to N.O. During World War I days he was with Papa Celstin and Joe Howard, at the Villa Cabaret. In 1919 worked in California with Ory. During the 20's he was on saxophone with Manuel Perez. Widely known for his ability to play trombone and trumpet simultaneously and in harmony.

MANGIAPANE, SHERWOOD (sb, tu, d, t, vo). b. N.O., Oct. 1, 1912. One of the all-time great N.O. bassists, began playing fifty-cent jobs at lawn parties before he was 12. Closely identified musically with Johnny Wiggs, Raymond Burke, and Dr. Edmond Souchon, with whom he has made many LP's. Known not only for superb musicianship, but also for his singing and whistling.

MANNONE, JOSEPH "WINGY" (t). b. N.O., Feb. 13, 1900. Wingy lost his right arm while hitching a trolley ride when he was nine years old. At the age of twelve he was playing kazoo in spasm bands on the streets of Storyville. Played very little trumpet in N.O. but was well known at the Gulf Coast resorts. Recorded for Okeh with the Arcadian Serenaders, a Mobile, Ala. band. Has appeared in several motion pictures and is widely recorded. His autobiography "Trumpet on the Wing," Doubleday, New York, has enjoyed an excellent sale.

WINGY MANONE

SHERWOOD MANGIAPANE

MANSION, HENRY (tb, bh). b. N.O., about 1898; d. N.O., Jan. 13, 1968. Best known as a brass band musician.

MARCOUR, MICKEY (p). b. N.O. ——; d. N.O., March 19, 1961. During 20's an active dixieland pianist. Played with the Halfway House Orchestra and in a quartet with Abbie Brunies, Buck Rogers, and Stalebread Lacoume at Bucktown tavern.

MARCOUR, OSCAR (v, l). b. N.O., July 1, 1895; d. N.O., Sept. 11, 1956. A formally trained violinist, brother of Mickey Marcour, who frequently worked in bands with top jazzmen.

MARES, PAUL (c, t). b. N.O., June 15, 1900; d. Chicago, Ill., Aug. 18, 1949. Played dance jobs around N.O. as a youth. Learned to play on his father's horn. (Joseph P. Mares, Sr., played in Tosso's Military Band at West End.) In 1920 was playing in Tom Brown's band. Led the N.O. Rhythm Kings in Chicago and became a national sensation. Co-composer of "Tin Roof Blues," "Farewell Blues," "Milneburg Joys," and other jazz standards. Retired from music in early 30's but began to fill concert dates in New York and Philadelphia during the late 40's.

MARGIOTTA, SAL (cl). b. N.O. about 1896; d. N.O., June 29, 1970. Police band. Played with all old-time dixieland stars. Led Triangle Band in 20's.

MICKEY MARCOUR

LAWRENCE MARRERO

PAUL MARES

MARRERO, BILLY (sb). b. N.O. about 1874; d. N.O. Superior Orchestra, 1910–13; Olympia Orchestra, 1913; Camelia Orchestra, 1918. Father of Eddie, John, Lawrence, Simon.

MARRERO, EDDIE (sb). b. N.O., Aug. 4, 1902. Son of Billy Marrero. Started professional career in brother

Lawrence's Young Tuxedo Orchestra, 1920. In mid-20's was playing with Chris Kelly's band.

MARRERO, JOHN (bjo). b. N.O. about 1895; d. N.O. about 1945. Began after World War I with Kid Rena. Son of Billy, brother of Lawrence, Simon, Eddie Marrero. During early 20's worked with Piron, Original Tuxedo Orchestra, Bebé Ridgley. Recorded with Original Tuxedo Orchestra in 1926.

MARRERO, LAWRENCE (bjo). b. N.O., Oct. 24, 1900; d. N.O., June 6, 1959. Started after World War I, with Wooden Joe Nicholas, Kid Rena, Chris Kelly. Formed own Young Tuxedo Orchestra in 1920. Sometimes played bass drum in marching bands, notably with George Lewis. Became famous as the rhythm keystone of the George Lewis Ragtime Jazz Band through the 40's and 50's at the height of Lewis' success.

MARRERO, SIMON (sb). b. N.O. about 1897; d. ——. Another of Billy's busy sons. Worked in Kid Rena's band in early 20's and with Papa Celestin's Original Tuxedo Orchestra with which he recorded in 1927. Joined King Oliver briefly in early depression years and moved to New York where he finished his playing days.

BILL MATTHEWS

ELERY MASER

MARTIN, ABRAHAM (bjo). A regular member of Evan Thomas' Black Eagles band in the 20's.

MARTIN, ALBERT (d). A member of the band that made the famous 1929 session under the name Jones-Collins Astoria Hot Eight.

MARTIN, CHINK. See Abraham, Martin.

MARTIN, "COOCHIE" (g. p). b. N.O. about 1887. d. about 1928. In the pre-World War I period played first with John Robichaux, 1911–12; with the Peerless Orchestra under Bab Frank in 1906 and later (1910) under A. J. Piron. In 1913 he organized his own combination, with himself on piano, and got the job at the 101 Ranch.

MARTIN, "FATS" (d). b. N.O. about 1900. Began his career in the first George Lewis band in the early 20's, but in later years moved into swing and then into modern deviations.

MARTIN, HENRY (d, g). b. N.O. about 1895; d. about 1932. Before World War I was the idol of many of the younger drummers. Played in the district with Kid Ory and with Oliver's band. Also was bass drummer with the Onward Brass Band about 1916. In 1917 he was leading his own small group. In the 20's played in Peter Bocage's Creole Serenaders.

MARTIN, MILTON (tb). b. Algiers, La., Nov. 24, 1896; d. N.O., 1977. Played for several years with Sam Ross Orchestra in Cut Off, La. He retired from music in 1913 at the age of 17.

MASER, ELERY (cl, s). b. N.O., May 12, 1904; d. N.O., Dec. 8, 1972. Played in bands of Happy Schilling, Johnny Bayersdorffer. Recorded with Johnny Hyman's Bayou Stompers, 1927. Later with Pinky Vidacovich, Pinky Gerbrecht, Leon Prima, Sharkey, Jules Bauduc.

MASINTER, LOUIS (sb, tu). b. N.O., Aug. 19, 1908. Frequently with the Primas in 30's.

MATTHEWS, LEWIS "CHIF" (c). b. Laplace, La. about 1885; d. ———. Began his career with Kid Ory about 1903 and stayed with him through 1908 when the band came to N.O. Lawrence Duhé left Ory to take the leader job at the 101 Ranch in 1909, and Matthews went along.

MATTHEWS, NATHANIEL "BEBÉ" (d). b. Algiers, La. about 1890; d. N.O., May 27, 1961. Pre-World War I drummer with Allen Brass Band, Onward Brass Band. Also played with Bebé Ridgley's orchestra. Brother of Bill Matthews.

PERCY McCAY

THOMPSON McCAY

MATTHEWS, RAMOS (d). b. Algiers, La. about 1886; d. N.O., Oct. 20, 1958. Popular parade drummer. Worked in Allen Brass Band from about 1912 to 1926. He also played in marching groups organized by Louis Dumaine. Brother of Bill and Bebé Matthews.

MATTHEWS, STONEWALL (bjo, g). b. Laplace, La., about 1889. Another charter member of the Kid Ory band that came to N.O. in 1908. Brother of Chif Matthews.

MATTHEWS, WILLIAM "BILL" (d, tb). b. Algiers, La., May 9, 1899; d. N.O., June 3, 1964. Youngest of the three Matthews drummers, Bill made his debut in 1917 with the Excelsior Brass Band and in the dance orchestra of Jack Williams. Worked with Desvigne in the district just before it closed, then odd jobs with Frankie Duson, Sam Morgan, Joe Howard.

Took up trombone in the early 20's, studied with Vic Gaspard and went west with Nat Towles orchestra in 1926. Toured with Jelly Roll Morton and went back to Desvigne on the steamship *Island Queen*. In 1927, again in N.O., played with Ridgley's section of the Original Tuxedo Orchestra and recorded with Papa Celestin. From 1945 to 1963, he kept quite busy at the Paddock on Bourbon St., usually with Celestin up to 1952.

MC CAY, PERCY (all string and wind instr.). b. N.O., Dec. 13, 1896. Talented amateur played with the all-string bands of N.O.—Invincibles, Six and 7/8, others.

MC CAY, THOMPSON (g, sb, mdl, v, tb, tu). b. N.O., Sept. 4, 1901; d. N.O., July 4, 1963. Brother of Percy McCay and well known for his work in all-string bands in early days of N.O. jazz.

GEORGE McCULLUM, SR.

MC CLEAN, RICHARD (sb, bjo, g). b. N.O., Jan. 25, 1898; d. N.O., 1968. Played with Papa Celestin, Octave Crosby bands. Was long a fixture on Bourbon St.

MC CLENNON, RUBE (bjo). During the 20's McClennon was closely associated with Buddy Petit, though for a short time, during an illness of Buddy's, he worked with Dejan's Black Diamond Orchestra. When Petit died in 1931, Rube took the leadership of the band and worked with it on the S.S. Madison.

MC CULLUM, GEORGE, SR. (c). b. N.O., July 27, 1885; d. N.O., Nov. 14, 1920. Marched in first parade at age 15. In 1909 joined Barnum & Bailey Circus band. Led regular brass band for the Jefferson City Buzzards. Played with Robichaux, Piron dance bands. Both Manuel Manetta and Sweet Emma Barrett played piano in his dance bands.

MC CULLUM, GEORGE, JR. (t). b. N.O., about 1906; d. N.O., 1938. Studied with his father and succeeded George, Sr. in the Robichaux orchestra in 1920. During the 20's, marched with the Excelsior and Tuxedo

brass bands and worked dance hall jobs under Eddie Jackson's leadership. In the mid-depression days was the solo trumpet in the WPA Brass Band led by Pinchback Touro.

MC CURDY, CHARLES (cl, s). b. N.O., about 1865; d. N.O., Oct. 4, 1933. A leading musician for over 50 years, McCurdy was a charter member of the Robichaux orchestra in 1894. In 1905 he was co-leader, with Bab Frank, of the Peerless Orchestra and marched with the Excelsior Brass Band before World War I. Went back with Robichaux in 1913. Later worked with Piron in the Olympia Orchestra and played with Fate Marable on the S.S. Capitol after the war. Rejoined Robichaux in the Lyric Theater, 1925–27, then in 1928 was in Peter Lacaze's NOLA Band. Until about 1934, was on the road working in tent show and circus bands, especially the show, "Silas Green from New Orleans."

MC NEAL, RICHARD (bjo). A member of Kid Rena Dixie Jazz Band, 1922.

MELLO, LEONCE (tb). b. N.O. about 1888; d. N.O. about 1941. One of the great trombones of early N.O. An occasional dance band musician, but best known for his performance with Jack Laine's Reliance Brass Band in the pre-World War I days. Also played in 1907 with the Fischer Brass Band. With Barocco brothers' band in 1919.

MELLO, MANUEL JOHN (c). b. N.O., June 18, 1886; d. N.O., Oct. 31, 1961. Made his parade debut with a five-piece marching band, The Big Five, that included his brother, Leonce, on trombone about 1903. Never recorded, he was an admirer of Manuel Perez' sound and strove to duplicate it. Was a mainstay of Jack Laine's ragtime bands from about 1908 and always a member of the No. 1 unit of the Reliance Brass Band.

MELLO, SANFORD (tb, d). b. N.O. about 1901. Played in Alfred Laine's band in the 20's. Brother of Leonce, Manuel.

MENDELSON, STANLEY (p). b. N.O., June 23, 1923. Played with Dukes of Dixieland, Sharkey, Phil Zito. Accompanied Lizzie Miles, Buglin' Sam Dekemel. In 60's soloist at cocktail lounge at the Sheraton-

LIZZIE MILES

PUNCH MILLER

Charles Hotel. Recorded with Tom Brown and Johnny Wiggs.

METOYER, ARNOLD (c, t). b. N.O., about 1876; d. N.O., 1935. A "legitimate" musician who spent most of his prime years playing in traveling tent shows, and was out of town much of the time. He was much respected by contemporaries for his technique. In 1921 was with Luis Russell at Anderson's Restaurant, and sometimes played dance jobs with jazzmen.

MILES, LIZZIE (vo). b. N.O., March 31, 1895; d. N.O., March 17, 1963. Popular N.O. singer who recorded in the 20's and experienced a revival during the 50's under the guidance of Joe Mares. Worked mainly at Davilla's Mardi Gras lounge and was in Los Angeles with Bob Scobey. Especially known in later years for renditions of a number of tunes in "gombo French."

MILLER, CHARLIE K. (tb). b. N.O., March 11, 1915; d. Thibodaux, La., Dec. 23, 1962. Worked in bands led by Irving Fazola, Augie Schellang, Leon Prima, Sharkey, and George Hartman. Member of WWL staff orchestra, The Dawn Busters.

MILLER, EDDIE (cl, s). b. N.O., June 23, 1911. In 1924 was a member of N.O. *Item* newsboy band. Joined the Owls in that band's latter days. Left town at the beginning of the depression, as tenor sax with Ben Pollack's orchestra, going to New York. A founding member of the Bob Crosby orchestra, active from 1935 to 1943, and became leader when Crosby began his film career. During the 50's settled in North Hollywood, Calif. Played a daily TV show during the 50's. Still visits N.O. occasionally, and during the early 60's played with a trio in Pete Fountain's club on Bourbon St. while Pete was on tour. Widely recorded on tenor sax, but his clarinet work with the Mound City Blue Blowers may have been his artistic peak.

MILLER, ERNEST "KID PUNCH" (t). b. Raceland, La., June 10, 1894; d. N.O., Dec. 3, 1971. Debuted in 1919 in N.O. after discharge as military band bugle corporal. First worked in band of Duck Ernest Johnson, then with Jack Carey, whom he left after two years to form his own band. He moved to Chicago in 1927, to a job with Francois' Louisianians (Francois Mosley of N.O.), then barnstormed with circus and carnival bands all over the U.S. Was in N.O. through early 60's leading his own band.

MILLER, JOHNNY (p). b. N.O. about 1897. With Johnny Bayersdorffer's most successful band, made

86

collector's item record with his own Johnny Miller's Frolickers.

MILLER, JAMES E. "SING" (p, bjo, vo). b. N.O., June 17, 1913. Veteran big band musician. Has worked in later years with George Lewis, Paul Barbarin, Earl Foster, Kid Thomas.

MILTON, ERNEST "KID" (t, d). b. N.O., June 14, 1905. An average trumpeter, with talent for finding jobs for a band. Always busy with his own dance groups since about 1918; he has employed many well-known N.O musicians during his active musical life.

MINOR, DONALD (cl). b. N.O., May 5, 1935. With Harold Dejan's Young Olympia Brass Band. Son of H. E. Minor.

MINOR, FRED "H. E." (bjo, g). b. N.O., Dec. 8, 1913. An active musician since early depression days in the Sidney Desvigne orchestra. During the 50's and early 60's was frequently seen with Paul Barbarin's band. In mid-60's, part of Noon Johnson bazooka trio.

MINOR, GEORGE (g). Guitar in Kid Sheik Band.

MIRANDA, JACK (cl). b. N.O., about 1908; d. N.O., about 1959. Dixielander who reached his peak working with Abbie Brunies in the 40's.

MITCHELL, ARTHUR (sb, bjo). A member of George Lewis' first band in 1923. As early as 1902 worked in a Buddy Bolden group, and in 1903 was in the district with Johnny Gould's string band playing guitar and banjo.

MITCHELL, EDNA (p, vo). b. N.O. ——. A gifted soloist who entertained in the cabarets as a piano-playing balladeer. She worked with Louis Armstrong at Anderson's Restaurant on Rampart St. in the early 20's. Wife of drummer, Albert Francis.

MITCHELL, LEONARD (bjo). Member of Louis Dumaine's Jazzola Eight that made the 1927 record session.

MOLIERE, ERNEST "KID" (cl). b. N.O., about 1902. In the early 20's, a member of Nat Towles' Creole Harmony Kings that toured the Southwest.

MONTEGUE, SIDNEY (d). b. N.O., Sept. 13, 1908; d. N.O., Jan. 31, 1969. Played on lake steamers with Leo Dejan.

MONTGOMERY, EURREAL "LITTLE BROTHER" (p, vo). b. Kentwood, La., about 1907. Played very little in N.O. but toured Louisiana with Clarence Desdunes' Joyland Revelers. Has long been a popular favorite in Chicago clubs. Recorded solo and with Lee Collins. Led his own band in Jackson, Miss., from 1931–38, with George Guesnon on banjo.

MOODY, DAN (tb). b. Mandeville, La., about 1890; d. N.O., June, 1959. A popular bandleader in the small resort towns on the shore of Lake Pontchartrain opposite N.O. in post-World War I days.

MOORE, CHARLIE (g, bjo). b. N.O.; d. Jan., 1961. A charter member of Jack Carey's Crescent Orchestra before World War I. Sometimes worked at Tom Anderson's.

MOORE, ROBERT "BUSTER" (tb). b. N.O., about 1898; d. Oct. 24, 1966. In the early 20's a member of Johnny Brown's band, Moore was little known until his comeback in the early 60's at Preservation Hall and with the Gibson Brass Band.

MOORE, SIDNEY (cl). With Reliance Brass Band about 1914.

MORAND, HERB (t, vo). b. N.O., 1905; d. N.O., Feb. 22, 1952. Self-taught. Half-brother of Lizzie Miles. First with Nat Towles' Creole Harmony Kings touring Southwest, 1923; same year made pioneer N.O. jazz radio broadcast. In 1924 was a sensation playing at a carnival in Mérida, Yucatan, Mexico. In mid-20's played with Cliff Jackson in New York; returned to N.O. and played for Chris Kelly. Went to Chicago in time for the crash and recorded with the brothers Dodds, Frank Melrose and the Harlem Hamfats. In 1941 returned to N.O., worked with George Lewis and played for several years in the lakefront resorts.

MORET, GEORGE (c). b. N.O., about 1870; d. N.O., 1924. Leader of the Excelsior Brass Band, 1905–22. A "legitimate" musician who sometimes filled in on a job with real jazzmen where reading was required.

HERB MORAND

EDDIE MILLER

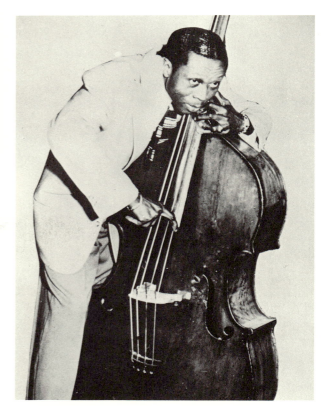

AL MORGAN

MORGAN, AL (sb, sou). b. N.O., Aug. 19, 1908; d. Los Angeles, April, 1974. Famed bass player; member of Morgan clan; seldom played in N.O. Spent most of his musical days on tour with Lee Collins in Florida, and with Fate Marable and Sidney Desvigne on the riverboats through the mid-20's. Bass on the Jones-Collins Astoria Hot Eight record session. Left N.O. in 1928; jobbed in New York and California with top name bands ever since.

MORGAN, ANDREW (cl, s). b. Pensacola, Fla., March 19, 1903. Professional career began in 1924 in the Young Superior Band with Leonard Bechet. In 1925 joined the Young Morgan Band led by brother, Isaiah. With same group under brother, Sam, in 1926 and made the famed record sessions. Worked through the 30's with Mike Delay, Kid Thomas, WPA Brass Band, ERA Orchestra; in 40's with Kid Rena at the Brown Derby; much work in Little Woods in late 40's, early 50's. Played in Young Tuxedo Brass Band and Preservation Hall.

MORGAN, ISAIAH (c, t). b. Bertrandville, La., April 7, 1897; d. May 16, 1966. Started his own Young Morgan Band in 1922. Studied with his brother, Sam. Played lead on the great recordings of the Sam Morgan jazz band, 1927. After Sam was incapacitated by a stroke, Isaiah held his brother's band together and kept it on tour, mainly through the Gulf Coast area. He settled in Biloxi, Miss., for many years. Returned to N.O. in the 50's.

ANDREW MORGAN

MORGAN, SAM (t). b. Bertrandville, La., 1895; d. N.O., Feb. 25, 1936. Oldest of the many brothers, Sam was a prime mover of jazz in N.O. His recordings are typical of Crescent City music of the mid-twenties. His career as a leader was interrupted by a stroke in 1925, but he made a comeback a year later. During the 30's the strain of being on the road was too much for him, and he died on Mardi Gras day in 1936. The Tulane Brass Band and Kid Howard Brass Band played for his funeral.

MORIN, EUGENE (d). b. Abita Springs, La., about 1880; d. about 1950. One of the earliest dixieland musicians. Played with the Abita Springs Serenaders Jazz Band in 1912–14.

MORRIS, EDDIE (tb). b. Algiers, La., July 19, 1896. With Punch Miller through the early 20's, to 1927; with Kid Rena, 1927–28; with Buddy Petit until latter's death in 1931. In mid-depression played for the ERA Orchestra and the WPA Brass Band. Led his own dance band and marched with the Gibson Brass Band.

JELLY ROLL MORTON

MORRIS, JOE (sb). b. N.O., about 1905; d. N.O., Jan. 13, 1961. Jobbed around with many bands, Kid Sheik's among them. Was in the big ERA Orchestra of the mid-thirties.

MORTON, FERDINAND JOSEPH LE MENTHE "JELLY ROLL" (p). b. N.O., Sept. 20, 1885; d. Los Angeles, Calif., July 10, 1941. Most famous of Storyville "professors." Left town permanently in 1915. One of the few great men of jazz. Composed classics—"Wolverine Blues," "King Porter Stomp," "Grandpa's Spells." Made 12 LP set of discs on jazz history for Library of Congress. Autobiography, aided by Alan Lomax, "Mr. Jelly Roll." Jelly Roll worked only in his own groups.

EDGAR MOSLEY

GUSSIE MUELLER

His many records remain as testimony to his creative genius. In selecting the most important single figure in jazz, Louis Armstrong could be considered his main rival.

MOSLEY, BAPTISTE "BAT" (d). b. Algiers, La., Dec. 22, 1893; d. N.O., Aug. 28, 1965. Began to play professionally in early 20's with Joe Harris' dixieland band. Was with the Kid Howard brass band irregularly; through the 30's worked with Kid Rena's brass band. Brother of Edgar.

MOSLEY, EDGAR (d). b. Algiers, La., Nov. 12, 1895; d. Los Angeles, Calif., 1962. During the 20's and 30's a leading bass drummer in the marching bands. Worked with the Kid Rena, Chris Kelly, George Lewis brass bands and recorded with Lewis dance band in 1943. In 1962 he was in a parade sponsored by the NOJC of Southern California.

MUELLER, GUSTAVE "GUSSIE" (cl, s). b. N.O., Apr. 17, 1890; d. North Hollywood, Calif., Dec. 16, 1965. Im-

portant early dixieland star. Composed "Wang Wang Blues" while with Paul Whiteman. As a youngster played with Papa Laine's Reliance Brass Band No. 1, the prime unit in the Reliance organization, 1903. Joined Tom Brown in Chicago in 1915. With Baron Long from 1918–20.

MUKES, DANIEL (sn). b. N.O. about 1901; d. N.O., March 17, 1956. Snare drummer for Eureka Brass Band.

MUMFORD, JEFF "BROCK" (g). b. N.O., about 1870; d. N.O., about 1914. Reportedly one of the great jazz rhythm men of all time. Played duets in the streets with Charlie Galloway as early as 1885. Played in Buddy Bolden's first band; from 1907 to 1914 with Frankie Duson's Eagle Band.

MURRAY, FRANCIS (s, cl, bjo). b. N.O., 1915; d. N.O., Jan. 21, 1963. Active dixielander, played under leadership of Johnny Wiggs, Dutch Andrus, Stuart Bergen, Abbie Brunies, Pete Fountain, Jack Delaney, and the Loyacano brothers. Also worked with Nick La Rocca, Tony Parenti, and Willie Guitar on various jobs. Was in the N.O. police band and in Clancy's Marching Band in Harahan, La. Was at times in the Leonard Ferguson Viscounts.

MUTZ, FRANK (p). b. about 1900. Participated in the first live jazz broadcast from N.O. with Ellis Stratakos, Ray Bauduc.

LOUIS NELSON

FRED NEUROTH

NAQUIN, BILL (t). b. N.O. about 1900. Member of the Melon Pickers in 30's.

NASH, LEMON (u, bjo, g, vo). b. Lakeland, La., April 22, 1898; d. N.O., Dec. 27, 1969. Started on banjo with Pete Williams' band. Worked with Noon Johnson trio. Mainly a solo entertainer and sometime teacher of strings at Morris Music Company.

NEELY, MAY (p). Pianist with John Robichaux orchestra at the Lyric Theater in 1925.

NED, LOUIS (tu, l) b. N.O., about 1858; d. N.O., about 1895. Early bandleader of the late 1870's who, along with Wallace Collins, was playing "skiffle" music in the streets of the city as early as 1869.

NELSON, DAVIDSON C. (p, t, arr). b. Donaldsonville, La., about 1906; d. April 7, 1946. Nephew of King Oliver. Accompanied Ma Rainey on discs. Toured with Jelly Roll Morton, Richard M. Jones. Led own combo in Chicago, 1927; with Jimmie Noone at Apex Club. In 1929 went to New York, worked with Luis Russell, Oliver. Organized original Mills Blue Rhythm Band. Recorded on Victor as Dave Nelson and the King's Men. In 1930 toured with Mae West show, "The Constant Sinner."

NELSON, GEORGE (s). b. N.O., about 1905. Brother of trombone player Louis Nelson. Played mainly on the lake steamers through the early 30's.

NELSON, LOUIS (tb). b. N.O., Sept. 17, 1902. Started with Joe Gable's band in Thibodaux. In the early 20's and 30's was with Original Tuxedo Orchestra, Kid Rena's band, and then for the next fifteen years with the Sidney Desvigne orchestra. During the depression he was in the WPA music program and joined Kid Thomas about 1944. Regularly at Preservation Hall especially with Percy Humphrey or Punch Miller during the 60's.

NELSON, "BIG EYE LOUIS." See Delisle, Louis Nelson.

NETTO, FRANK (sb, tu, tb). Dixielander, played with late version of Owls, 1925–27.

NEUMANN, FREDDIE (p.). b. N.O., July 20, 1904. Dixielander of the 20's, played with most of top bands. Also with dance bands of Joe Capraro and Angelo Capra (Capraro).

NEUROTH, FREDDIE (c). b. N.O., about 1892; d. Chicago, Ill., about 1923. Active with Jack Laine's Reliance Brass Band about 1910–12. With Morgan's Euphonic Syncopators in Chicago during pre-World War I days.

91

ALBERT NICHOLAS

WOODEN JOE NICHOLAS

NEWMAN, DWIGHT (p). b. N.O., 1902; d. N.O., about 1942. Early 20's with the Young Tuxedo Orchestra. Later played dance hall jobs with Eddie Jackson. Joined the A. J. Piron Orchestra in 1928. Played with Peter Bocage's Creole Serenaders through the 30's. Occasionally worked with George Lewis.

NEWTON, WILLIE (sb). b. N.O., about 1885; d. N.O., about 1921. With Tig Chambers about 1905. Later with Kid Milton.

NICHOLAS, ALBERT (cl). b. N.O., May 27, 1900; d. Paris, Oct. 2, 1973. Pupil of Lorenzo, Tio, Jr., 1910. Nephew of Wooden Joe Nicholas. At 14 worked with Buddy Petit, the Marreros, Arnold Depass. November, 1916, joined U.S. Navy; spent war in Caucasian band on U.S.S. *Olympia*. He joined Maple Leaf Or-

chestra in 1919 and went into the Cadillac Cabaret with Depass in 1921. In 1922 worked at Oasis Cabaret with Manuel Perez. Took his own band into Tom Anderson's on Rampart St. for a year, 1923–24. Joined King Oliver in Chicago in 1924; stayed until 1926 then went to Shanghai's Plaza Hotel band. In 1927 he barnstormed home through East Indies, Java, and the Middle East, spending a year in Cairo. Back in New York, 1928, with Luis Russell, then Louis Armstrong and Jelly Roll Morton. During late 30's, 40's he played only with small groups in New York jazz spots and concerts in New York and Philadelphia. Made his home in Europe and recorded extensively in Paris.

NICHOLAS, JOSEPH "WOODEN JOE" (c, t, cl). b. N.O., Sept. 23, 1883; d. N.O., Nov. 17, 1957. One of best

JIMMIE NOONE

known bandsmen of the red-light district until 1917, as a clarinetist. Practiced on King Oliver's cornet on the bandstand during Oliver's frequent "coffee breaks." Organized his Camelia Dance Band and Camelia Brass Band in 1918. Usually Buddy Petit played second cornet in the brass band. Remained

musically active into the 40's and was recorded on both clarinet and trumpet by American Music. Also occurs on wax with Johnny St. Cyr and Raymond Burke. He was an uncle of Albert Nicholas.

NICKERSON, PHILIP (g, bjo). b. N.O., about 1886. A son of the celebrated music teacher, Professor William J. Nickerson. Played regularly in the early 1900's with the Silver Leaf Orchestra.

NOLAN, POREE (p). a Storyville "professor" between 1905–13.

NOLAN, WALTER (d). with Jimmie Noone in 1915.

NOONE, JIMMIE (cl). b. Cut Off, La., April 23, 1895; d. Los Angeles, Calif., April 19, 1944. Studied with Sidney Bechet, Lorenzo Tio, Jr. First real job with Freddie Keppard in 1912 in Storyville. Led a band jointly with Buddy Petit until 1917. Worked irregularly with Kid Ory or Papa Celestin in the district until it closed permanently. Vaudeville tour with Original Creole Orchestra. Migrated to Chicago; played with Joe Oliver, Doc Cook, Zutty Singleton; led own band at Apex Club. Recorded for Decca, Capitol just before his death. Was a brother-in-law of Paul Barbarin, Freddie Keppard.

NUNEZ, ALCIDE "YELLOW" (cl). b. N.O., about 1892; d. N.O., about 1933. Pioneer dixieland star with Reliance Brass Band 1912 to 1916. Went to Chicago with what became the Original Dixieland Jazz Band, though he missed out on the chance to make the historic first jazz records. Joined Anton Lada in The Louisiana Five, then returned to N.O. After 1927, played with the N.O. police band.

OGDEN, DAVE (d). b. N.O., about 1888; d. N.O., Mar. 18, 1963. Played with Maple Leaf Orchestra. One-time leader of this group. Also in ERA bands.

OGLE, ARTHUR (d). b. N.O., about 1895; d. N.O., April 7, 1959. Respected drummer in the Eureka Brass Band. Earlier was in the Camelia Brass Band. His career as a jazz drummer dates back to about 1918. In 1920 was with Lee Collins in The Golden Leaf Orchestra. Plays on the rare Pax record of the Eureka Brass Band.

KING OLIVER

KID ORY

OLIVER, JOSEPH "KING" (c). b. Abent, La., Dec. 19, 1885; d. Savannah, Ga., April 8, 1938. Began about 1904 as a substitute with the Onward Brass Band. To about 1910 was with Allen Brass Band, the Original Superior Orchestra, the Eagle Band, and the Magnolia Band, usually filling in for famed horn-men Manuel Perez, Bunk Johnson. After 1910 worked regularly with Richard M. Jones Four Hot Hounds at Abadie's, and then as leader at Pete Lala's. Left for Chicago and world renown in 1918, where his band at the Lincoln Gardens became the sensation of the early 20's. Louis Armstrong made his debut outside N.O. with this band. A poor business-man, he failed to capitalize on his reputation, and his career declined steadily until he was near starvation during the days just before his death. Oliver's story may be read in *King Joe Oliver*, by Brian Rust and Walter C. Allen; and in *King Oliver*, by Martin Williams. There is a chapter on him in *Jazzmen*, by Frederic Ramsey and Charles E. Smith.

OLIVIER, ADAM (c). b. N.O., about 1865; d. before W W I. Full-time barber and part-time bandleader of the 90's until about 1910; he was first to employ both Bunk Johnson and Tony Jackson.

"OLLIE PAPA" (sb). b. N.O., about 1900. Always active job musician. Played with most N.O. jazz stars, notably with Kid Howard, Burnell Santiago, Joe Robichaux. Still working in 1960's. Legal name, Charles Thomas.

ORY, EDWARD "KID" (tb). b. Laplace, La., Dec. 25, 1886; d. Jan. 23, 1973. Led hometown band in his teens and brought it into N.O. about 1908, where it promptly split up. From 1913 to 1919, Ory was one of the most prominent "hot" bandleaders in town, work-ing mainly in the district at Pete Lala's. Left for Los Angeles in 1919, never to return to N.O. In Chicago in the mid-twenties, he made discs with Louis Arm-strong's Hot Five and with Oliver. Is perhaps the most important influence on jazz trombone playing. In the forefront of the jazz revival of the 40's he produced some of the period's finest recordings and remains musically active on the West Coast. As late as 1963 he was seen on a telecast from Disneyland with Johnny St. Cyr and again in 1965 with Ed Sullivan. Among his composition credits are the evergreen "Muskrat Ramble" and "Ory's Creole Trombone."

WILLIE PAJEAUD

ROY PALMER

TONY PAPALIA

OUILLIBER, EMILE (tb). b. N.O., 1921; d. N.O., Sept. 13, 1964. Dixielander who played with most of the best-known musicians of his period.

OXLEY, DAVE (d, vo). b. N.O., May 1, 1910; d. N.O., July 20, 1974. Regular with George Lewis Band. Played with Papa Celestin, Joe Robichaux, Kid Howard, Henry Hardin. Toured with Bessie Smith.

PADRON, BILL (t). b. N.O., July 15, 1903; d. N.O., April 9, 1959. Played with N.O. Owls and other 1920 bands. Only records are with Owls.

PAGE, ANTHONY (vt). b. N.O., before Civil War; d. N.O., about 1905. Charter member of the Excelsior Brass Band, 1880.

PAJEAUD, WILLIE (c, t). b. N.O., 1895; d. N.O., May 12, 1960. Regularly with the Eureka Brass Band until his death. One of the city's best "readers." Professional since 1915. Worked with Tuxedo Brass Band, 1919; with Maple Leaf Orchestra, John Robichaux, Sam Morgan. In 1929 he was the leader at the Alamo dime-a-dance palace. Worked regularly with his own groups during the depression. Pupil of Manuel Perez.

PALAO, JAMES A. (v, s, ah). b. N.O., about 1880. d. about 1925. With the Imperial Orchestra in 1906. Active in the district to 1912, especially at 101 Ranch and Villa Cabaret. Left to tour in vaudeville with the Original Creole Orchestra. In 1919, played in Chi-cago in the Deluxe Cafe. His 1916 business card has the word "jaz" printed on it in several places.

PALISIER, JOHN "PUJOL" (cl). b. N.O., about 1885; d. N.O. ———. In band led by Bill Gallaty, Sr., cousin of Tony Fougerat. Usually misspelled "Pallachais."

PALMER, ROY (tb). b. N.O., 1892; d. Chicago, Ill., 1964. With Richard M. Jones, Sidney Desvigne before moving to Chicago in 1914. With Lawrence Duhé in Original Creole Orchestra in 20's. Also with Johnny Dodds and King Oliver, Jelly Roll Morton. Strong influence on George Brunies.

PALMISANO, ANGELO (g). Late version of New Orleans Owls, Halfway House Orchestra.

PAPALIA, ANTHONY "TONY" (s, cl, l). b. N.O., 1905; d. N.O., Jan. 25, 1974. Long a well-known society orchestra leader. In early days did lots of theater work and was in Tony Parenti's orchestra.

95

TONY PARENTI

SLOW DRAG PAVAGEAU

RUSS PAPALIA

PAPALIA, RUSS (tb, sb, l). b. N.O., 1903; d. N.O., Oct. 27, 1972. Led society dance orchestra for many years. Early career with Tony Parenti, Johnny De-Droit, Irving Fazola, Johnny Bayersdorffer.

PAPIN, PETER (bjo, vo, l). b. N.O., Sept. 17, 1898. Played in Chris Kelly's band in 20's. Popular as a singer and entertainer.

PARENTI, TONY (cl). b. N.O., Aug. 6, 1900; d. New York City, April 17, 1972. Child prodigy, was an established bandsman at twelve. At fourteen he played with ragtime bands and turned down offer to go north with Original Dixieland Jazz Band be-cause of his youth. In N.O. worked with Jack Laine units and played excursions on the steamer *Majestic* on Lake Pontchartrain. Also was in the Triangle and Alamo theaters, the Pup Cafe and with Johnny De-Droit's band. Became a leader at an early age with both a "symphonic" dance orchestra and a jazz band. In 1925 he formed his Liberty Syncopators which played at the Liberty Theater and the Lavida Ball-room. This band was recorded on Columbia. In the 20's, left N.O. to become a world-renowned jazz star. Remains a major attraction into the 60's, playing on Broadway, mainly at the Metropole and Jimmy Ryan's. Outstanding recordings of rags on Circle, Riverside, G.H.B.

PARKER, GEORGIE (p, l). b. N.O., about 1905; d. N.O., Sept. 25, 1959. Led small groups during 20's and 30's, often featuring George Guesnon, Clarence Tisdale, Cornbread Thomas, Elmer Talbert.

PARKER, WILLIE (cl, bd). b. N.O., March 4, 1875; d. N.O., Aug. 31, 1965. With Jimmy Palao, Terminal Brass Band in early 1900's. Became a founding member of Eureka Brass Band, 1920. During the late 20's was in the Lyons Brass Band.

PASHLEY, FRANK (bjo). Member of Nat Towles' Creole Harmony Kings in the 20's. Migrated to St. Louis in 1924. Played with Kid Ory and Bunk John-son in 40's in Calif.

96

SANTO PECORA

SAMMY PENN

PAUL, CASIMIR (g). b. N.O. ——. With Harold Dejan, Lester Santiago on the lake cruisers in the early 30's.

PAUL, EMANUEL (v, bjo, s). b. N.O., Feb. 2, 1904. First learned music in a church-organized orchestra of 17 pieces. His instrument has been the saxophone through his professional years since the depression, although during the 20's he played banjo on dance jobs. Frequently worked on jobs for T-Boy Remy in 1940–42 and started with the Eureka Brass Band about that time. Joined the Kid Thomas band about 1942 and has remained with these two groups for over 20 years.

PAVAGEAU, ALCIDE "SLOW DRAG" (g, b). b. N.O., March 7, 1888; d. N.O., Jan. 19, 1969. Known to traditional fans as the Grand Marshal of the Second Line. Winner of many dance contests in pre-World War I years. He won his musical reputation as the driving bass man of the Bunk Johnson and George Lewis bands through the 40's and 50's. Photogenic and charming, he is the target of tourist and press photographer alike and has frequently been seen on network TV, albeit anonymously.

PAYEN, JOE (ah). b. N.O., about 1875; d. N.O., 1932. Alto horn in the Excelsior Brass Band, also managed

the organization for some twenty years. When he died, the band collapsed.

PAYNE, RICHARD (g). b. N.O., about 1880. With Original Superior Band in 1910.

PECCOPIA, PETE (c). d. about 1950. A highly regarded musician of the period from 1905–30. Much used by Jack Laine dance units and in the Reliance Brass Band. In Susquehanna Band, early 20's.

PECK, BERT (p). b. N.O., July 15, 1906. Now prominent in politics. Was popular dixieland piano man in 20's. With Princeton Revellers, Bayersdorffer, Leon Prima at various times.

PECORA, SANTO (tb, l). b. N.O., March 21, 1902. The true maestro of the dixieland tailgate style. Played and recorded with N.O. Rhythm Kings in 1925. Spent 17 years barnstorming with both large swing bands, Buddy Rogers, Ben Pollack, Will Osborne; and small dixieland groups, Sharkey, Wingy Manone. Since 1942 has worked steadily in Louisiana, first in and around Baton Rouge, and more recently, in N.O. at the Famous Door on Bourbon St.

PECORARO, SANTO (d). b. N.O., Sept. 26, 1906. Nephew of Santo Pecora. Worked frequently with

MANUEL PEREZ

Johnny Wiggs in the days prior to Wiggs's temporary retirement about 1962.

PELLEGRINI, PETE (c). b. N.O., about 1885; d. N.O., 1940. With Reliance Brass Band.

PENN, ERNEST (bjo).

PENN, SAMMY (d, vo). b. Morgan City, La., Sept. 15, 1902; d. Florida, Sept. 18, 1969. First job in hometown band of Jake Johnson. Came to N.O. in 1921; with Chris Kelly Brass Band, Kid Rena Brass Band, Eureka Brass Band. Was showy personality, a mainstay of the Kid Thomas band for a quarter-century. In mid-50's he took a group of his own to Chicago as Penn and His Five Pennies, but was soon back at his post with Thomas.

PENN, WILLIAM (bjo). b. N.O. ——; d. N.O., about 1946. Popular solo performer of 20's, widely known as a specialty act of great virtuosity and repertoire. Cousin of Ernest Roubleau.

PEQUE, PAUL (cl, s). b. N.O., about 1906. Played with Brownlee band in 20's.

JOSEPH PETIT

PEREZ, MANUEL (c). b. N.O., 1873; d. N.O., 1946. A titan of early jazz. Organized his own Imperial Orchestra in 1900. Joined the Onward Brass Band in 1899 and stayed with it until it broke up 30 years later. Made a brief visit to Chicago in 1915 to play at the Arsonia Cafe but returned to N.O. quickly. Was one of the "big name" leaders of Storyville, mainly at Rice's Cafe. After World War I, he played on the S.S. *Capitol* and was fairly busy thereafter until depression.

PERKINS, DAVE (tb, d, t, eu). b. N.O., about 1868; d. N.O., 1926. Active brass band musician from 1895 to about 1912, working with the Reliance Brass Band and the Toca Brass Band. Became one of the great music teachers in N.O. for both trombone and drums.

ONE-EYE BABE PHILIP

PETERSON, HAROLD (d). b. N.O., about 1900. Pre-World War I dixielander, cousin of Raymond Burke.

PETIT, BUDDY (c). b. N.O., 1887; d. N.O., July 4, 1931. Actual name, Joseph Crawford. Contemporaries acclaim Petit as the equal of Armstrong. In 1916 was co-leader of a band with Jimmy Noone. Preferred to job around on one night stands, advertising wagons, and dance dates. Roamed the Gulf Coast from Galveston to Mobile; dedicated himself more to high living than music, financing his peccadilloes with his horn. Played for a while on the riverboats and lake steamers about 1931 and died, according to accounts, from the effects of overeating at a July 4 picnic.

PETIT, JOSEPH (tb, l). b. N.O., about 1880; d. N.O., 1946. Started playing about 1896. Was in Olympia Orchestra about 1900. Led Security Brass Band, Terminal Orchestra during WW I years. Was in Camelia Orchestra and Brass Band in early 20's. Usually played in Jefferson City Buzzards' Mardi Gras parades. Stepfather of Buddy Petit.

PEYTON, HENRY (acc). Leader of the string trio that played for the opening of Tom Anderson's Annex on Basin St., and, reportedly, in 1899 with a group at the Big 25.

PFLUEGER, SIDNEY (bjo, g.), b. N.O., about 1905. Has been playing jobs in N.O. for more than 40 years. Was associated in his early days with Burnell Santiago.

PHILIP, JOSEPH "ONE-EYE BABE" (sb). b. N.O., 1879; d. N.O., 1960. Active bassist of early 20's. Yank Johnson's band, 1920; Foster Lewis' jazz band, 1922; Chris Kelly band, 1923. Jobbed around during late 20's and 30's. During 40's and early 50's was often seen at Mama Lou's and the Happy Landing. Worked for a time with the Kid Thomas band, with which he recorded for AM in 1951.

PHILIP, JOSEPH, JR. (bjo). b. N.O., 1912; d. N.O., 1968. Played in 1929–30 with Buddy Petit. Son of One-eye Babe Philip.

PHILLIPS, JOE (t). b. N.O., 1893. Worked with Joe Oliver in 1915.

PHILLIPS, JOHN HENRY, SR. (cl, l). b. N.O., May 28, 1877; d. N.O., Oct. 9, 1948. Known as Johnny Fischer. One of the prominent turn-of-the-century brass band and dance band leaders. Also worked at times with the Brunies and with Anton Lada. Five Southern Jazzers. Original N.O. Jazz Band in 1916. Along with Papa Laine and Happy Schilling, dominated the dixieland scene for 15 years.

99

FATS PICHON

ALPHONSE PICOU

PHILLIPS, WILLIE (c, d). b. N.O., about 1885. Played with Joe Oliver in the Melrose Brass Band, 1907, on drums. In later years played cornet; occasionally during World War I.

PICHON, WALTER "FATS" (p). b. N.O., 1905; d. N.O., Feb. 26, 1957. Best known as cocktail piano player during many years at the Absinthe House. In the early 20's he played band piano for Amos Riley. He led his own band in the mid-20's, mainly spot jobs. He played with Sidney Desvigne on the *Island Queen* from 1927 into the 30's. In 1937 he spent a short time with A. J. Piron. He led band on S.S. *Capitol* in mid-30's.

PICOU, ALPHONSE (cl). b. N.O., Oct. 18, 1880; d. N.O., Feb. 4, 1961. Known as the creator of a celebrated chorus in "High Society." Musical career began in 1892 in a band led by Bouboul Valentin. A year later he organized his own Accordiana Band and, in 1897, the Independence Band. In 1899 he played for Oscar Duconge, with Keppard's Olympia Orchestra in 1906, and with the Excelsior Brass Band. From 1916

to the mid-twenties he played in the Tuxedo Brass Band, with time out to play in the Camelia Orchestra and with John Robichaux. In the late 40's he was to be seen at times with the Celestin band, and frequently worked in the Paddock on Bourbon St. His funeral during Mardi Gras of 1961 was one of the biggest in N.O. history.

PIERCE, BILLIE (p, vo). b. Marianna, Fla., June 8, 1907; d. N.O., 1974. Boogie-woogie piano player and blues shouter. Worked with husband Dee Dee Pierce. Sister of Sadie Goodson who played in Buddy Petit's band.

PIERCE, JOSEPH DE LA CROIX "DEE DEE" (t, vo). b. N.O., Feb. 18, 1904; d. N.O., Oct. 29, 1973. Played until he lost his sight with Young Tuxedo Brass Band. With Abby Williams. In late 50's was regularly at Luthjen's. Frequently at Preservation Hall in 60's. Known for his songs in Creole French.

PIERSON, EDDIE (tb). b. Algiers, La., 1904; d. N.O., Dec. 17, 1958. Mainly associated with Oscar Celestin

100

DEE DEE PIERCE   BILLIE PIERCE

ARMAND J. PIRON

ARTHUR PONS

from 1951 until Celestin's death; he took over leadership of the band's remnants in 1954. Played for Sidney Desvigne on the riverboats in early 30's, and worked in a group that included Louis Barbarin and Emanuel Sayles. With the Sunny South, A. J. Piron, Barbarin, Young Tuxedo orchestras, Great Lakes Naval Station band.

PINERO, FRANK (p). b. N.O., about 1906; d. N.O., 1967. Dixieland piano man; with Happy Schilling band in 20's. Worked with Leon Prima-Sharkey All-Stars and was on the road in the Louis Prima band.

PINNER, CLAY (tu, sb). b. N.O., 1895; d. N.O., June 7, 1969. With Owls, Happy Schilling, and the police band.

PIRON, ARMAND J. (v, l). b. N.O., 1888; d. N.O., 1943. Crippled at age 7 by accident, unable to walk for many years. Studied violin and began to play professionally with the Peerless Orchestra about 1912. Played in many dance bands. In 1915, with Clarence Williams, formed publishing company where many jazz standards made their debuts. From 1917 until his death, remained one of the most popular leaders in N.O. Well remembered especially for his years at Tranchina's Restaurant at Spanish Fort. Composer of many outstanding melodies.

PONS, ARTHUR (g). b. N.O., Dec. 19, 1913; d. N.O., Nov. 29, 1973. Virtuoso soloist, but also played

BONNIE POTTLE

LEON PRIMA

with prominent dixielanders in 30's, 40's, 50's. Was with bands led by Irving Fazola. Played with Armand Hug, Monk Hazel, Julian Laine.

POREE, ERNEST (s). b. N.O., Nov. 9, 1908. Mainly brass band musician, has played for many years with the George Williams Brass Band. Was in the ERA Orchestra during the mid-thirties.

"PORK CHOP." See Smith, Jerome.

PORTER, JOHN (bh, ah, sb). b. N.O., about 1890; d. N.O., Nov. 2, 1958. Well-known brass band musician; started with Holmes Brass Band, Lutcher, La., 1910. Played with Tuxedo Brass Band, Allen Brass Band, Louis Dumaine Brass Band.

POTTLE, BONNIE (sb). b. N.O., about 1910; d. N.O., 1940's. Popular dixieland drummer, recorded with late version of N.O. Rhythm Kings (George Brunies, Wingy Manone, Sidney Arodin).

POWERS, EDDIE (s). b. N.O., about 1900; d. N.O., about 1955. Participated in first jazz broadcast from N.O. under Pinky Gerbrecht. Played with Ellis Stratakos Jung Hotel roof orchestra.

PREDONCE, JOHNNY (b). b. N.O., about 1895; d. N.O., about 1939. Led the Silver Leaf Orchestra, 1918, and

always had jobs under his own leadership through 1919–23. In 1923 he worked for a while with Chris Kelly and then retired from music to pursue an active and profitable career as a bartender at the Big 25 Club on Franklin St.

PRESCOTT, DEWEY (p). b. N.O. Most of musical life in Calif.

PRICE, FONCE (v). Pre-World War I dixieland musician.

PRIMA, LEON (t). b. N.O., July 28, 1907. Led own bands for many years and was co-leader, with Sharkey, of a swing band in the 30's. During the 40's, 50's, and 60's, a successful night club operator and led combos in his own spots. Brother of Louis Prima.

PRIMA, LOUIS (t, vo). b. N.O., Dec. 7, 1911. In 1923 led his own "kid's band" which featured 10-year old Irving Fazola. Went to work in the Saenger Theater pit band in 1928; became popular in mid-thirties as leader of large swing band. Made several films. Produced several outstanding discs on Brunswick and Vocalion with small combo. Composer of "Sing, Sing, Sing."

ALTON PURNELL

SNOOZER QUINN

PROVENZANO, JOHNNY (p, v, g, vo). b. N.O., about 1878; d. N.O., about 1962. One of the earliest dixieland piano players. Heard in the 1900's with Johnny Lala, Tony Giardina, and the Brunies clan. Played solo piano in cabarets of the "tango belt" (a group of cafes surrounding the Storyville district) from 1905–25.

PURNELL, ALTON (p). b. N.O., about 1911. Best known for his recordings with Bunk Johnson in 1945 and for his years in the George Lewis band during the late 40's and early 50's. Now resides in California.

PURNELL, THEODORE (s, cl); b. N.O., about 1903; d. N.O., Nov. 25, 1974. With David Jones at Lavida Ballroom, 1925. On the historic Jones-Collins Astoria Hot Eight session in 1929. In 1932 he was working riverboats with Disney Desvigne. Sometimes seen in street parades; played at the Paddock occasionally into the 50's.

QUINN, EDWIN MC INTOSH "SNOOZER" (g, v, vo). b. McComb, Miss., Oct. 18, 1906; d. N.O., in 1952. As a very young child played professionally in a local trio at Bogalusa, La. In his teens, worked with Paul English Traveling Shows, then joined Claude Blanchard's orchestra and the Jack Wilrich band before working with Johnny Wiggs in Peck Kelly's Jazz Band at Houston, Texas, 1924. Jobbed around N.O. for a few years. Went on tour with Paul Whiteman, 1928. Cut four sides with Bix Beiderbecke and Frank Trumbauer on Columbia which were lost. Recorded in 1931 with hillbilly singer Jimmy Davis later Governor of Louisiana. Early 50's made four sides issued by Johnny Wiggs. In his later professional years, played guitar and violin, sang scat vocals with Earl Crumb's band at Beverly Gardens. Considered by some prominent N.O. jazzmen to have been the greatest guitarist of all time.

HENRY RAGAS

EBLEN RAU

RAGAS, HENRY W. (p). b. N.O., 1897; d. New York City, Feb. 18, 1919. Original pianist of the Original Dixieland Jazz Band. Jobbed around N.O. from 1910, playing solo in the "tango belt." From about 1913, was associated with Johnny Stein's band. Left town with Stein and the Original Dixieland Jazz Band men to start his months of glory. Made the first Original Dixieland Jazz Band discs. Succumbed in flu epidemic as band was preparing to go to Europe.

RAGAS, HERMAN (sb). b. N.O. ——. Early dixielander played in Jack Laine dance bands. Brother of Original Dixieland Jazz Band's Henry Ragas.

RAMOS, FLORENZO (s). b. Mexico, D.F., about 1865; d. N.O., July 7, 1931. Came to U.S. with Mexican band for Sugar and Cotton Exposition, 1885, and remained. One of founders of musicians union. Introduced saxophone to N.O. Played with everyone, from the band at the French Opera House to Stalebread Lacoume.

RAMOS, "SOU SOU" (g). Played with Stalebread's Spasm Band, 1904–1908.

RANDO, DOC (cl). b. N.O., 1910. Played with the Bob Crosby orchestra.

RANKIN, "HUGHIE" (sb, tu).

RANKINS, SAM (g). b. N.O., d. N.O., Feb. 17, 1971. Member of Noon Johnson bazooka trio in 50's.

RAPHAEL, BERNARD (tb). b. N.O., about 1883; d. N.O. ——. A member of the Melrose Brass Band in 1907. Worked in the district until about 1913. Also in the Excelsior Brass Band in 1913.

RAPP, BUTLER "GUYÉ" (tb, g, bjo). b. N.O., about 1898; d. N.O., 1931. Played trombone with Onward Brass Band in early 20's; banjo with Sam Morgan until 1925. Worked in late 20's with Chris Kelly, the Magnolia Orchestra, and Eddie Jackson.

RAU, J. EBLEN (v). b. N.O., Sept. 3, 1898. Entire musical career linked with Invincibles String Band, which became N.O. Owls. Gave up music as a profession as soon as the group took "professionalism" seriously.

RAY, PHIL (sb). b. N.O., about 1888. Pre-World War I dixielander.

LIONEL REASON

KID RENA

RAYMOND, HENRY (s, cl). b. N.O., about 1895; d. July 24, 1949. With Johnny DeDroit, Ellis Stratakos.

REASON, LIONEL (p). b. N.O., about 1909. Played very little in N.O. though has worked all over U.S. with N.O. bands, including Ory on the West Coast and King Oliver in the mid-West. In 1932 was on tour in large band led by Paul Barnes.

REED, HOWARD (t). b. N.O., March 27, 1906. Started in 1922 with Extra Half Jazz Band. Through 20's, 30's, played in Dixola novelty band and was with Fazola in the 40's. Led own band for short time in early 50's before retiring from music.

REINER, JULES (p). b. N.O. ———. An early dixieland pianist associated with Jack Laine dance groups before World War I.

REININGER, JOHNNY (s, cl). b. N.O., Aug. 19, 1908. Popular dance band leader. Was one of Dawn Busters on N.O. station WWL for many years. During early 30's played with Ellis Stratakos at the Jung roof, and frequently with Leon Prima. Had house band at L'Enfant's during early 50's.

REMY, DOMINIQUE "T-BOY" (t). b. N.O., about 1886. Played many dance jobs during the 40's and became leader of the Eureka Brass Band about 1946. Migrated to Los Angeles in early 50's.

RENA, HENRY "KID" (t). b. N.O., Aug. 30, 1898; d. N.O., April 25, 1949. With Louis Armstrong at the Waif's Home, Rena was taught by Armstrong's teacher, Peter Davis; later studied with Manuel Perez. Rival to Buddy Petit and Chris Kelly, he worked for a while for Kid Ory. Then put together his own Dixie Jazz Band which worked steadily in N.O. during the 20's and made successful trips to Chicago on several occasions. Later played in Tuxedo Brass Band and during depression led his own brass band. He had a group, including Alphonse Picou and Alec Bigard, which played at the Brown Derby, a dime-a-dance palace. He made only one disc session, 1940, on the Delta label, but contemporaries agree he did not sound at his best. Forced to quit music because of ill-health and died two years later.

RENA, JOSEPH (d). b. N.O., March 11, 1897; d. N.O., Dec. 26, 1973. Jobbed with brother Kid Rena in his

105

JEFF RIDDICK

BEBÉ RIDGLEY

teens. Was in Wesley Don's Liberty Bell Orchestra in 1920 and was with his brother's Dixie Jazz Band in 1923 and 1924. Made the Delta session with his brother in 1940 and stayed with him until about 1945, when he retired from music to become an Evangelical Baptist preacher.

RICHARDSON, EDDIE (t). b. N.O., April 18, 1903. Paraded with Kid Rena's brass band. Played in Mandeville with Earl Foster in 1929–30 and was in the WPA and ERA music programs in the mid-depression years. Recorded with Eureka Brass Band for Pax. Played in Gibson Brass Band.

RIDDICK, JEFF (p). b. N.O., June 3, 1907. Long-time mainstay of Sharkey's best band. Leads small groups of his own on dance jobs and performed at the Famous Door through the early 50's with a memorable trio including Ray Burke, Sherwood Mangiapane. Infrequently recorded. Brother of Johnny Riddick.

RIDDICK, JOHNNY (p). b. N.O., Nov. 12, 1901. Member of the two great recording bands of the mid-20's centered in Mobile—the Arcadian Serenaders, the Crescent City Jazzers. Brother of Jeff Riddick.

RIDDICK, TOM (p). b. N.O., March 19, 1900. Played with most of the leading early dixieland groups of the 20's. Lives in Indianapolis, Ind.

RIDDICK, RICHARD "DICK" (h). b. N.O., Feb. 1, 1904. Worked steadily with Borrah Minevitch Harmonica Rascals, won a "World Harmonica Championship" in Berlin (1950).

RIDGLEY, WILLIAM "BEBÉ" (tb). b. N.O., Jan. 15, 1882; d. N.O., May 28, 1961. Founder of the Tuxedo Brass Band and the Original Tuxedo Orchestra in which he worked for many years, sometimes with, sometimes separate from, Papa Celestin. Started with the Silver Leaf Orchestra about 1907. Remained musically active until 1936 when he retired because of ill health. Made his last public appearance at the age of 79 as a mourner at the funeral of Alphonse Picou.

RILEY, AMOS (t). b. N.O., about 1879; d. N.O., 1925. Organizer and leader of the long-popular Tulane Orchestra, one of the best known pre-World War I dance bands.

106

AMOS RILEY

HENRY ROBERTSON

ZUE ROBERTSON

RILEY, THEODORE (t). b. N.O., May 10, 1924. With George Williams Brass Band in 1950's. In 1965, took over leadership of band following Williams' death. Son of Amos Riley.

ROBERTSON, HENRY "SLEEPY" (d). b. N.O., about 1890. Long-time parade bass drummer last seen in 1960's with the Young Excelsior Brass Band.

ROBERTSON, C. ALVIN "ZUE" (tb). b. N.O., March 7, 1891; d. Watts, Calif., 1943. Pupil of cousin, Baptiste Delisle. During his few Crescent City years worked in Storyville with Joe Oliver, John Robichaux, A. J. Piron, Richard M. Jones, Clarence Williams. Frequently at Pete Lala's in the district. Drafted in 1918, discharged the following year. Worked in carnivals and circuses.

ROBICHAUX, JOE (p). b. N.O., March 8, 1900; d. N.O., Jan. 17, 1965. Much influenced by Steve Lewis, Burnell Santiago. Before World War I sometimes played solo for private parties. Joined Tig Chambers in Chicago in 1917; soon returned to N.O. Joined the Black Eagles on the "country circuit," 1922–23. Recorded in 1929 with Jones-Collins Astoria Hot Eight. Short stint with Willie O'Connell at the Music Box, then organized own band for Entertainers Club. Made session for Vocalion. Invaded big band market in 30's, increasing to 15 pieces. During 40's and 50's frequently accompanied blues singers. In mid-50's was at Davila's behind Lizzie Miles. Ultimately replaced Alton Purnell in George Lewis band.

ROBICHAUX, JOHN (v, sb, d, acc, l). b. Thibodaux, La., Jan. 16, 1866; d. N.O., 1939. Began career as bass drummer for the Excelsior Brass Band in 1891.

JOE ROBICHAUX

JIM ROBINSON

From 1893 to 1939 was the most continuously active dance band leader in N.O. history. Led band at Lyric Theater, 1918–27. La Louisiane restaurant.

ROBICHAUX, JOHN (d). b. N.O., May 16, 1915. Nephew of famed band leader of same name. Played with Kid Shots in 1944. During 50's was at times with Kid Thomas.

ROBINSON ED "RABBIT" (d). b. Laplace, La., about 1882. Drummer in Kid Ory's first band.

ROBINSON, FRANK (tu , sou). b. N.O. ——. During the 20's, bass man for the Excelsior Brass Band.

ROBINSON, ISAIAH "BIG IKE" (tb). b. Thibodaux, La., March 16, 1892. d. N.O., 1962. Played guitar in local Thibodaux band, 1911. With Kid Milton band, 1920, and in the Camelia Brass Band and Orchestra. Studied with Dave Perkins on trombone and joined Chris Kelly in 1924, remaining until the latter's death in 1927. Worked for a while in dance halls and with Kid Rena's brass band. Retired about 1938.

ROBINSON, NATHAN "JIM" (tb). b. Deer Range, La., Dec. 25, 1892; d. N.O., May 4, 1976. Studied guitar as a kid, but took up trombone while in the army. On return to N.O. in 1919 was good enough to join Sam Morgan band in which he was a fixture for a dozen years. Studied with Sunny Henry and worked with Lee Collins in the Golden Leaf Band. Stayed active through depression mainly with Kid Howard and was a regular in the George Lewis band. Recorded with Sam Morgan in the 20's; was in on the Kid Rena Delta session in 1940; is also on most of Bunk Johnson records.

ROBINSON, OSCAR (sb). b. N.O., about 1888. With Silver Leaf Orchestra, 1909.

ROBINSON, SAM (s). Alto sax man of the 20's. Worked with Young Morgan Band and with Kid Howard.

ROUBLEAU, ERNEST (bjo). b. N.O., about 1897; d. June 7, 1973. Cousin of celebrated William Penn. Worked with all contemporary traditional groups.

RODDY, RUBEN (as). b. Joplin, Mo., May 5, 1906; d. N.O., 1960. Joined Eureka Brass Band in 1946 after career with Count Basie, Bennie Moten, and Walter Page. Played in 50's in dance bands led by Kid Thomas.

ROGERS, EMMETT (d). b. N.O., about 1898; d. N.O., about 1947. Legal name, John McCloskey. One of

ERNEST ROGERS EMMETT ROGERS LEON ROPPOLO

the big names among dixieland drummers. Worked steadily at Halfway House in Abbie Brunies' band, and was usually considered the Brunies' drummer. Played at the Doghouse with Harry Shields about 1940. Nephew of Buck Rogers.

ROGERS, ERNEST (d). b. N.O., April 19, 1891; d. N.O., Aug. 26, 1956. Began career with Edward Clem, 1910. In 1913 was in the Crescent Orchestra. Joined Silver Leaf Orchestra and stayed until World War I. Was with the Lions Brass Band from its inception; and played through the 30's and 40's in other brass bands, including the Young Tuxedo. Worked at Luthjen's in the 40's. Made records with Bunk Johnson, Big Eye Louis Nelson, 1949.

ROGERS, EVERETT "BUCK" (p, d). b. N.O., Apr. 18, 1891; d. N.O., Aug. 28, 1952. Worked with Abbie Brunies, Johnny Wiggs. First drummer with Dukes of Dixieland. Uncle of Emmett Rogers.

ROPPOLO, LEON (cl, s, g). b. Lutheran, La., March 16, 1902; d. N.O., Oct. 5, 1943. His family name is often incorrectly spelled Rappolo. Among jazz immortals though career spanned less than a decade. At age 14 left N.O. with Bee Palmer vaudeville troupe. Back home, joined Brunies brothers' band. Played with Halfway House Orchestra. Famed through play with

N.O. Rhythm Kings in Chicago during early 20's. Shares composer credit for "Tin Roof Blues," "Farewell Blues." Spent 18 years in a sanitarium before succumbing to various ills.

ROSE, FREDDIE (p). b. N.O., about 1892. A dixieland pianist associated with Merritt Brunies, Emile Christian, with whom he worked in the New Orleans Jazz Band before World War I.

ROSS, SAM (c, l). b. Algiers, La., about 1878; d. Algiers, La., 1921. An early bandleader who was first to employ Jimmie Noone. His group was active for eleven years, playing only dances.

ROTIS, JOE (tb). b. N.O., Oct. 30, 1917; d. Apr. 24, 1965. Came to national attention during the 50's with the Basin Street Six. Also worked extensively with Sharkey, Phil Zito.

ROUCHON, TETE (sb, tu). b. Algiers, La., about 1860; d. N.O., about 1932. Member of the Pickwick Band about 1882 and the Algiers Brass Band. Played with Henry Allen before 1910; in 1916 worked with Elton Theodore. His final professional jobs were with Chris Kelly in the late 20's.

ROUSE, MORRIS (p, vo). b. N.O. ——. Member of Louis Dumaine's Jazzola Eight recording band.

JIMMY RUTH

JOHNNY ST. CYR

ROUSSEAU, AUGUST (tb). b. N.O., about 1894; d. N.O., about 1956. Member of the Original Tuxedo Orchestra before World War I. Sometimes played alto horn in the Tuxedo Brass Band.

ROWLING, RED (cl). b. N.O., about 1894. Pre-World War I Dixielander. Played frequently in bands with the Brunies family. In Chicago in 1916 with Morgan's Euphonic Band.

RUSS, HENRY (d, t, sb). b. N.O., Aug. 7, 1903. During the late 20's a bandleader at the dime-a-dance halls or worked with Peter Lacaze's NOLA Band. During the depression switched to trumpet and worked with WPA and ERA groups. During World War II was in the Algiers Naval Station Brass Band.

RUSSELL, BUD (sb). b. N.O. ——. Played with Golden Leaf Band in 1920 and led own band in later 20's.

RUSSELL, LUIS (p, l). b. Careening Cay, Panama, Aug. 5, 1902; d. New York City, about 1962. Played at Tom Anderson's in 1920 with Al Nicholas, Paul Barbarin. To Chicago in 1925 with Doc Cook, Joe Oliver. Led own band until 1948, touring the country and recording. It was Russell's band that Louis Armstrong fronted from 1935 to 1943.

RUTH, JIM (mdl). b. N.O., about 1880; d. N.O., 1957. Pioneer rhythm man, half-brother of the Shields family. Played with earliest dixieland groups, including Ernest Giardina's band, Jack Laine, the Barrocco brothers, Alex "King" Watzke.

ST. CYR, JOHNNY (bjo, g). b. N.O., April 17, 1889; d. Los Angeles, Calif., June 17, 1966. Led his own band, the Young Men of New Orleans, on the miniature river steamer *Mark Twain* at Disneyland. A first magnitude star of jazz. Worked in 1917 with Piron. On the S.S. *Capitol* under Fate Marable. In the mid-20's made the fabulous Armstrong Hot Five and Hot Seven discs. Worked with King Oliver, Jelly Roll Morton, and all the top names of his era.

SANTIAGO, BURNELL (p). b. N.O., Sept., 1915; d. Jan. 6, 1944. Billed himself "King of Boogie Woogie" in the 30's, but was skilled musician, held by many contemporaries as finest of his era. Worked mainly as soloist or in a trio including Ollie Papa, string bass, and Sidney Pflueger, guitar. Brother of Lester, nephew of Willie Santiago.

SANTIAGO, LESTER "BLACKIE" (p). b. N.O., Aug. 14, 1909; d. N.O., Jan. 18, 1965. Began career in late 20's with Arnold Depass. Mainly associated with Paul Barbarin; led groups and recorded extensively. Sometimes did vocals in Creole patois. Nephew of Willie, brother of Burnell.

SANTIAGO, WILLIE (bjo, g). b. N.O., about 1887; d. N.O., 1945. One of the great rhythm men of N.O.

110

BURNELL SANTIAGO

LESTER SANTIAGO

Was with the top Storyville bands and in 1919–20 with the Maple Leaf Orchestra. Uncle of Lester and Burnell Santiago. Played with Louis Armstrong at Anderson's in 1920, later with Arnold Metoyer, Paul Barbarin. Worked at the Bungalow, 1925–31. Is on the Kid Rena Delta recordings.

SAYLES, EMANUEL bjo, g). b. Donaldsonville, La., Jan. 31, 1905. Studied violin, viola with Dave Perkins. Son of banjoist George Sayles. Joined band in Pensacola, Fla. 1923; returned to a stint with Ridgley's Tuxedo Orchestra at the Pelican Hall, 1925. Worked the riverboats with Fate Marable, and on the S.S. "J. S." under A. J. Piron. Member of famed Jones-Collins Astoria Hot Eight disc session. Played with Sidney Desvigne at the Knights of Pythias roof garden. From 1939 to 1949, led own group, mainly in Chicago. Worked with George Lewis band, 1959. In recent years has been recorded extensively on Atlantic, Riverside, and other labels. In 1966 at Jazz, Ltd., in Chicago.

SAYLES, GEORGE (g, bjo). b. N.O., about 1880. Played with Silver Leaf Orchestra before Spanish-American War. After war, continued with same band until 1918, when it disbanded. Retired from music soon after. Father of Emanuel.

SBARBARO, TONY (d, kazoo). b. N.O., June 27, 1897; d. N.Y., Oct. 29, 1969. Known also as Tony Spargo. Youngest member of Original Dixieland Jazz Band; considered by many to be the greatest dixieland drummer. Replaced Johnny Stein in Original Dixieland Jazz Band at Chicago in June, 1916. Had already worked in N.O. with Brunies brothers at the Tango Palace and was a member of Ernest Giardina's ragtime band. Played kazoo mounted in large horn. In latter years was seen frequently at Nick's and on jobs with the Phil Napoleon band.

SCAGLIONE, NUNZIO (cl). b. N.O., about 1890; d. N.O., May 12, 1935. Early dixielander, veteran of Papa Laine groups. Recorded on famous Bayersdorffer sides for Okeh.

SCHELLANG, AUGUST (d). b. N.O., March 1, 1905; d. N.O., Oct. 16, 1958. Played with most of top dixieland and dance bands during 20's and 30's, including Ellis Stratakos, the Prima-Sharkey orchestra, the N.O. Rhythm Masters, Wingy Manone. Nephew of Tony Parenti.

EMANUEL SAYLES

TONY SPARGO (Tony Sbarbaro)

TONY SCHIRO

SCHILLING, GEORGE, SR. "HAPPY" (tb, g, l). b. N.O., April 26, 1886; d. N.O., Feb. 28, 1964. Important early dixieland influence. Led own brass band and dance orchestra. He and another noted leader, Johnny Fischer, used to play in each other's bands. Also led the band at Heineman's ball park for N.O. Pelicans' games.

SCHILLING, GEORGE, JR. (s, cl). b. N.O. ——. Son of Happy Schilling. Played with dad's orchestra and brass band. Also was with Slim Lamar's Argentine Dons.

SCHIRO, LUKE (cl). b. N.O., about 1903. Seldom-heard N.O. clarinetist. Rarely worked professionally, but was seen frequently during the fifties at the NOJC. Taught Irving Fazola.

SCHIRO, TONY (g, bjo). b. N.O., Apr. 18, 1899. Veteran dixielander studied with John Marrero, Johnny St. Cyr. Played in Triangle Band from 1917–25. Later with Sharkey.

SCIAMBRA, JACOB (p, cl). b. N.O., Sept. 23, 1910. Well-known attorney, active with Johnny Wiggs during the late 50's.

112

BUD SCOTT

JAKE SCIAMBRA

SCIONEAUX, LOUIS (tb). b. N.O., about 1931. Became popular as trombonist with George Girard's New Orleans Five during the 50's. For many years with Sam Butera's Witnesses, a rock-and-roll act occasionally fronted by Louis Prima.

SCOTT, ALEX (sb). b. N.O., about 1895; d. N.O., about 1943. Active bassist began about 1915 with the Tulane Orchestra but was mostly active during the 20's with George Lewis, Earl Humphrey, Lee Collins.

SCOTT, ARTHUR "BUD" (g, bjo, vo). b. N.O., Jan. 11, 1890; d. Los Angeles, Calif., July 2, 1949. Between 1905–12 played mainly in the district with Freddie Keppard, Kid Ory. Also worked with Buddy Bolden's and John Robichaux's orchestras. Recorded with Oliver. From 1927, worked in Chicago with Erskine Tate, Oliver, Jimmie Noone. Moved to California at beginning of depression and worked frequently with Mutt Carey and Kid Ory. Was with Ory when he died in 1949.

SEELIG, ARTHUR, SR. (sb). b. N.O., Apr. 8, 1908. Dixieland and dance musician, active especially during 30's. At Famous Door with Santo in 1966.

SEELIG, ARTHUR, JR. (p). b. N.O., Apr. 9, 1929. Younger dixieland musician, played with Dukes of Dixieland, George Girard.

SHANNON, HARRY (t). b. N.O., about 1885. Dixieland trumpet player of early 1900's. Played in Fischer's Brass Band, about 1905.

SHANNON, TONY (tu, sou). b. N.O. ——. Original tuba player in Fischer's Brass Band.

SHARKEY. See Bonano, Joseph.

SHIELDS, BERNARD SAXON (g, md, bjo, z, org). b. N.O., May 6, 1893. Began playing with Six and 7/8 String Band about 1910 and still makes every public appearance of the group. Had long vaudeville career. Not related to other Shieldses listed.

SHIELDS FAMILY. A large uptown family of musicians and music teachers of which only the most prominent jazzmen are listed here. Among the brothers was half-brother Jimmy Ruth.

SHIELDS, EDDIE (p). b. N.O., 1896; d. N.O., 1938. Brother of Larry and Harry. Played with members of Original Dixieland Jazz Band before they went north.

ARTHUR SEELIG, SR.

HARRY SHIELDS

EDDIE SHIELDS

LARRY SHIELDS

114

OMER SIMEON

SHIELDS, HARRY (cl, bs). b. N.O., June 30, 1899; d. N.O., Jan. 18, 1971. One of the greats of N.O. clarinet. Played baritone sax in Norman Brownlee band after World War I; clarinet with Johnny Wiggs, Sharkey, Tom Brown. Brother of Larry, Eddie Shields. Much recorded.

SHIELDS, LARRY (cl). b. N.O., Sept. 13, 1893; d. Hollywood, Cal., Nov. 21, 1953. Celebrated clarinetist of the Original Dixieland Jazz Band. Star of the very first jazz record date. Also played with Tom Brown's Five Rubes in vaudeville. Shares composer credit for "Tiger Rag," "Original Dixieland One-Step," "Clarinet Marmalade," "Lazy Daddy," and others.

SHIELDS, PAT (g). b. N.O., about 1891. A member of Alex "King" Watzke's dixieland band in 1904–08. Played with his many brothers.

SIMEON, OMER (cl). b. N.O., July 21, 1902; d. New York, N.Y., Sept. 17, 1959. Pupil of Lorenzo Tio, Jr. Probably never worked in N.O. In Chicago in 20's with Charlie Elgar, King Oliver, Erskine Tate. Played and recorded with Jelly Roll Morton. Played in the pit at the Regal Theater in 1931. Six years with Earl Hines until 1937; also, till 1940 with Walter Fuller, Horace Henderson, Coleman Hawkins. 1942–50 with the Jimmy Lunceford orchestra. 1951–58 with Wilbur DeParis at Jimmy Ryan's in N.Y. Much recorded; last for Audiophile 3 weeks before his death.

MONK SMITH

SIMPSON, DUKE (d). b. Algiers, La. ——; d. ——. Snare drummer with Pacific Brass Band before World War I.

SIMS, GEORGE (bh). b. Algiers, about 1872. d. ——. Manager and baritone horn, Pacific Brass Band from about 1900 to about 1910.

SINGLETON, ARTHUR "ZUTTY" (d). b. Bunkie, La., May 14, 1898; d. New York City, July 14, 1975. Tuxedo Brass Band, 1916; Maple Leaf Band, 1916; John Robichaux orchestra, 1917. With Big Eye Louis Nelson, Steve Lewis trio, before 1920. On riverboats with Charlie Creath, Fate Marable, early 20's. In Chicago with Doc Cook, Carroll Dickerson, Louis Armstrong, Jimmie Noone, Dave Peyton. Remained in forefront of jazz drummers through 30's and 50's.

SMALL, FREDDIE "BLIND FREDDIE" (cl, har). b. N.O., about 1898. Worked bars with trio or duet for many years. In 1920's worked with Wesley Don's Liberty Bell Orchestra. Seen in 1966.

SMILIN' JOE. See Joseph, Pleasant.

SMITH, JEROME "PORK CHOP" (d). b. Dec. 26, 1895. Played in the 20's with Sam Morgan, Kid Rena.

Moved to Chicago about 1928. Played with Lee Collins, Eurreal Montgomery, Natty Dominique.

SMITH, JOHN (p, bjo). b. N.O., Oct. 21, 1910. Played with Wooden Joe Nicholas' Camelia Orchestra in late 1920's. Nephew of trumpeter Sugar Johnny Smith. Played at Preservation, Dixieland halls in 1965.

SMITH, JOHN "SUGAR JOHNNY" (c). b. N.O., about 1880; d. Chicago, Ill., 1918. Worked in group with Lorenzo Staulz in the district in 1902. Later led small band at Groshell's Dance Hall; and worked in Richard M. Jones's Four Hot Hounds, at Abadie's in 1913–14. Went to Chicago in 1917, played briefly in vaudeville act with Lawrence Duhé's band, then worked for Duhé at the Deluxe Cafe. Succumbed to pneumonia in 1918.

SMITH, LESTER "MONK" (g, cl, s, l). b. N.O., May 23, 1898; d. Bay St. Louis, Miss., Sept. 5, 1952. Member of Invincibles String Band 1912–20. A founder and once leader of the N.O. Owls.

SNAER, ALBERT (t). b. N.O., 1902; d. 1962. One of the best technicians on brass N.O. ever produced. Played in Excelsior Brass Band and between 1926–28 led Moonlight Serenaders. His later career was spent touring with big swing bands, Andy Kirk, Horace Henderson, Edgar Hayes. In the 50's he was doing studio work in Los Angeles.

SON, BABE (bjo). b. N.O., about 1897; Banjo with Kid Rena in 1918–19, playing dances and advertising wagons. In mid-20's active with Chris Kelly's band. During depression worked taxi dance halls with Willie Pajeaud.

SONGIER, LEO (bjo). b. Covington, La. ——. With Foster Lewis Jazz Band in 20's.

SOUCHON, EDMOND, M.D. (bjo, g, vo). b. N.O., Oct. 25, 1897; d. N.O., Aug. 24, 1968. In his teens helped organize Six and 7/8 String Band. One of the most recorded jazz musicians, he appeared on wax with many of the great N.O. jazzmen. For many years was editor of the magazine *The Second Line*.

SPARGO, TONY (d). See Sbarbaro, Tony.

ELMER TALBERT

SPEARS, A. B. (s). b. N.O. ——; d. N.O., Aug. 24, 1965. Sax player and manager of the Gibson Brass Band.

SPITLERA, JOSEPH P., JR. "PEE WEE" (cl). b. N.O., about 1938. An animated youngster frequently seen in the "kid bands" of the 50's, especially under the leadership of George Girard, Murphy Campo. Now regular clarinetist with Al Hirt.

STAULZ, LORENZO (g, bjo). b. N.O., about 1880; d. N.O., about 1928. Highly regarded but erratic. Played irregularly in the Bolden band in early 1900's. With Buddy Petit in the Eagle Band, 1916. Worked in the district first with Freddie Keppard, then with Kid Ory at Lala's until 1918. Finished his active career about 1925 with Bob Lyons' Dixie Jazz Band.

STEIN, JOHNNY. b. N.O., June 15, 1891; d. N.O., Sept. 30, 1962. Legal name John Philip Hountha. Organizer, first leader of Original Dixieland Jazz Band but lost leadership before band scored its big success, because of personality conflicts. Organized original N.O. Jazz Band for Jimmy Durante. Played in New York and Chicago for most of career.

STEPHENS, JOE (d). b. N.O.; d. N.O., 1974. Son of the great drummer "Ragbaby" Stephens. Joe was active during the 30's, especially in a band led by Henry Bellis, and featuring Raymond Burke.

STEPHENS, MIKE "RAGBABY" (d). b. N.O., about 1885; d. Richmond, Ind., about 1927. Sometimes called the "father of dixieland drums"; he was a fixture in Jack Laine units and in the Reliance Brass Band.

STEVENS, ARTHUR (tb). b. N.O. ——. Manager and trombone for the Bulls Club Brass Band in the early 20's.

STEVENSON, BURKE (sb, tu, t). b. Plaquemine, La., Aug. 14, 1899. Pupil of Professor Jim Humphrey. Played trumpet with Eclipse Brass Band, Deer Range Brass Band. Came to N.O. in 1917; played mostly for dances, frequently with Little Dad Vincent, Walter Decou. Was in Kid Rena's brass band. Was in ERA Orchestra as trumpet in mid-thirties. Worked in Kid Thomas band for many years.

STEWART, GEORGE (cl). With Camelia Orchestra in 20's. Earlier in Excelsior Brass Band.

STRATAKOS, ELLIS (tb). b. N.O., Dec. 1, 1904; d. Gulfport, Miss., Jan. 25, 1961. Early dixieland contemporary of DeDroit brothers, Tony Parenti, Johnny Wiggs. Fronted dance band at the Jung Hotel roof for many years. Popular along Mississippi Gulf Coast. Recorded on Vocalion.

SUMMERS, EDDIE (tb). b. N.O., Sept. 15, 1903. Began in neighborhood bands. Joined Augustin-Snaer Moonlight Serenaders in late 20's; then worked with same group under leadership of A. J. Piron. Was with Eureka and Young Tuxedo brass bands.

SURGI, STANLEY (d). b. N.O., Sept. 18, 1907. Active in 30's, 40's, 50's. Longtime standby at New Orleans Jazz Club. In early years was frequently with Tony Fougerat's band.

TALBERT, ELMER "COO COO" (t). b. N.O., Aug. 8, 1900; d. N.O., Dec. 13, 1950. Did not begin career until 1929 with Arnold Depass dance orchestra. Trained by Kid Rena; sometimes worked in Rena's brass band. Worked with the George Lewis band. In 1935 he was with Paul Barnes. Worked his last jobs in 1950 with Albert Jiles group.

TARANTO, JOE (g). Dixielander of 1900's.

TERVALON, CLEMENT (sb, tb). b. N.O., Nov. 13, 1915. Most frequently seen in 40's and 50's at the Paddock under Octave Crosby's leadership or with the Young Tuxedo Brass Band. Led band on Bourbon Street in 60's.

THEODORE, ELTON (bjo, s). b. Algiers, La., about 1897; d. N.O., Sept. 11, 1972. Popular bandleader of 20's "across the river" with whom Kid Thomas played.

THOMAS, BOB (tb). b. N.O., about 1898; d. N.O., Feb. 26, 1960. Worked in early 20's with Evan Thomas' (no relation) Black Eagles band, touring Louisiana and East Texas. Long a popular jazzman, he was seen most frequently in later years with Paul Barbarin, with whom he recorded and went on frequent tours.

THOMAS, EVAN (t). b. Crowley, La., about 1890; d. Rayne, La., Nov. 21, 1931. Reportedly equal to Arm-

BOB THOMAS

117

strong, Thomas never played in N.O., preferring to lead his Black Eagles band, manned with N.O. jazz stars, through the hinterlands. Stabbed to death on a bandstand.

THOMAS, GEORGE W. (p, l). b. N.O., about 1885. d. ———. Bandleader of the World War I period who composed the "New Orleans Hop Scop Blues." Played at Fewclothes Cabaret in the district. Had music publishing firm on Franklin St.

THOMAS, JOE "BROTHER CORNBREAD" (cl). b. N.O., Dec. 3, 1902. Cornbread worked in Joe Harris Dixieland Band in the mid-twenties and spent a lot of time on tour in the late 20's and 30's. In 1951 he joined the Papa Celestin band and continued with the group after Papa's death, first under the leadership of Eddie Pierson, then Albert French.

THOMAS, KID. See Valentine, Thomas.

THOMAS, SON (bjo). b. N.O., about 1903; d. N.O., about 1933. Played with Young Eagles Band, 1918–19, and through mid-20's with Kid Rena's dixie jazz band.

THOMAS, WORTHIA "SHOWBOY" (tb). b. Napoleonville, Feb. 26, 1907. Called Showboy because he's always been ready to leave town with any circus or tent show that came along. Usually seen, when in N.O., with the George Williams Brass Band. Sometimes works dance jobs.

TILLMAN, CORNELIUS (d). b. N.O., about 1887. One of Buddy Bolden's favorite rhythm men.

TILLMAN, WILBERT (s, t, tu, sb). b. N.O., March 31, 1898; d. Feb. 11, 1967. Best known of present-day brass band bassists. With Eureka Brass Band; Young Tuxedo Brass Band. During depression years was in ERA music program and in 40's led a band jointly with Joe Avery. Still active in 1965 at Preservation Hall.

TIO, LORENZO, SR. (cl). b. Mexico, D.F., about 1865; d. Jackson, Miss., about 1920. Played in Excelsior Brass Band in 1880's. Organized dance band with Anthony Doublet, which was active until about 1892. Active as a teacher until the early 1900's. Brother of Luis, father of Lorenzo, Jr.

WILBERT TILLMAN

TIO, LORENZO, JR. (cl). b. N.O., 1884; d. New York, N.Y., Dec. 1, 1933. Most famed as teacher of Jimmie Noone, Albert Nicholas, Barney Bigard, Omer Simeon, Emile Barnes, Albert Burbank, Louis Cottrell, Jr., Johnny Dodds, Wade Whaley. Worked in 1910 with Onward Brass Band and in 1913 with Celestin's Original Tuxedo Orchestra. First as concert musician under his father and Theogene V. Baquet. Went to Chicago with Manuel Perez, 1915–16. Back to Celestin in 1917–18. In 1918 began long stand with A. J. Piron Orchestra with whom he made his only recordings. Son of Lorenzo, Sr. Nephew of Luis Tio.

TIO, LUIS "PAPA" (cl). b. Mexico, D.F., about 1863; d. N.O., 1927. With Excelsior Brass Band in the 1880's. Mainly concert musician, he turned to jazz after 1910, working in the district with Manuel Manetta, Peter Bocage, Henry Peyton. He also played in dance bands with John Robichaux, A. J. Piron.

TISDALE, CLARENCE (g, bjo). b. N.O., about 1900. Usually associated with Kid Rena, especially in the 30's. Sometimes played with trios for dancing.

LAWRENCE TOCA

TOCA, LAWRENCE (t). b. N.O., about 1900; d. N.O., July 2, 1972. Worked with Bill Hamilton's Oriental Orchestra during the 20's. During the depression was with many small groups, notably Kid Milton, Paul Barnes in Little Woods and at Harmony Inn through mid-40's; later at Happy Landing with Albert Jiles, Emma Barrett. Played for a short time with George Lewis. Recorded with Dee Dee Pierce in 1951. Retired about 1955.

TODD, CAMILLA (p). b. N.O., about 1888; d. N.O., 1969. Prominent piano teacher. Played mainly with concert groups, but was a member of the Maple Leaf Orchestra, 1919–20. Played in NOLA Band.

TOMS, RICKY (tb). Dixielander of pre-World War I era. Played with Nick La Rocca, Yellow Nunez, and Laine groups.

TORTORICH, TONY (d). b. N.O., about 1900. With Dixola Jazz Band in 1920's.

TOURO, PINCHBACK (bh, g, v). b. St. James Parish, La., about 1870; d. early 1940's. Always a bandleader, Touro invariably called his many outfits by the name of The Lincoln Band. Was most active during the depression, when he headed the WPA Brass Band.

TOWLES, NAT (sb). b. about 1900. During the early 20's was leader of the Creole Harmony Kings.

TREPAGNIER, ERNEST "NINESSE" (d). b. N.O., about 1885; d. N.O., April 11, 1968. Started with Olympia Orchestra in 1909. Worked before 1920 with Robichaux, Celestin, and the Gaspards. In 1916 joined the Tuxedo Brass Band and stayed with it until 1928, winning his reputation as the greatest bass drummer of them all. During the depression he was in the ERA Orchestra and the WPA Brass Band.

TREVEQUE, JACK (bjo). b. N.O. about 1899. During the 20's worked with Alfred's Laine's orchestra.

TSCHANTZ, EDDIE (d). b. N.O., Jan. 7, 1911. Popular dixieland drummer. Nephew of Tom Brown. Frequently leads small combinations for dancing.

TUJAGUE, JOE (sb, gu, g). b. N.O. ——. Pre-WW I dixielander.

TUJAGUE, JON (sb). b. N.O. ——. Pre-WW I dixielander.

TURNER, BENNY (p). b. N.O., about 1908; d. N.O., Oct. 8, 1973. Worked during 30's with Kid Rena. During 40's was frequently at Luthjen's; worked many small group dance jobs in 40's and 50's. Seen in 60's at Preservation Hall.

TURNIS, ARTHUR (bd). b. N.O. ——. Lyons Brass Band in late 20's.

119

NINESSE TREPAGNIER

EDDIE TSCHANTZ

VACHE, ALPHONSE (tu). Played in Melrose Brass Band with Joe Oliver in 1907.

VALENTIN, BOUBOUL (vt). b. N.O., about 1870; d. N.O., about 1925. Led Accordiana Band in 1894. In 1897 played in Alphonse Picou's Independence Band. Sometimes worked with Henry Peyton. Sat in frequently with the bands on Iberville St. in the district.

VALENTIN, PUNKIE (c). b. N.O., about 1866; d. Calif., about 1951. A part-time musician (he was a dentist), Valentin, older brother of Bouboul, was a virtuoso. Frequently marched with the Excelsior, Onward, and Melrose brass bands. Moved to Calif. in the 40's.

VALENTINE, THOMAS (t). b. Reserve, La., Feb. 3, 1896. Known as Kid Thomas. Played in the Hall's family band at home until about 1923, when he joined the Elton Theodore band in Algiers. Has led his own band actively since 1926.

VECA, LAWRENCE (c). b. N.O., 1889; d. N.O., 1911. Considered by many contemporary musicians the greatest of the dixieland cornetists. Veca was leader of Papa Jack Laine's No. 1 Ragtime Band and a star

of the Reliance Brass Band. Played all instruments. Name usually misspelled "Vega."

VERRET, IRVING "CAJUN" (tb). b. Alexandria, La., about 1906. Verret has been an outstanding big band musician and studio star for many years. Played with Sidney Arodin. He is of particular interest because of his discs with Wingy Manone.

VERRETT, HARRISON (bjo, g). b. N.O., Feb. 27, 1907; d. Oct. 18, 1965. Pupil of Dave Perkins. Made debut in 1924 with Johnny Brown's band. During late 20's worked taxi dance places, N.O. and Mississippi; in 30's continued with own group at Fern Cafe. Worked with Celestin, 1945–51; made successful tour with Fats Domino. Best known in last years as part of Noon Johnson bazooka trio.

VIDACOVICH, IRVINE "PINKY" (cl). b. N.O., 1905; d. N.O., July 5, 1966. Known to a generation of Orleanians as the voice of Cajun Pete in a popular radio commercial. Was with N.O. Owls and earlier Princeton Revellers. Was a member of WWL staff band, Dawn Busters, and recorded recently for Southland.

120

KID THOMAS VALENTINE

LAWRENCE VECA

CAJUN VERRET

PINKY VIDACOVICH

VIGNE, JOHN (d). b. N.O., about 1865. Dance band drummer in turn-of-century days. Played with Olympia Orchestra in 1901; with Peerless Orchestra under Bab Frank, 1903–08; and also under A. J. Piron until about 1912. Also worked with Golden Rule Orchestra and about 1906 with the Imperial Orchestra.

VIGNE, JOHN "RATTY" (d). b. N.O., about 1885. Played with Jack Carey, about 1912, and on jobs in the district with Clarence Williams in 1913. He was

121

ALBERT WARNER

LOUIS WARNICK

also at Fewclothes Cabaret with Keppard in the same year, and played with Joe Oliver at Pete Lala's cafe in 1915.

VIGNE, SIDNEY (cl). b. N.O., about 1903; d. N.O., Dec. 24, 1925. A promising young clarinetist who played with the Golden Leaf Band, Bob Lyons' Dixie Jazz Band, the Maple Leaf Orchestra in the early 20's. Killed by a truck on Christmas Eve, 1925.

VINCENT, CLARENCE "LITTLE DAD" (bjo). b. Baton Rouge, La., 1899; d. N.O., 1960. Lilliputian Little Dad was barely four feet tall. Was well known for work with Buddy Petit and Chris Kelly before he was twenty. Played at West End in Amos White's New Orleans Creole Jazz Band, 1923–24. In 20's joined Herb Morand to work in Yucatan, Mexico. During depression worked at times with Louis Dumaine and with Octave Crosby.

VINSON, EDDIE (tb). b. N.O., about 1885. In 1910, Vinson was a member of the Olympia Orchestra and the Excelsior Brass Band. He left N.O. with the Original Creole Orchestra, led by Bill Johnson, for a vaudeville tour. He remained up north thereafter.

WALDE, BILL (sb). b. N.O., 1892; d. N.O., 1959. Dixielander worked frequently with Abbie Brunies. Also with Albert Artigues' French Market Gang. Brother of Henry Walde.

WALDE, HENRY (g). b. N.O., Aug. 10, 1902; d. N.O., June 14, 1975. One-time leader of the Melon Pickers. Worked with Alfred Laine and Leon Prima.

WALTERS, ALBERT (t). b. N.O., July 19, 1905. Began musical career about 1929. In 1931 organized, with Albert Jiles, the Crescent City Serenaders, which was active through the early depression years. Has played with most of the best bands in town since and was frequently in parades, especially with the George Williams Brass Band.

WARD, BENNY (p). A Storyville "professor."

WARNER, ALBERT (tb). b. N.O., Dec. 31, 1890. Known almost exclusively as a brass band musician. Was with Kid Rena's brass band, the Young Tuxedo Brass Band, and since 1932 with the Eureka Brass Band. In the early 40's he recorded with Bunk Johnson. In earlier days, he played in dance bands, notably with Big Eye Louis Nelson.

WARNER, WILLIE (cl). b. N.O., about 1865; d. N.O., about 1908. Member of the original Buddy Bolden band. Also played with Charlie Galloway and with the Pelican Brass Band.

JOE WATKINS

EDDIE WATSON

WARNICK, LOUIS (s, cl). b. N.O., about 1890. Warnick played jobs in brass bands in his teens. In 1918 he joined A. J. Piron for a ten-year stand at Spanish Fort; he recorded with the orchestra, 1923–25. In 1928 he played with the Creole Serenaders which was one of the city's most successful bands; broadcast regularly over station WWL.

WASHINGTON, EDMOND (cl, as, vo). An active member of the Kid Thomas band through the late 40's, early 50's.

WASHINGTON, EDWARD "SON WHITE" (d). b. Natchez, Miss., Oct. 12, 1902; d. N.O., 1964. Known mainly as a brass band drummer, especially with the George Williams Brass Band. He was also a dance drummer who studied with Dave Perkins in 1920 and went to work for the Foster Lewis band. In later years he was associated with Joe Avery and with Wilbert Tillman.

WASHINGTON, FRED (p). b. N.O., 1888. A Storyville "professor." Moved to California in 1919. Played, irregularly, for many years. Recorded on first Ory session.

WASHINGTON, GEORGE (tb). b. N.O., about 1900; d. N.O., about 1942. First job in Joe Lindsey's kid band,

alongside Louis Armstrong, 1916. Later identified with Buddy Petit in early 1920 period.

WATKINS, JOE. See Mitchell Watson.

WATSON, EDDIE (g). b. Pass Christian, Miss., July 13, 1904. One of Edmond Souchon's early teachers. Began with his three brothers in a spasm band which later merged with the Handy band led by John Handy.

WATSON, JOSEPH (cl). b. N.O., about 1895; d. N.O., about 1925. A member of Sam Morgan's first band in 1916.

WATSON, MITCHELL (d. vo). b. N.O., Oct. 24, 1900; d. N.O., Sept., 1969. Known as Joe Watkins. Internationally known drummer in George Lewis band during its peak years. In 1964 he toured Japan with the band and was a frequent performer at Preservation Hall. Nephew of Johnny St. Cyr. Stopped playing in 1966 because of failing health.

WATZKE, ALEX "KING" (v, l). b. N.O., about 1880; d. N.O., 1918. Led popular band before 1908. Another claimant to composer credit for "Tiger Rag" which he actually played in 1904, calling it "No. 2." Died in flu epidemic.

WHALEY, WADE (cl). b. N.O., 1895; d. before 1916 at the Bungalow. Another protégé of the Tios. Before he left N.O. in 1919 he had worked in the bands of A. J. Piron, John Robichaux, Manuel Perez, Manuel

WADE WHALEY

JOHNNY WIGGS (John Wigginton Hyman)

Manetta, Jack Carey. In California he worked with Jelly Roll Morton and Kid Ory; led own band in California from mid-20's until the depression. Recorded with Bunk Johnson in 1944.

WHITE, AMOS (c). b. Kingstree, S.C., Nov. 6, 1889. Came to N.O. in 1919 after army discharge. Played first at Cadillac Bar with Harrison Verrett, then joined Celestin's Tuxedo Brass Band. Worked on boats with Fate Marable and is on Marable's Okeh disc, 1924. Organized his N.O. Creole Jazz Band in 1924 which played for dancing opposite Tranchina's. As late as 1960 White played a concert in California, where he has settled.

WHITE, BENJAMIN "BENJY" (cl, s, v). b. N.O., Aug. 30, 1901. Played with Invincibles String Band before taking up reeds, clarinet, saxophone. Was one of the original group of N.O. Owls. Never played with anyone else; when group disbanded, he quit music.

WICKER, CHESTER (p). b. N.O., 1904; d. N.O., Dec. 21, 1970. With Tony Fourgerat, Tony Almerico, Irving Fazola, Julian Laine from about 1919.

WIGGS, JOHNNY. See Hyman, John Wigginton.

WILLIAMS, ABBY (d). b. N.O., Sept. 22, 1906. Still active drummer, mainly with pickup groups. Led Square Deal Social Club Brass Band in late 20's.

WILLIAMS, ALFRED (d). b. N.O., Sept. 1, 1900; d. N.O., April 30, 1963. First job playing snare drum in the Tuxedo Brass Band in 1920. In early 20's worked in the Sam Morgan band. From 1925–27 was with Manuel Perez; joined A. J. Piron on the S.S. *Capitol* in 1929. Left N.O. in 1936; returned in 1951, playing small dance jobs and marching with the Eureka

124

ABBY WILLIAMS

ALFRED WILLIAMS

Brass Band. Was frequently at Preservation Hall before his death.

WILLIAMS, "BLACK BENNY" (d). b. N.O., about 1890; d. N.O., in 1924. Though better known as an underworld character, was quite a drummer. Played bass drum for the Onward Brass Band before World War I. Sometimes marched with the Tuxedo Brass Band or sat in with Louis Armstrong on a job. Stabbed to death by a woman.

WILLIAMS, CLAIBORNE (c, l). Leader of early concert orchestra and brass band, mainly in Baton Rouge area in early 1900's.

WILLIAMS, CLARENCE (p, vo, l). b. Plaquemine, La., Nov. 8, 1893; d. New York, N.Y., Nov. 6, 1965. Began playing in Storyville brothels in about 1914 and occasionally had a job with Piron. Went to Texas with Sidney Bechet via boxcar, but the trip proved unproductive. Went into music publishing business with Piron in 1915. Migrated to Chicago about 1917 and became an important factor in the publishing and recording business. Through the 20's and 30's produced great records on Okeh and Columbia, including the famous Blue Five discs that brought Louis

Armstrong and Sidney Bechet together on wax. For more than 20 years operated a hobby shop in Harlem.

WILLIAMS, DAVE (p). b. N.O., La., Aug. 26, 1920. Occasional performer at Preservation, Dixieland halls during the 60's.

WILLIAMS, FREDDIE, (d). b. N.O., about 1887; d. April 30, 1963. Early dixielander; an official in the New Orleans police department. Played with Emile Christian, George and Merritt Brunies in pre-World War I era.

WILLIAMS, GEORGE (bd). b. N.O., Oct. 25, 1910; d. N.O., Aug. 27, 1965. Leader of the George Williams Brass Band, active in N.O. for the past 20 years. Worked at the Paddock with Bill Matthews in 50's.

WILLIAMS, GEORGE (c). Before World War I played in Excelsior Brass Band.

WILLIAMS, GEORGE (g). Worked in the district about 1910–13, mainly with the Primrose Orchestra.

SPENCER WILLIAMS

WILLIE WILSON

WILLIAMS, NOLAN "SHINE" (d). b. N.O., about 1902; d. N.O., about 1942. First major job with the Sam Morgan band in 1926–27; recorded with the band in spring, 1927. Went on to work in Clarence Desdunes Joyland Revelers, mainly traveling through Louisiana and nearby states.

WILLIAMS, NORWOOD "GIGGY" (g). b. about 1880. Member of Bill Johnson's Original Creole Orchestra that left N.O. for history-making Pantages vaudeville tour.

WILLIAMS, SPENCER (p). b. N.O., Oct. 14, 1880; d. New York, N.Y., July, 1965. Reared by the notorious madam, Lulu White, he worked as a "professor" for a while in his early years. Is best known as a composer. Wrote "Basin St. Blues," "Mahogany Hall Stomp," "Tishomingo Blues," and "Shim-Me-Sha-Wabble."

WILLIGAN, BILL (d). b. N.O. ——. Early drummer in Buddy Bolden's band.

WILLIGAN, JIM (d). b. N.O., about 1902; d. N.O., about 1930. One of the best of the N.O. drummers. First noted in 1923 with Towles' Creole Harmony Kings and then with Papa Celestin's Original Tuxedo Orchestra. Selected by Dumaine for the celebrated Jazzola Eight session of 1927. Joined Lee Collins just before the depression.

WILLIS, JOSHUA F. "JACK" (t, mel, ah). b. Galena, Ill., April 15, 1920. Active member of marching bands in recent years, Young Tuxedo Brass Band, George Williams Brass Band. Played with George Lewis, and at Preservation and Dixieland halls.

WILSON, ALFRED (p). One of the best musicians among the Storyville bordello "professors."

WILSON, JOHNNY (bh). Charter member of the Eureka Brass Band. Brother of Willie Wilson.

WILSON, UDELL (p). Though not a Louisianan, Wilson was active in the district as a band piano man before World War I, working at Fewclothes Cabaret, with Big Eye Louis Nelson, and at 101 Ranch. Worked with Maple Leaf Orchestra, 1919, and with Manuel Perez, 1922. Replaced Luis Russell at Anderson's in 1924.

WILSON, WILLIE (t). b. N.O., about 1890. Founder of the Eureka Brass Band. Worked in the ERA program during the depression.

FREDDIE WILLIAMS

BOOTS YOUNG

WINKLER, MARTIN "BULL" (d). b. N.O., about 1890; d. N.O., about 1955. Dixieland drummer with the Jack Laine, Bill Gallaty, Frank Christian bands.

WINSTEIN, DAVE (s). b. N.O., Dec. 18, 1909. Active in the late 20's and early 30's. Worked with the Sharkey-Leon Prima All-Stars and with Louis Prima. Is now president of local 174 of the AFM.

WOLFE, JOE (p). b. N.O., 1892; d. Dec. 13, 1961. Most noteworthy connections—Johnny Bayersdorffer in the 20's, Ellis Stratakos in the 30's.

WOODS, ALVIN (d). b. N.O., Feb. 1, 1909. With Kid Sheik, Narvin Kimball. Played with Joe Robichaux orchestra in late 30's. Also with Willie Joseph.

WYNN, ALBERT (tb). b. N.O., July 29, 1907; d. Chicago, 1975. Never played in N.O., but career was closely associated with the jazz of his native city. Although he lived in Chicago, he played for over 40 years with the most celebrated Crescent City jazzmen.

YOUNG, AUSTIN "BOOTS" (tb, tu, sb). b. N.O., about 1885; d. N.O., about 1954. With his brother Sport, sax, Willie Pajeaud, trumpet, formed nucleus of dance group that worked dance halls from the late 20's through the depression years. He recorded in 1942 with Bunk Johnson for American Music in 1945 and 1949.

YOUNG, SPORT (s). Brother of Boots Young. Worked with his brother Boots and Willie Pajeaud in taxi dance halls for 15 years.

YSAGUIRRE, ROBERT (tu, sb). b. N.O., about 1895. Long-time bassist with A. J. Piron Orchestra.

CHESTER ZARDIS

ROY ZIMMERMAN

ZANCO, MANUEL "MOOSE" (c). b. N.O., Feb. 12, 1929. Regular with The Last Straws.

ZARDIS, CHESTER (sb). b. New Iberia, La., May 27, 1900. Outstanding bassist with Buddy Petit in Mandeville in 1920. Saw duty with Chris Kelly, Kid Rena, Kid Howard. Was with Desvigne in 1930–31, then had his own band from 1935 to 1938. He recorded with the George Lewis band in 1943. Regular performer at Preservation Hall.

ZENO, HENRY (d). b. N.O., about 1880; d. N.O., about 1918. Early drummer with the Buddy Bolden band, 1900. Worked frequently with Edward Clem, Manuel Manetta in the years around 1906–07; joined Duson's Eagle Band in 1908. Played in the Olympia Orchestra with A. J. Piron in 1913–14 and was at Pete Lala's with King Oliver in 1916. Just before his death he was working with the Original Tuxedo Orchestra.

ZIMMERMAN, GUS (c). b. N.O., about 1887. Member of Reliance Brass Band. With Barocco brothers in 1919.

ZIMMERMAN, ROY (p). b. N.O., Oct. 23, 1913; d. Gulfport, Miss., July 7, 1969. Best known as pianist with Basin Street Six during 50's. Often seen with Sharkey. Was with Pete Fountain and his Three Coins.

ZIMMERMAN, TOM (p). b. N.O., about 1886; d. Dec. 4, 1923. Considered by many the greatest ragtime piano player of the "tango belt." Apprenticeship as movie house musician. He was a popular soloist in cabarets for most of his active days. In the 20's he played with Tony Parenti and with the Johnny De-Droit orchestra.

ZITO, PHIL (d). b. N.O., Aug. 8, 1914. Active bandleader of the late 40's and early 50's. Recorded with own band called the International Dixieland Express.

A JAZZ BAND BALL

Here is a cavalcade of New Orleans bands that made jazz history. They came in all sizes and varieties, with as many approaches to the music as there were leaders. All of those listed and pictured are not purely jazz bands. Some are, of course, but others, not similarly oriented, nevertheless *sometimes* played the real jazz.

A word of explanation is necessary about our use of terms to describe these musical groups.

First, when we use the term "jazz band" we mean a group of musicians playing in 2/4 or 4/4 time, improvising collectively on any theme. Usually these bands emphasized counterpoint rather than conventional harmony.

By a "dixieland band" we mean a group of from five to eight musicians consisting of a front line of cornet or trumpet, clarinet and trombone, plus a rhythm section. The group will have memorized certain parts of each tune in their fixed repertoire. (This is what is called a "head arrangement.") It includes some collective improvisation, but usually is more occupied with "hot" solos. Sometimes there is a saxophone in a dixieland band.

When we say "dance orchestra" in the New Orleans jazz sense, what we mean is any group of musicians employed to play for dancing which is capable of reading written scores. However they are all supplied with a number of tunes which they play *without* music in the dixieland tradition.

A "novelty orchestra" is one that depends largely on showmanship, odd or homemade instruments, slapsticks, and other items of "skiffle" origin. Fre-

quently, however, such groups are of excellent jazz quality.

String bands, of course, are just what the name specifies. Brass bands are a big enough classification to be covered elsewhere in this volume as a separate group.

Our first knowledge of an organized jazz band using conventional instruments dates back to 1889 when a group headed by guitarist Charlie Galloway played for dances and social activities. However, the authors disclaim, here and now, any implication that this was, in truth, the first jazz band. In fact, we are convinced that the development of jazz was so gradual as to make specious any such claim as related to an individual or group.

ACCORDIANA BAND (1894), dance orchestra. Nucleus: Henry Peyton, acc, l; Alphonse Picou, cl; Punkie Valentin, c; Bouboul Valentin, vt.

ALBERT, TOM (1910), jazz band. Tom Albert, t, v, l; Eddie Atkins, tb; Albert Gabriel, cl; Manuel Manetta, p, v; Skeeter Jackson, g; Lutzie Rubean, b; Son Hamilton, d.

AMERICAN STARS (1908–17), jazz band. Willie Hightower, c, l; Roy Palmer, tb; Wade Whaley, cl; Robert Smith, g; Udell Wilson, p; Baby Dodds, d. Sometimes a violin was added.

ANDRUS, DUTCH, dance orchestra. Varied personnel. Frequently employed on steamer *President*. Dutch Andrus, t, l.

ARCADIAN SERENADERS (mid-20's), dixieland band. Mainly Orleanians, active on Gulf Coast, especially Mobile, Ala. Wingy Manone or Stirling Bose, t;

Avery Loposer, tb; Cliff Holman, cl, s; John Riddick, p; Slim Hill or Bob Marvin, bjo; Felix Guarino, d.

BANJO BUMS (50's), string band. John Chaffe, Malcolm Genet, bjo; Edmond Souchon, g; Sherwood Mangiapane, sb.

BANNER BAND (20's), jazz band. Traveling band in Louisiana country towns. Varied personnel, usually including: Gus Fortinet, v, l; Bunk Johnson, t; Lawrence Duhé, cl; Joe Avery, tb; George Hamilton, bar. h; Chester Zardis, b.

BARBARIN, PAUL (early 40's to present), jazz band. Partial collective personnel: John Brunious, Ernie Cagnolatti, Albert Walters, t; Bob Thomas, Frog Joseph, Clement Tervalon, tb; Willie Humphrey, (younger), Louis Cottrell, Jr., cl; Lester Santiago, Joe Robichaux, p; Danny Barker, bjo; Paul Barbarin, d, l.

130

Happy Schilling's Orchestra (1915). Left to right, kneeling, are Fred Dantagnan, Don Sanderson. Others are Johnny Frisco, Happy Schilling, Bob "One-leg Robbie" Aquilera, Johnny Lala, Henry Knecht, Jack Pipitone, John Goety, Lefty Eierman.

Stalebread Lacoume's band at West End in 1906. Stalebread (extreme right) brought his Razzy Dazzy Spasm Band to the lake at old West End in 1906 to play for this family picnic. Of the other musicians, only Sou Sou Ramos, the mandolin player, is identified. Members of this gang were usually tagged with such bizarre nicknames as "Warm Gravy," "Chinee," "Family Haircut," and "Cajun."

The Original Tuxedo Orchestra in 1924. In front seated, left to right, are Paul Barnes, Joe Strohter, whose local fame was based more on his playing of the slide whistle than on his drumming, Bebé Ridgley, Oscar Celestin, John Marrero. Standing, left to right, are Henry Pajeaud, Simon Marrero, Manuel Manetta, and Kid Shots Madison.

The Louisiana Shakers in the mid-20's. Seated, left to right, are Roy Evans, Lionel Ferbois, Kid Keifer, Edmund Bottley, unknown. Standing, left to right, are George Clark, Sidney Pflueger John Handy, Benny Clark, Henry Kimball.

The Eagle Band (Feb. 28, 1916). Left to right are Big Eye Louis Nelson, Chinee Foster, Frankie Duson, Buddy Petit, Lorenzo Staulz, Dandy Lewis.

Revised Original Dixieland Band (1956). Making an appearance with Garry Moore on the "I've Got a Secret" program are, left to right, Russel Robinson, Tony Parenti, Phil Napoleon, Eddie Edwards, Tony Spargo.

Superior Orchestra (1910). Seated, left to right, are Walter Brundy, Peter Bocage, Richard Payne. Standing, Buddy Johnson, Bunk Johnson, Big Eye Louis Nelson, Billy Marrero.

BASIN STREET SIX (50's), dixieland-comedy band. Co-op group. George Girard, t, vo; Joe Rotis, tb; Pete Fountain, cl; Roy Zimmerman, p; Bunny Franks, b; Charlie Duke, d.

BAYERSDORFFER, JOHNNY (20's–30's), dixieland band. Partial collective personnel: Johnny Bayersdorffer, t, l; Tom Brown, Charlie Hartmann, tb; Nunzio Scaglione, Lester Bouchon, Harry Shields, Ellery Maser, Bill Creger, cl, s; Johnny Miller, Joe Wolfe, p; Nappy Lamare, Freddie Loyacano, Steve Loyacano, bjo, g; Martin Abraham, Sr., b; Leo Adde, Ray Bauduc, d.

BIENVILLE ROOF ORCHESTRA (1928), dixieland band. Sharkey, t; Sidney Arodin, cl; Hal Jordy, s; Freddie Neumann, p; Joe Capraro, g; Luther Lamar, b; Monk Hazel, d, ml, t, l.

BLACK AND TAN ORCHESTRA (20's), jazz band. Buddy Petit, t, l; George Washington, tb; Edmond Hall (later, Pill Coycault), cl; Sadie Goodson, p; Buddy Manaday, bjo; Chester Zardis, sb; Eddie "Face-O" Woods (later, Chinee Foster), d.

BLACK DEVILS (20's), jazz band. Played in and around Plaquemine, La. Leader, Dennis Williams, sb (father of pianist Clarence Williams).

135

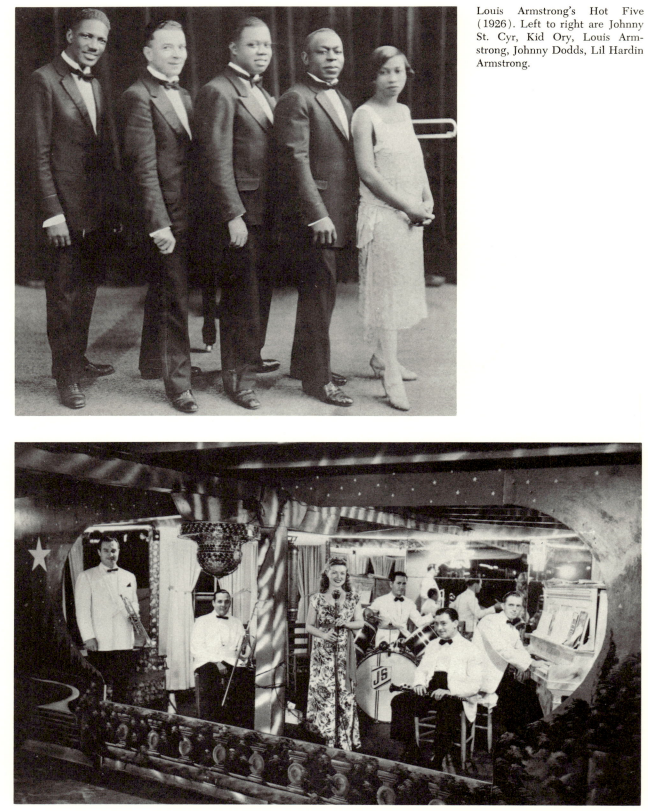

Louis Armstrong's Hot Five (1926). Left to right are Johnny St. Cyr, Kid Ory, Louis Armstrong, Johnny Dodds, Lil Hardin Armstrong.

The Henry Belas Orchestra (1930's). Left to right are Henry Belas, Al Moore, Joe Stephens, Raymond Burke, "Pee Wee"—.

Papa Celestin's Band (1950's). Left to right are Happy Goldston, Papa Celestin, Octave Crosby, Alphonse Picou, Roger Wolfe (disc jockey, mc), Ricard Alexis Bill Matthews.

The Crawford-Ferguson Night Owls (1963). Left to right, seated, are Edmond Souchon (not a regular member), Bill Humphries, Leonard Ferguson. Standing, Paul Crawford, Jack Bachman, Hank Kmen, Sherwood Mangiapane.

137

BLACK DIAMOND ORCHESTRA (30's), dance orchestra. Albert Walters, t; Frank Crump, s; Eddie Summers, tb; Clifford Bigeou, bjo; George Henderson, d, l.

BLACK EAGLES (1921–33), jazz band. Partial collective personnel: Evan Thomas, t, l; Bunk Johnson, c; Bob Thomas, Kid Avery, Harrison Brazlee, tb; Lawrence Duhé, George Lewis, Sam Dutrey, Jr., cl; Robert Goby, s; Abraham Martin, bjo; Walter Thomas, Abbey Foster, d.

BOLDEN, CHARLES "BUDDY" (1893–1907), ragtime band. Flexible personnel, according to nature of job. Played for dances, parades, parties. Partial collective personnel: Buddy Bolden, t, l; Bunk Johnson, t; Willie Cornish, Frank Duson, Vic Gaspard, tb; Frank Lewis, Willie Warner, Big Eye Louis Nelson, Sam Dutrey, Sr., cl; Manuel Manetta, Alcide Frank, James A. Palao, v; Bab Frank, pc; Charlie Galloway, Brock Mumford, Lorenzo Staulz, g; Jimmy Johnson, Bob Lyons, Albert Glenny, Bebé Mitchell, sb, tu; Bill Willigan, Henry Zeno, John McMurray, Cornelius Tillman, d.

TOM BROWN'S BAND FROM DIXIELAND (1915). As it left for Chicago in 1915: Ray Lopez, t; Tom Brown, tb, l; Gus Mueller, cl; Deacon Loyacano, sb, p; Billy Lambert, d. Larry Shields replaced Mueller, cl, in late 1915.

BROWNLEE, NORMAN (20's), dixieland, novelty band. Collective partial personnel: Emmett Hardy, Johnny Wiggs, Sharkey, George Barth, c, t; Tom Brown, George Barth, tb; Harry Shields, Lester Bouchon, cl, s; Billy Braun, ml, s; Norman Brownlee, p. s, l; Behrman French, Bill Eastwood, Freddie Loyacano, bjo; Alonzo Crombie, tb, d; Frank Christian, tu; Paul Peque, s.

BRUNIES NEW ORLEANS JAZZ BAND (about 1918). See Original New Orleans Jazz Band.

CAMELIA DANCE ORCHESTRA (1917–mid-20's). Same as Camelia Brass Band, but Ike Robinson switches to guitar and Joe Parone, string bass, replaces Buddy Luck. Billy and Lawrence Marrero, string bass and banjo, respectively, sometimes played in the band.

CHRISTIAN RAGTIME BAND (about 1910–18). Partial collective personnel: Harry Nunez, v; Ernest Giardina, v, vo; Frank Christian, t, tu, l; Emile Christian, c; Charlie Christian, tb; Bill Gallaty, vt; Yellow Nunez, Achille Baquet, Tony Giardina, Leon Goureaux, cl; Manuel Gomez, g; Willie Guitar, sb; Kid Totts Blaise, Martin "Bull" Winkler, d.

COLUMBUS BAND (1898), jazz band. Tig Chambers, t, l; Willie Humphrey (elder), cl; Willie Cornish, tb; Bob Lyons, sb; Bill Willigan, d.

CREOLE HARMONY KINGS (1922–27), jazz band. Herb Morand, t; Bill Matthews, tb; Kid Moliere, cl; Wallington Hughes, s; Frank Pashley, bjo; Nat Towles, sb, l; Louis Mahier (later Bill Willigan), d.

CREOLE SERENADERS (from 1928), dance orchestra. Peter Bocage, t, v, l; Henry Bocage, t; Lorenzo Tio, Jr., cl; Louis Warnick, s; Steve Lewis, Dwight Newman, p; John Marrero, Charlie Bocage, bjo; Paul Barbarin, Cié Frazier, Henry Martin. Since 1928 all Bocage-led groups have been called Creole Serenaders.

CRESCENT CITY JAZZERS (mid-20's). Name only used for recording purposes. Same personnel as Arcadian Serenaders plus Eddie Powers, s, and minus Wingy Manone, t.

CRESCENT CITY SERENADERS (1931–34), dance orchestra. A group of changing personnel built around a four-man nucleus, according to the size of the job. The basic four: Albert Walters, t; Frank Crump, s; Clifford Bigeou, bjo; Albert Jiles, d.

CRESCENT ORCHESTRA (1913–20), jazz band. Partial collective personnel: Mutt Carey, Punch Miller, t; Jack Carey, tb, l; Wade Whaley, Willie Humphrey (elder), Georgia Boy Boyd, cl; Charles Moore, Tom Benton, g; Wiley King, Pops Foster, sb, tu; Li'l Mack Lacey, Tubby Hall, Baby Dodds, Ernest Rogers, Ram Hall, d.

CROSBY, OCTAVE (1940's to 1963), jazz band. House bandleader at the Paddock on Bourbon St. for many years. In his band have been: Alvin Alcorn, Oscar

138

Sharkey and His Kings of Dixieland (1949). Left to right are Santo Pecora, Monk Hazel, Martin Abraham, Sharkey, Jeff Riddick, Lester Bouchon.

Johnny Wiggs Orchestra (1950). Left to right are Edmond Souchon, Ray Bauduc, Johnny Wiggs, Stanley Mendelson, Harry Shields, Tom Brown, Sherwood Mangiapane.

Celestin, Lee Collins, Thomas Jefferson, t; Bill Matthews, Frog Joseph, Bob Thomas, Clement Tervalon, tb; Alphonse Picou, Albert Burbank, Willie Humphrey (younger), Ted Purnell, cl; Octave Crosby, p, l; Ricard Alexis, Narvin Kimball, Richard McClean, bjo; Happy Goldston, Alfred Williams, George Williams, d.

DEDROIT, JOHNNY (1917 to late 50's), dance orchestra. Johnny DeDroit, t, l; Russ Papalia, Ellis Stratakos, tb; Tony Parenti, Henry Raymond, cl, s; Rudolph Levy, as; Frank Cuny, Tom Zimmerman, p; George Potter, bjo; Paul DeDroit, d; Frank Froeba, p.

DEJAN'S MOONLIGHT SERENADERS (early 30's), dance orchestra. Early version of rock-and-roll band. Leo Dejan, t, l; Harold Dejan, s; Sidney Cates, bjo; Arnaul Thomas, d.

CLARENCE DESDUNES JOYLAND REVELERS (1927–31), dance orchestra. Usual personnel: Clarence Desdunes, v, l; Alvin Alcorn, George McCullum, Jr., George Montgomery, t; Ray Johnson, Ray Brown, tb; Oliver Alcorn, cl, ss; Lucien Johnson, Harold Dejan, s; Harry Fairconnetue, bjo; Henry Kimball, sb; Ransom Knowling, tu; Little Brother Montgomery, p.

DESVIGNE, SIDNEY (1925–31), dance orchestra. Worked on Streckfus line. This partial collective personnel includes only musicians from New Orleans: Sidney Desvigne, t, l; Henry Allen, Jr., Gene Ware, t; Bill Matthews, Big Eye Louis Nelson, tb; Adolphe Alexander, Jr., Ted Purnell, Henry Julian, Eddie Cherie, s; Sam Dutrey, Sr., s, cl; Walter Pichon, William Houston, p; Pops Foster, Sylvester Handy, Albert Morgan, Ransom Knowling, sb, tu; Emanuel Sayles, Rene Hall, Fred Minor, Johnny St. Cyr, g, bjo; Louis Barbarin, d.

DIXIE RHYTHM BAND (1930–36), dance orchestra. Small group playing on lake steamers, led by saxman, Harold Dejan and including Casimir Paul, bjo; Lester Santiago, p.

DIXIE JAZZ BAND (1918–25), jazz band. Ricard Alexis, c; Sidney Vigne, later Louis Nelson Delisle, cl; Ernest Kelly or Paul Ben, tb; Lorenzo Staulz, bjo;

Little Dad Vincent, g; Little Joe Lindsey, d; Bob Lyons, b, l.

DIXIELAND ROAMERS (20's). In 1923 this group made the first live jazz broadcast from New Orleans, from the Joe Uhalt station atop the Southern Electric Company building next to the DeSoto Hotel. Pinky Gerbrecht, t, l; Ellis Stratakos, tb; Eddie Powers, s; Frank Mutz, p; Ray Bauduc, d; Ed McCarthy, vo.

DIXOLA JAZZ BAND (mid-20's, early 30's), dance orchestra. Howard Reed, t; Chick Johnson, Elwood Taylor, s; Count Comes, p; Tony Tortorich, d; Leo Donegan, d; Harold Wirth, bjo; Axson Riley, tu.

DUKES OF DIXIELAND (1950 to present), dixieland-novelty. One of the nation's "big-name" bands built around the Assunto family. Papa Jac plays bjo, tb; son Frank is t, l; Freddie, tb, now deceased. New Orleans musicians who have at times worked in the band: Harry Shields, Tony Parenti, Raymond Burke, Pete Fountain, cl; Stanley Mendelson, Arthur Seelig, Jr., p; Willie Perkins, Buck Rogers, Roger Johnston, d; Tony Balderas, g; Henry Barthels, Martin Abraham, Jr., sb.

LOUIS DUMAINE JAZZOLA EIGHT (1927–29), jazz band. Collective personnel: Louis Dumaine, t, l; Earl Humphrey, Yank Johnson, tb; Willie Joseph, cl; Clarence Gabriel, g; Leonard Mitchell, bjo; Morris Rouse, p; Joe Howard, sb, tu; Willie Lebet, Jim Willigan, d.

DUMAINE-HOUSTON JAZZ BAND (30's), dance orchestra. Joint leadership band. Louis Dumaine, t; Fats Houston, d. They booked jobs and hired musicians to fill them. Willie Joseph, cl, was a steady employee.

EAGLE BAND (1900–17), jazz band. Partial collective personnel: Bunk Johnson, Tig Chambers, Joe Johnson, Joe Oliver, Frank Keelin, Edward Clem, Buddy Petit, t; Frank Duson, tb, l; Willie Parker, Frank Lewis, Sidney Bechet, Johnny Dodds, Big Eye Louis Nelson, cl; Dandy Lewis, Bill Johnson, Pops Foster, Bob Lyons, sb, tu; Lorenzo Staulz, Brock Mumford, g; Henry Zeno, Abbey Foster, Baby Dodds, d.

The Dixola Novelty Orchestra (1924). In the "Tip-Top Room" at the Grunewald Hotel are, left to right, Howard Reed, Leo Donegan, Axson Riley, Count Cómes, Harold Wirth, Henry "Chick" Johnson, Elwood Taylor.

The Irving Fazola Orchestra. At Tony's Cafe on Canal Boulevard. Left to right are Joe Rotis, Howard Reed, Irving Fazola, Charlie Duke, Ogden Lafaye.

Dejan's Original Moonlight Serenaders (about 1921). Left to right: Arnaul Thomas, Leo Dejan, Harold Dejan, Henry Casenave, Sidney Cates.

The Jazzola Six (1918). Left to right are Roscoe Legnon, Bill Braun, Johnny Beninate, Johnny Bayersdorffer, Paul Cinquemano, Buster Klein.

Pop Hamilton's Band (1930). Patty Whisker at the piano. The others, standing, left to right, are leader Lumas Hamilton, Andrew Johnson, Dave——, Al Smith, Pop Hamilton, Lenex "Pinky" Alberts, ——Johnson (emcee), ——Kelley.

Jelly Roll Morton's Red Hot Peppers (1920's). Seated, Jelly Roll. Standing, left to right, are Omer Simeon, Andre Hillaire, John Lindsay, Johnny St. Cyr, Kid Ory, George Mitchell. All except Mitchell are native Orleanians.

143

EMERGENCY RELIEF ADMINISTRATION ORCHESTRA (mid 30's). Some 90 musicians on a federal anti-depression project. Led first by Pinchback Touro, later by Louis Dumaine. As many as possible of the musicians are identified on the photograph in this volume.

FIVE SOUTHERN JAZZERS (about 1919–24). This band played in Chicago. Frank Christian, t, l; Frank L'Hotag, tb; Johnny Fischer, cl; Ernie Erdman, p; Anton Lada, d. L'Hotag and Erdman are midwesterners.

FOUGERAT, TONY, dixieland band. This bandleader has been supplying music to Orleanians for forty years. Some of those who have worked in his bands are Nappy Lamare, g; Charlie Christian, tb; Willie Guitar, sb; Lester Bouchon, Harry Shields, cl.

FOUR HOT HOUNDS (1909–11), jazz band. A Storyville group usually at Abadie's. Sugar Johnny Smith, c; Wooden Joe Nicholas, cl; Richard M. Jones, p, l; Ernest Rogers, d. Sometimes Joe Oliver replaced Smith.

BUDDY GEHL AND HIS EIGHT WINDS. A college-boy band of the 20's composed mainly of Tulane students. Most of its members have become New Orleans business or professional men. Played many dance and theater dates over a five-year span. Its steadiest members were: Herman Kohlmeyer, Dick Mackie, t; Gerald "Skinny" Andrus, Dede Newman, cl, s; Louis Kohlmeyer, tu; Preacher Wadsworth, p; Rene Gelpi, bjo; Buddy Gehl, d, l.

GOLDEN LEAF BAND (1920–21), jazz band. Lee Collins, t; Jim Robinson, tb; Sidney Vigne, cl; Sidney Brown, v; Bud Russell, sb; Arthur Ogle, d, g; Jesse Jackson, bjo, l. Sometimes Punch Miller, t, and Happy Goldston, d, substituted.

GOLDEN RULE ORCHESTRA (1905), dance orchestra. Alcide Frank, v, l; Adolphe Alexander, Sr., t; Big Eye Louis Nelson, cl; James Brown, sb; Joe Brooks, g; Jean Vigne, d. A revival of the band in 1920 included Dennis Harris and Louis Cottrell, Jr., cl, s; Lawrence Marrero, bjo; Cié Frazier, d.

HALFWAY HOUSE ORCHESTRA (1923–28), dance orchestra. Partial collective personnel: Abbie Brunies,

c, l; Leon Roppolo, Charles Cordilla, Sidney Arodin, cl, s; Joe Loyacano, as; Merritt Brunies, vt; Bill Eastwood, Angelo Palmisano, bjo; Mickey Marcour, Red Long, p; Deacon Loyacano, Chink Martin, Bud Loyacano, sb; Monk Hazel, d, mel, c; Leo Adde, Emmett Rogers, d.

POP HAMILTON BAND (1930's). Lumas Hamilton, l, t; Andrew Johnson, d; Dave ——, bjo; Al Smith, ts; Pop Hamilton, tu; Pinky Alberts, t; —— Johnson, mc; —— Kelly, as; Patty Whisker, p.

HIGHTOWER, WILLIE (see American Stars)

HILL CITY BAND (1906), dance orchestra. Andrew Kimball, c; John Hime, Hamp Benson, tb; Charles McCurdy, cl; Charles Pierson, sometimes Cootchie Martin, g; Cato, d.

HOLLYWOOD ORCHESTRA (1929–31), dance orchestra. A large dance band headed by Mike Delay, c, featuring Louis Nelson, tb, and Andrew Morgan, cl, s.

JOHNNY HYMAN BAYOU STOMPERS (1927), dixieland recording band. Johnny Wiggs, c, l; Charlie Hartman, tb; Ellery Maser, cl; Alvin Gautreaux, h; Horace Diaz, p; Nappy Lamare, g; Monk Hazel, d.

IMPERIAL ORCHESTRA (1901–08), dance orchestra. Partial collective personnel: Manuel Perez, c, l; George Filhe, Buddy Johnson, tb; George Baquet, Big Eye Louis Nelson, cl; James A. Palao, v; Adolphe Alexander, Sr., bh; Rene Baptiste, g; Jimmy Brown, sb; John Vigne, John MacMurray, d.

INVINCIBLES STRING BAND (1912–21). This group evolved into the New Orleans Owls. Collective personnel: Johnny Wiggs, Eblen Rau, Frank Ferrer, Benjy White, Ed Pinac, Donald Coleman, v; Bill Kleppinger, mdl; Fred Overing, bjo-mdl; Ernest Guidry, 6-string bjo; Rene Gelpi, 5-string bjo; Charles Hardy, tar; Monk Smith, g, uk; Rollo Tichenor, Lorimer Naff, g; Red Mackie, sb, g, bjo; Mose Ferrer, p; Earl Crumb, d.

JAZZOLA SIX (1919–21), dixieland band. Johnny Bayersdorffer, c, l; Paul Cinquemano, tb; Johnny Beninate, cl; Bill Braun, p; Roscoe Legnon, sb; Buster Klein, d.

144

The Peerless Orchestra (about 1911). In City Park, New Orleans. Front row, left to right, are John Vigne, Charles McCurdy, Armand J. Piron, Coochie Martin. Back row, left to right, Vic Gaspard, Andrew Kimball, Oak Gaspard.

The Sam Morgan Jazz Band. Left to right are Nolan Williams, Isaiah Morgan, Jim Robinson, Sam Morgan, Earl Fouché, Andrew Morgan (seated, sax), Sidney Brown, string bass, Johnny Dave.

JONES-COLLINS ASTORIA HOT EIGHT (1927). Organized for a single recording session. Lee Collins, t, co-leader; Sidney Arodin, cl; Ted Purnell, as; David Jones, ts, co-leader; Joseph Robichaux, p; Emanuel Sayles, bjo; Al Morgan, b.

ALFRED LAINE ORCHESTRA (late 20's, early 30's), dixie-land band. Alfred Laine, t, c, l; Sanford Mello, tb; Red Lagman, cl, s; Bud Loyacano, sb, tu; Jack Treveque, bjo; Charlie Kuhl, p; Jimmy Cozzens, d. Sometimes Harry Shields or Raymond Burke, cl, joined the band.

LAST STRAWS (1950's–60's). Moose Zanco, c; Nick Gagliardi, tb; Bris Jones, cl; Bill Lee, ss; Bob Casey or Frank de la Houssaye, p; Al Lobre or John Chaffe, bjo; Bob Ice, sb, tu, l; Bob McIntyre or John Joyce, d.

FOSTER LEWIS JAZZ BAND (early 20's). Dude Foster, t; Zeb Lenares, cl; Tink Baptiste, p; Leo Songier, bjo; One-Eye Babe Philip, sb; Foster Lewis, d, l.

GEORGE LEWIS RAGTIME JAZZ BAND (from early 40's). Partial collective personnel: Percy Humphrey, Thomas Jefferson, Elmer Talbert, Kid Howard, Punch Miller, t; Jim Robinson, Albert Warner, Louis Nelson, tb; George Lewis, cl, l; Alton Purnell, Joe Robichaux, Charlie Hamilton, p; Lawrence Marrero, Emanuel Sayles, Creole George Guesnon, g, bjo; Slow Drag Pavageau, Papa John Joseph, sb; Joe Watkins, Baby Dodds, Edgar Mosley, d.

LIBERTY BELL ORCHESTRA (1919–20), jazz band. Wesley Don, t, l; Jack Blount, v, mgr; Freddie Miller, tb; William Dimes, cl; Little Dad Vincent, bjo; Eddie Gilmore, sb; Joe Rena, d. Sometimes Jim Robinson, tb; Freddie Small, cl, har.

LINCOLN BAND (30's), large semi-concert dance orchestra. This title was always used for bands led by Pinchback Touro, v, l. Willie Pajeaud, t; Sunny Henry, tb, were mainstays. Sometimes Lawrence Duhé played clarinet.

KID LINDSEY'S JAZZ BAND (1917–18). Louis Armstrong, t; Maurice French, tb; Louis Prevost, cl; Son Carr, b; Joe Lindsey, d, l; various guitarists, banjoists.

LOUISIANA FIVE (early 1919), dixieland band. This band never played in N.O. and was organized just to make phonograph records. Its two Orleanians were Yellow Nunez, cl, Anton Lada, d, l.

LOUISIANA SHAKERS (early 30's), rock-and-roll band. A forerunner of today's mechanized, commercial groups organized by sax player John Handy and including his bassist brother Sylvester.

MAGNOLIA ORCHESTRA (1909–14), dance orchestra. Partial collective personnel: Emile Bigard, v, l; Joe Oliver, c; Big Boy Goudie, Dave Depass, Lorenzo Tio, Sr., George Baquet, cl; Zue Robertson, Honore Dutrey, tb; Louis Keppard, Johnny St. Cyr, g, bjo; Pops Foster, Tom Copland, sb; Arnold Depass, Happy Goldston, d.

MAGNOLIA SWEETS (1910), jazz band. Tig Chambers, c, l; Ernest Kelly, tb; Zeb Lenares, cl; various rhythm sections. Sometimes Yank Johnson, tb, in place of Kelly.

MAPLE LEAF ORCHESTRA (1918–late 20's), dance orchestra. Collective personnel: Emile Bigard, v; Hippolyte Charles, Willie Pajeaud, Sidney Desvigne, t; Vic Gaspard, tb; Lorenzo Tio, Jr., Albert Nicholas, Sidney Vigne, Sam Dutrey, Sr., cl; Willie Bontemps, Willie Santiago, bjo; Camilla Todd, Steve Lewis, Udell Wilson, p; Oak Gaspard, sb, l; Louis Cottrell, Sr., Alec Bigard, Dave Ogden, d.

MARABLE, FATE (1910–25), dance orchestra. Streckfus Steamship lines band. Sometimes called Marable's Ten Gold Harmony Kings; The S.S. Capitol Harmony Syncopators; Marable's Cotton Pickers; Marable's Capitol Revue Orchestra. This is a partial collective personnel including only the New Orleans musicians in the Marable orchestras: Louis Armstrong, Red Allen, Peter Bocage, Manuel Perez, Joe Howard, Amos White, Albert Duconge, Sidney Desvigne, t; Honore Dutrey, Bebé Ridgley, Bill Matthews, tb; Walter Brundy, Willie Humphrey (younger), Johnny Dodds, Sam Dutrey, Sr., cl; David Jones, s, mel; Fate Marable, p, l; Willie Foster, g; Johnny St. Cyr, bjo; Pops Foster, Albert Morgan, Henry Kimball, Wellman Braud, sb, tu; Baby Dodds, Walter Brundy, Zutty Singleton, d.

The Jimmy Palao Band (about 1900). Front row (not including children), left to right, are Edward "Chico" Claiborne, trombone; Louis Rodriguez, cornet; Joe Smith, violin; Rene Babtiste, guitar. Back row, left to right, are Willie Parker, clarinet; James A. Palao, violin; Toby Nuenutt, string bass.

The Original Tuxedo Orchestra (about 1928). Left to right are Bill Matthews, Guy Kelly, leader Papa Celestin, Jeanette Salvant, Narvin Kimball, Joe Lawrence, Chinee Foster, Joe Rouzon, Simon Marrero, Clarence Hall.

Sidney Desvigne's S.S. *Capitol Orchestra* (about 1931). Left to right are Louis Nelson, Eugene Porter, Gene Ware, Emanuel Sayles. Adolphe Duconge, leader Sidney Desvigne, Marcellus Wilson, Ransom Knowling, Tats Alexander, Jr., Ted Purnell, Walt Cosby.

Prima-Sharkey Orchestra (1930). At the Little Club are, front row, left to right, Charlie Hartman, Sharkey, Leon Prima, Irving Fazola, Dave Winstein, Nino Picone. Back row, Augie Schellang, Louis Masinter, Freddie Loyacano, Frank Pinero.

148

Don Albert's Orchestra (about 1933). Left to right are Ferdinand Dejan, Arthur Derbigny, Albert Martin, Jimmy Johnson, Hiram Harding, Don Albert, Herb Hall, Louis Cottrell, Jr., Frank Jacky, Albert Freeman, Sidney Hansell.

The Woodland Band (1905). Kid Ory's first band, at LaPlace, Louisiana. Left to right are Edward Robinson, Kid Ory, Chif Matthews, Raymond Brown, Stonewall Matthews, Foster Lewis.

Frank Christian's New Orleans Jazz Band (1921 or 1922). Chicago, Illinois. Left to right are Anton Lada, Frank L'Hotag, Frank Christian, Johnny Fischer, Ernie Erdman.

Alfred Laine's Orchestra (1920's). Left to right, seated, are Jimmy Cozzens, Red Legnon, Alfred Laine, Charlie Kuhl. Standing are Sam Mello, Bud Loyacano, Jack Treveque.

Johnny Bayersdorffer's Orchestra (about 1922). At Tokyo Gardens at Spanish Fort. Left to right are Martin Abraham, Tom Brown, Johnny Bayersdorffer, Leo Adde, Johnny Miller, Steve Loyacano, Nunzio Scaglione.

New Orleans Owls (early 1920's). Left to right are Monk Smith, leader Earl Crumb, Benjy White, Mose Ferrer, Rene Gelpi, Eblen Rau, Dick Mackie.

Original New Orleans Jazz Band (1916–17). In Chicago. Left to right are Johnny Fischer, Fred Rose, Merritt Brunies, Emile Christian, Fred J. Williams.

New Orleans Owls (1928). Left to right, standing, are Johnny Laporte, Eddie Miller, Frank Netto, Armand Hug, Bill Padron. Seated, Angelo Palmisano.

Happy Schilling's Orchestra (about 1924). Happy Schilling is seated holding the euphonium. Others, left to right, are Elery Maser, Monk Hazel, Johnny Wiggs, Clay Pinner, Freddie Loyacano, George Schilling, Jr., Frank Pinero.

Norman Brownlee Orchestra (about 1921). Left to right, standing, are Alonzo Crombie, Emmett Hardy, Billy Braun, Norman Brownlee, George Barth. Seated is Bill Eastwood.

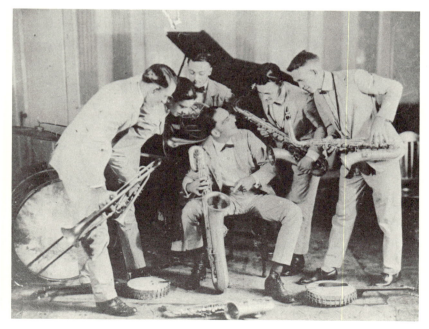

Tony Parenti's Symphonic Dance Orchestra (1922–23). At "The Cave" in the Grunewald (now Fairmont) Hotel. Left to right are Johnny Bayersdorffer, George Traiy, Charlie Hartmann, Wilbur Dinkel, Tony Parenti, Sam LaNasa, Bill Miller, Joe Hartman.

The Melon Pickers (1930's). Left to right are leader Henry Walde, John Bell, Raymond Burke, Al Doria, Bill Naquin, Julius Chevez.

The Elton Theodore Band (1921). Algiers, Louisiana. Seated, left to right, are Tommy Henderson, Steve Angrum, Kid Thomas. Standing, Loochie Jackson, Elton Theodore, Tete Rouchon.

Red Bolman Orchestra (1931). The Little Club. Left to right are Julian Laine, Luther Lamar, Steve Brue, Red Bolman, Monk Hazel, Gene Meyer, Joe Wolf, Nino Picone, Sal Scorsone.

MELODY MASTERS. Band that played for dancing on the steamer *Greater New Orleans*. Leon Prima, Sharkey, t; Julian Laine, tb; Charlie Cordilla, cl, s; Nino Picone, Joe Loyacano, s; Freddie Neuman, p; Freddie Loyacano, bjo; Chink Martin, sb, tu; Leo Adde, d.

MELON PICKERS (late 20's, early 30's), dance orchestra. Bill Nacquin, t; Raymond Burke, cl; Julius Chevez, p; Henry Walde, g, l; John Bell, sb; Al Doria, d.

JOHNNY MILLER FROLICKERS (1927–28), Sharkey, t; Sidney Arodin, cl; Hal Jordy, s; Johnny Miller, p, l; Steve Brue, bjo; Martin Abraham, b; Leo Adde, d.

PUNCH MILLER JAZZ BAND (1920), jazz band. Punch Miller, c, l; Eddie Morris, tb; Georgia Boy Boyd, cl; Walter Preston, bjo; Joe Gable, sb; Arnold Depass, d.

MOONLIGHT SERENADERS (1926–35), dance orchestra. Originally led by George Augustin, sb, bjo, later by Armand J. Piron, v. Among its regulars: Albert Snaer, t; Eddie Summers, tb; Alfred Williams, d.

MORGAN, SAM (1920's), dance orchestra. Collective personnel: Sam Morgan, t, l; Isaiah Morgan, t; Jim Robinson, Yank Johnson, tb; Joseph Watson, cl; Andrew Morgan, cl, ts; Earl Fouché, cl, as; Tink Baptiste, Walter Decou, p; Sidney Brown, Tom Copland, sb; Johnny Dave, Guyé Rapp, Creole George Guesnon, g, bjo; Nolan Williams, Alfred Williams, Rudolph Bodoyer, Roy Evans, d.

MORGAN'S EUPHONIC BAND (1917). This band played together in Chicago. All but the pianist are Orleanians. Fred Neuroth, c; Emile Christian, tb; Red Rowling, cl; Ernie Erdman, p; Billy Lambert, d.

NAYLOR'S SEVEN ACES (1920's), recording group. Oliver Naylor, v, p, l; Pinky Gerbrecht, c; Charles Hartman, tb; Jerry Richel, s; Jules Bauduc, bjo; Ray Bauduc, d.

NEW ORLEANS CREOLE JAZZ BAND (1925), dance orchestra. Played for dancing at Spanish Fort. Amos White, t, l; Willie Willigan, c; Sunny Henry, tb; Barney Bigard, cl; Willa Bart, p; Bob Ysaguirre, sb; Red Dugie, p.

NEW ORLEANS HARMONY KINGS (1920's), dixieland band. Sharkey, t; Sidney Arodin, cl; Freddie Neuman, p; Joe Capraro, bjo; Chink Martin, tu; Augie Schellang, d.

NEW ORLEANS JAZZ BAND (1918–22), dixieland band. Co-op band. Frank Christian, c; Frank L'Hotag, tb; Achille Baquet, cl; Jimmy Durante, p; Johnny Stein, d. Durante (the comedian) and L'Hotag are not from N.O.

NEW ORLEANS OWLS (1922–29), dance orchestra. Collective personnel: Dick Mackie, Red Bolman, Johnny Hyman, Bill Padron, c; Frank Netto, tb; Jimmy Rush, Pinky Vidacovich, Eddie Miller, cl, s; Johnny Carughi, Eblen Rau, Benjy White, v; Siegfried Christensen, Mose Ferrer, Armand Hug, p; Dan Leblanc, Red Mackie, tu, sb; Rene Gelpi, Monk Smith, Nappy Lamare, Angelo Palmisano, bjo, g; Johnny Laporte, d; Earl Crumb, d, l.

NEW ORLEANS RHYTHM KINGS (early 20's), dance orchestra. Also known as Friar's Society Orchestra. Partial collective personnel: Paul Mares, c, l; Wingy Manone, t; George Brunies, Santo Pecora, tb; Leon Roppolo, Charles Cordilla, cl, s; Red Long, p; Steve Brown, Arnold Loyacano, Bonnie Pottle, Chink Martin, sb, tu; Leo Adde, Monk Hazel, d.

NOLA BAND (1920's), dance orchestra. Peter Lacaze t, l; Ricard Alexis, t; Henry Russ, t, c; Mercedes Fields, p; Charles McCurdy or Alphonse Picou would frequently play clarinet. The other musicians were "pickup" depending on the occasion.

NOONE-PETIT ORCHESTRA (1916), jazz band. Buddy Petit, c, co-l; Honore Dutrey, tb; Jimmie Noone, cl, co-l, were the front line men. Rhythm sections added as convenient.

ADAM OLIVIER ORCHESTRA (1892-1910), dance orchestra. Many small dance groups played under this name, led by cornetist, violinist Olivier. Most of the musicians were not jazzmen, but both Bunk Johnson and Tony Jackson, cornet, piano, respectively, made their debuts in this band.

OLYMPIA ORCHESTRA (1900–14), dance orchestra. Partial collective personnel: Freddie Keppard, c, l; King Oliver, c; Joseph Petit, Zue Robertson, Eddie

The Princeton Revelers (about 1922). Seated, left to right, are Vic Leglise, Steve Brue, Bert Peck. Standing, left to right, are Bill Padron, Paul Peque, Pinky Vidacovich.

The New Orleans Harmony Kings (1920's). Left to right are Freddie Neumann, Martin Abraham, Sharkey, Augie Schellang, Sidney Arodin, Joe Capraro.

Atkins, Eddie Vinson, tb; Big Eye Louis, Alphonse Picou, Lorenzo Tio, Jr., Sidney Bechet, Charles McCurdy, cl; Armand J. Piron, v, l (1912); Louis Keppard, Willie Santiago, Bud Scott, g, bjo; Steve Lewis, Clarence Williams, p; John Lindsay, Billy Marrero, sb; John Vigne, Louis Cottrell, Sr., Ernest Trepagnier, Henry Zeno, d.

OLYMPIA ORCHESTRA (2) (1927–32), jazz band. Basic personnel: Elmer Talbert or Dee Dee Pierce, t; George Lewis, cl; Lester Santiago, p; Arnold Depass, d.

ORIENTAL ORCHESTRA (1928–38), jazz band. Lawrence Toca, t; Eddie Summers, tb; Melvin Frank, cl; Bill Hamilton, g, l; Albert Jiles, d.

ORIGINAL CREOLE ORCHESTRA (about 1913–17), vaudeville band. Collective personnel: Freddie Keppard, c; James A. Palao, v; Eddie Vinson, George Filhe, tb; George Baquet, Jimmie Noone, Big Eye Louis Nelson, cl; Bill Johnson, sb, l; Giggy Williams, g; Dink Johnson, d.

ORIGINAL DIXIELAND JAZZ BAND (1915 through early 20's). Collective personnel: Nick La Rocca, Sharkey, c, t; Eddie Edwards, Emile Christian, tb; Yellow Nunez, Larry Shields, cl; Henry Ragas, p; Johnny Stein, Tony Sbarbaro, d. This band made the first jazz records.

ORIGINAL NEW ORLEANS JAZZ BAND (about 1918). Merritt Brunies, c, l; Emile Christian, tb; Johnny Fischer, cl; Freddie Rose, p; Freddie Williams, d.

ORIGINAL TUXEDO ORCHESTRA. Partial collective personnel: Papa Celestin, t, vo, l; Guy Kelly, Kid Shots Madison, Ricard Alexis, t; Bill Matthews, Eddie Pierson, tb; Clarence Hall, Cecil Thornton, Cornbread Thomas, Tats Alexander, Alphonse Picou, cl, s; Mercedes Fields, Emma Barrett, Jeanette Kimball, Lester Santiago, Joe Robichaux, p; Sidney Brown, Ricard Alexis, sb; Albert French, Narvin Kimball, bjo; Louis Barbarin, Happy Goldston, d; Joe Strohter, d and slidewhistle.

PEERLESS ORCHESTRA (1905–13), dance orchestra. Collective personnel: Andrew Kimball, Nenny Coycault, c; Vic Gaspard, George Filhe, Hamp Benson, tb; Charles McCurdy, cl; Armand J. Piron, v, l (1910); Peter Bocage, v; Bab Frank, pc; Coochie Martin, g; Oak Gaspard, Bill Johnson, sb; Walter Brundy, John Vigne, Bebé Matthews, d.

A. J. PIRON ORCHESTRA (1918–28), dance orchestra. Partial collective personnel: Peter Bocage, Willie Edwards, c, t; John Lindsay, tb; Lorenzo Tio, Jr., Louis Warnick, cl, s; Charles Bocage, John Marrero, Johnny St. Cyr, bjo, g; Steve Lewis, Arthur Campbell, p; John Lindsay, Bob Ysaguirre, Henry Bocage, sb, tu; Louis Cottrell, Sr., Paul Barbarin, Cié Frazier, Bill Matthews, d; A. J. Piron, v, l.

PRIMROSE ORCHESTRA (1912), dance orchestra. A small band that worked in Storyville cabarets. Herb Lindsay, v, l; Joe Johnson, c; Hamp Benson, tb; George Williams, g, bjo; "Cato," d.

RAZZY DAZZY SPASM BAND (1890's). A skiffle band made up of teenage boys under the leadership of Stalebread Lacoume.

RELIANCE BAND (about 1892–1913), dixieland band, dance orchestra. Sometimes as many as six units of this Jack Laine-owned and -operated organization were working simultaneously. Front lines were drawn from members of the Reliance Brass Band. Others added for dance units follow. Partial listing: Henry Ragas, Norman Brownlee, Johnny Provenzano, Jules Reiner, Tom Zimmerman, p; Dominick Barocco, Joe Guiffre, Stalebread Lacoume, Jim Ruth, g, bjo; Joe Barocco, Steve Brown, Jules Cassard, John Guiffre, Willie Guitar, Arnold Loyacano, Bud Loyacano, sb, tu; Dave Perkins, Tim Harris, Buster Klein, Anton Lada, Buddy Rogers, Emmett Rogers, Tony Sbarbaro, Johnny Stein, Diddie Stephens, Mike "Ragbaby" Stephens, d.

RIDGLEY'S TUXEDO ORCHESTRA (1925), dance orchestra. A group that split from the Celestin-led Tuxedo Orchestra. Partial collective personnel: Kid Shots Madison, Ricard Alexis, t; Bebe Ridgley, tb, l; Kaiser Joseph, cl, s; Emma Barrett, p; Willie Bontemps, bjo; Simon Marrero, sb, tu; Bill Willigan, Bebe Matthews, d.

ROBICHAUX, JOHN (1895–1927), dance orchestra. Partial collective personnel: John Robichaux, v, l; Wendell MacNeil, v; Arnold Metoyer, James Mac-

Ellis Stratakos Orchestra (1929). Left to right are Louis Masinter, Johnny Reininger, Irving Fazola, Augie Schellang, Ellis Stratakos, Frank Federico, Freddie Neumann, Louis Prima, Dave Winstein.

Original Dixieland Jazz Band (1916). Left to right are Tony Spargo, Daddy Edwards, Nick La Rocca, Yellow Nunez, Henry Ragas.

159

The Halfway House Orchestra (1923). Left to right are Charlie Cordilla, Mickey Marcour, Leon Roppolo, Abbie Brunies, Bill Eastwood, Joe Loyacano, Leo Adde.

Buddy Bolden's Band (about 1902). Standing, left to right are Willie Warner, Willie Cornish, Buddy Bolden, Jimmy Johnson. Seated are Frank Lewis, Brock Mumford. This is the only known photograph of Bolden. It has been published twice before, printed backward each time because the photographer posed the bass and guitar players playing left-handed. *Photo, courtesy Mrs. Bella Cornish.*

160

New Orleans Rhythm Kings (about 1922). Orleanians in this group are George Brunies, trombone; Paul Mares, trumpet, leader; Leon Roppolo, third from left, front; Steve Brown, string bass, sousaphone. Others are Ben Pollack, drums, rear; Mel Stitzel, piano; Volly De Faut, clarinet, saxophone; Lew Black, banjo.

The Olympia Band (1915). Left to right are Joe Alexis, Ricard Alexis, Peter Alexis. *Photo, courtesy Danny Barker*.

Johnny Stein's Original Dixieland Jazz Band (1916). Chicago. Left to right are Yellow Nunez, Daddy Edwards, Henry Ragas, Nick La Rocca, leader Johnny Stein. *Photo, courtesy Mrs. John P. Hountha.*

The Original Creole Orchestra (about 1914). Front row, left to right, are Dink Johnson, leader James Palao, Norwood Williams. Back row, Eddie Vinson, Freddie Keppard, George Baquet, Bill Johnson.

162

Frank and McCurdy's Peerless Orchestra (1906). Left to right are John Vigne, George Filhe, Charles McCurdy, Andrew Kimball, Bab Frank, Coochie Martin.

Stalebread's Spasm Band (1899). Second from left is Emile "Stalebread" Lacoume. *Photo, courtesy Mrs. Anna Lacoume.*

The Imperial Orchestra (about 1905). Left to right are John MacMurray, George Filhe, James A. Palao, Big Eye Louis Nelson, Rene Baptiste, Manuel Perez, Jimmy Brown.

The Original Dixieland Jazz Band in England (1919). Left to right are Tony Spargo, Emile Christian, Nick La Rocca, Larry Shields, and English pianist Billy Jones. *Photo, courtesy Harry Shields.*

Nat Towles's Creole Harmony Kings (1926). Left to right are Bill Matthews, Herb Morand, Louis Mahier, Wallingford Hughes, Frank Pasley, Nat Towles.

Buddy Petit's Jazz Band (1920). Mandeville, La. Left to right are Leon René with megaphone, Eddie "Face-O" Woods, George Washington, Buddy Petit, Buddy Manaday, Edmond Hall, Chester Zardis. *Photo, courtesy George Hoefer.*

First Live Musical Broadcast from New Orleans. Station WOWL. Left to right are Frank Mutz, Ed McCarthy, Pinky Gerbrecht, Eddie Powers, Ellis Stratakos, Ray Bauduc.

Johnny Bayersdorffer Orchestra (1924). Tokyo Gardens. Left to right are Charlie Hartman, Ray Bauduc, Johnny Bayersdorffer, Joe Wolfe, Nappy Lamare, Lester Bouchon, Bill Creger.

Johnny Dodds's New Orleans Jazz Band (1939). Chicago. Left to right are Baby Dodds, Natty Dominique, Johnny Dodds, Rudolph Reynaud, Lonnie Johnson, Lillian Hardin Armstrong. All except the last named are from New Orleans. *Photo, courtesy Duncan Schiedt.*

King Oliver's Creole Jazz Band (early 1920's). Kneeling in foreground playing slide trumpet is Louis Armstrong. His future wife, Lillian, is at the piano. The others, left to right, are Honore Dutrey, Baby Dodds, King Oliver, Bill Johnson, Johnny Dodds. *Photo, courtesy George Hoefer.*

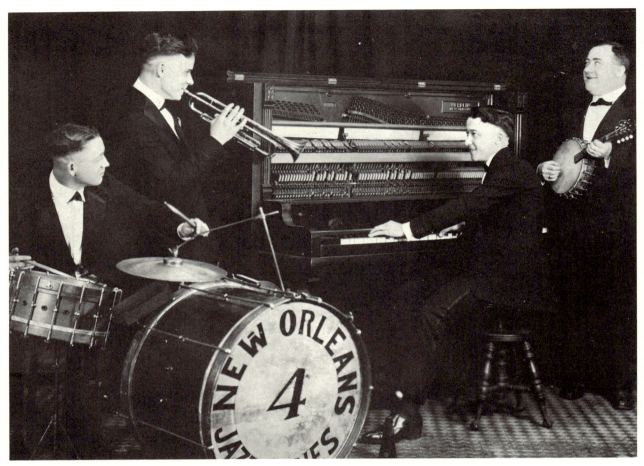

Four New Orleans Jazz Babies (about 1920). At the Halfway House. Left to right are Buck Rogers, Abbie Brunies, Mickey Marcour, Stalebread Lacoume. *Photo, courtesy Mrs. Anna Lacoume.*

The Crescent City Jazzers (about 1926). Johnny Riddick is at the piano. The others, left to right, are Felix Guarino, Stirling Bose, Avery Loposer, Slim Leftwich, Cliff Holman.

The Invincibles (about 1916). Front row, left to right, are Fred Overing, Bill Kleppinger, Monk Smith, Ernest Guidry. Back row, Lorimer Naff, Frank Ferrer, Rollo Tichenor.

Ridgley's Original Tuxedo Jazz Band (about 1925). Standing is Jesse Thoma. The others, left to right, are Bill Matthews, Bebé Ridgley, Kid Shots Madison, Willie Joseph, Emma Barrett, Arthur Derbigny, unknown saxophonists, Robert Hall, Willie Bontemps.

Armand J. Piron's Society Orchestra (about 1923). Seated, left to right, are Bob Ysaguirre, Charles Bocage, Armand J. Piron, Steve Lewis, Louis Warnick. Standing are Lorenzo Tio, Jr., Louis Cottrell, Sr., Peter Bocage, John Lindsay.

Five Southern Jazzers (1921 or 1922). Left to right are Frank L'Hotag (not from N.O.), Frank Christian, Anton Lada, Ernie Erdman, Johnny Fischer. *Photo, courtesy John Arlt.*

Johnny DeDroit Orchestra (about 1918–26). Johnny DeDroit is seated at the piano. The others, left to right, are Paul DeDroit, Henry Raymond, Frank Froeba, Ellis Stratakos, George Potter.

A New Orleans jazz band, 1947, in Chicago. Left to right are Little Brother Montgomery, Lonnie Johnson, Bill Johnson, Oliver Alcorn, Pork Chop Smith, Lee Collins, Preston Jackson. *Photo, courtesy George Hoefer.*

Neil, James Williams, Andrew Kimball, Charlie Love, George McCullum, Sr., c, t; Baptiste Delisle, Harrison Barnes, Vic Gaspard, Honore Dutrey, John Lindsay, tb; Charles McCurdy, Alphonse Picou, Lorenzo Tio, Jr., Sam Dutrey, Sr., Wade Whaley, George Baquet, cl; Henry Kimball, Oak Gaspard, Paul Domingues, Sr., George Augustin, Albert Glenny, sb; Bud Scott, Coochie Martin, g; Lawrence Marrero, bjo; Albert Carroll, Paul Beaulieu, p; Dee Dee Chandler, Happy Bolton, Cie Frazier, Alec Bigard, Louis Cottrell, Sr., Walter Brundy, Zutty Singleton, d.

ROSS, SAM ORCHESTRA (1910–1921). This band from "over the river" was distinguished mainly by the presence of Jimmie Noone who started his career playing in it at Cut Off, Louisiana, his home town. Personnel at its peak period consisted of Sam Ross, c, l; Milton Martin, tb; Jimmie Noone, cl; Jackson Butler, b; Skeeter Jackson, g; Sonny Hampton, d.

SCHILLING, HAPPY (1910–26), dance orchestra. Partial collective personnel: Johnny Wiggs, Richie Brunies, Johnny Lala, Henry Knecht, Arnold Metoyer, c, t; Monk Hazel, c, mel, d; Bob Aquilera, tb; Happy Schilling, tb, l; Achille Baquet, George Schilling, Jr., Johnny Fischer, Ellery Maser, cl, s; Clay Pinner, tu; Frank Pinero, p; Freddie Loyacano, g, bjo; Johnny Frisco, d.

SECURITY ORCHESTRA (1900's), dance orchestra. A small, short-lived group, organized, led, and managed by trombonist Joseph Petit.

SILVER LEAF ORCHESTRA (1897–1917), dance orchestra. Hippolyte Charles, c; Henry Lambert, vt; Sam Dutrey, cl; Albert Baptiste, v, l; Oscar Robinson, bjo, g; Johnny Predonce, sb; Ernest Rogers, d. Others who sometimes played instead of regulars: Honore Dutrey, tb; Phil Nickerson, bjo; George Sayles, g; Paul Barbarin, d.

SIX AND 7/8 STRING BAND (from 1911). Original group: Bob Reynolds, g; Harry Reynolds, mdl; Hilton "Midget" Harrison, Roland Rexach, v; Charlie Hardy, uk, tara; Bill Gibbens, g, mdl; Bernie Shields, bjo, mdl, steel g, z; Shields O'Reardon, mdl; Edmond Souchon, 12-str. g. Combined collective personnel included: Earl Crumb, bjo, d; Albert Moustier, uk;

Wilfred Sancho, mdl, v, uk; Howard McCaleb, g, vo; Alton Nall, g, uk; Bill Kleppinger, mdl; Red Mackie, sb; Percy McCay, g, sb; Thompson McCay, g, sb; Marie Souchon, p, vo; Ed Pinac, v; Ruth Hardy, p, vo.

ELLIS STRATAKOS ORCHESTRA (late 20's, early 30's), dance orchestra. Partial collective personnel: Johnny Wiggs, Louis Prima, Howard Reed, c, t; Ellis Stratakos, tb, v, l; Irving Fazola, Dave Winstein, Johnny Reininger, Joe Loyacano, Eddie Powers, cl, s; Joe Wolfe, Freddie Neuman, p; Frank Federico, Al Hessemer, Freddie Loyacano, g, bjo; Freddie Chretien, v; Louis Masinter, Don Peterson, tu, sb; August Schellang, Von Gammon, d.

SUPERIOR ORCHESTRA (about 1908–13), dance orchestra. Collective personnel: Bunk Johnson, Nenny Coycault, c; Buddy Johnson, tb; Big Eye Louis Nelson, George Baquet, cl; Adolphe Alexander, Sr., bh; Peter Bocage, v, l; Richard Payne, g; Billy Marrero, sb, mgr; Walter Brundy, d.

THE SUSQUEHANNA BAND (1923–25). Worked on the lake steamer *Susquehanna*. Its basic members were: Pete Peccopia, t; Benny Deichman, tb; Johnny Palisier, cl; Bill Farrell, p; Dominick Barocco, g, bjo, mdl, l; Joe Barocco, sb, tu; Ferdie Knecht, d.

ELTON THEODORE ORCHESTRA (Algiers, La. early 1920's), jazz band. Kid Thomas Valentine, t; Loochie Jackson, tb; Steve Angrum, cl; Elton Theodore, bjo, l; Tete Rouchon, sb, tu; Tommy Henderson, d.

TIO-DOUBLET ORCHESTRA (1888–90), dance orchestra. Charles Doublet, c; Anthony Doublet, v; Anthony Page, tb; Lorenzo Tio, Sr., Papa Tio, cl; Dee Dee Chandler, d.

TIO-DOUBLET STRING BAND (1889), dance quartet. A. L. Tio, Anthony Doublet, v; Professor William J. Nickerson, vla; Paul Domingues, Sr., sb.

TRIANGLE BAND (1917–25). Dominated the jazz activities in the Irish Channel during its period. Basic personnel: Tony Margiotta, c; Charles Christian, tb; Sal Margiotta, cl, s; Tony Schiro, g, bjo; Bud Loyacano, sb, tu; Louis Stephens, d.

Dejan's Black Diamond Orchestra (1928). Seated, left to right, are leader Leo Dejan, Alvin Mc-Neal, Eddie Johnson, Herb Leary, Reese Cobette, Harold Dejan. Standing are Sherman Cook, Eddie Pierson, Sidney Montegue, Rube McClennon, August Lanoix. *Photo, courtesy Harold Dejan.*

The Creole Serenaders (1930). Left to right are leader Peter Bocage, Henry Bocage, Louis Warnick, Dwight Newman, Henry Martin, Charlie Bocage. *Photo, courtesy Danny Barker.*

TULANE ORCHESTRA (1906–19), jazz band. Loosely organized group which played irregularly, led by Amos Riley, t. Usually included Alcide Landry, t; Kid Avery, tb; Sam Dutrey, Sr., cl; Alex Scott, sb; "Big Cato," bjo; "Cato," d.

TUXEDO ORCHESTRA (started 1913), dance orchestra. Partial collective personnel: Papa Celestin, t, l; Ricard Alexis, Kid Shots Madison, Guy Kelly, Kildee Holloway, Joe Howard, t; August Rousseau, Yank Johnson, Bebé Ridgley, George Filhe, Bill Matthews, Eddie Pierson, tb; Paul Barnes, Sidney Carriere, Clarence Hall, Cecil Thornton, Joe Rouzon, Adolphe Alexander, Jr., Willard Thoumy, Joe "Brother Cornbread" Thomas, cl, s; Jeannette Kimball, Emma Barrett, Mercedes Fields, Lester Santiago, p; John Marrero, Willie Bontemps, Johnny St. Cyr, Albert French, g, bjo; Simon Marrero, Narvin Kimball, Jim Little, sb, tu; Henry Zeno, Abbey Foster, Happy Goldston, Louis Barbarin, d.

WATZKE, ALEX "KING" (1903–08), dixieland band. Played lots of original material by the leader. None of the tunes had names—just numbers. Basic personnel: Alex "King" Watzke, v; Jimmy Kendall, t; Freddie Burns, cl; Buzz Harvey or Emile Bizard, sb; Jimmy Ruth or Pat Shields, g. Sometimes Larry Shields played with this band.

JOHNNY WIGGS AND HIS NEW ORLEANS MUSIC (from about 1949). Wiggs's legal name is John Wigginton Hyman. His early bands are listed under either Johnny Hyman or The Bayou Stompers. Partial collective personnel: Johnny Wiggs, c, l; Tom Brown, Julian Laine, Santo Pecora, Charlie Miller, Emile Christian, Paul Crawford, tb; Raymond Burke, Harry Shields, Boojie Centobie, Lester Bouchon, Irving Fazola, cl; Armand Hug, Stanley Mendelson, Julius Chevez, Jeff Riddick, Jake Sciambra, p; Edmond Souchon, g, bjo; Martin Abraham, Sr., Arnold Loyacano, Sherwood Mangiapane, sb, tu; Ray Bauduc, Von Gammon, Buck Rogers, Freddie King, Eddie Tschantz, Santo Pecoraro, d.

YOUNG EAGLES BAND (1918), jazz band. Lee Collins, t; Earl Humphrey, tb; John Casimir, cl; Son Thomas, bjo; Pops Foster, sb, tu; Joe Casimir, d.

YOUNG MORGAN BAND (1921–25), dance orchestra. Isaiah Morgan, t, l; Jim Robinson, tb; Andrew Morgan, cl; Earl Fouché, Sam Robinson, s; Johnny Dave, bjo; Sidney Brown, sb, tu; Rudolph Bodoyer, d.

YOUNG OLYMPIANS (1917–18), jazz band. Band led by Buddy Petit, c.

YOUNG SUPERIOR BAND (early 20's), jazz band. Arthur Derbigny, t; Leonard Bechet, tb, l; Andrew Morgan, cl; Whitey Arcenaux, bjo; Tommy Hudson, sb, tu; Arthur Joseph, d.

YOUNG TUXEDO ORCHESTRA (1920), dance orchestra. Bush Hall, t; Paul Ben, Bob Thomas, tb; Louis Cottrell, Jr., Paul Barnes, Henry Julian, c, s; Dwight Newman, p; Lawrence Marrero, bjo, l; Eddie Marrero, sb; Cié Frazier, Milford Dolliole, d.

Bunk Johnson's Band (1944). Left to right are Jim Robinson, Bunk Johnson, Baby Dodds, Lawrence Marrero, George Lewis, Slow Drag Pavageau.

Manuel Perez' Jazz Band (1923). Pythian Roof. Left to right are Alfred Williams, Earl Humphrey, Tats Alexander, Maurice Durand, Osceola Blanchard (kneeling), Manuel Perez, Caffrey Darensburg, Eddie Cherie, Jimmy Johnson.

The Dominos (about 1929). Nappy Lamare's brother Jimmy, a non-musician, is seated at the piano just for the picture. The others, left to right, are Tony Burrella, Charles Christian, Tony Fougerat, Lester Bouchon, Willie Guitar, Nappy Lamare. *Photo, courtesy Raymond Burke.*

Johnny DeDroit's Jazz Band (1920). Kolb's Restaurant. Left to right are Tony Parenti, Johnny DeDroit, Paul DeDroit, Mel Berry, Tom Zimmerman.

Preservation Hall All-Star Jazz Band (1963). This band toured Japan for four months in the summer of 1963. Left to right are Papa John Joseph, Louis Nelson, Joe Watkins, Kid Thomas (did not make the trip), Kid Punch Miller, Joe Robichaux, George Lewis.

Clarence Desdunes Joyland Revelers (about 1929). Lined up left to right, next to the band's bus, are Harry Fairconnetue, Harold Dejan, George McCullum, Jr., Nolan Williams, Ray Brown.

Jimmie Noone's Orchestra (1930's). Plenty of New Orleanians could be found in Chicago during the depression. Here with Noone (clarinet) are Baby Dodds, John Lindsay, Lee Collins, Preston Jackson, and John Henley. *Photo, courtesy Duncan Schiedt.*

Six and 7/8 String Band of New Orleans, Louisiana, at a concert, Royal Orleans Hotel, May 24, 1964. Seated, left to right, are Charles J. Hardy (deceased), Bill Kleppinger, and Bernie Shields. Standing, left to right, are Edmond Souchon, M.D., and Frank "Red" Mackie. This group probably holds the record for having "played together and stayed together" longer than any other. Its members began playing as a group in 1912 or 1913!

The Last Straws (1963). Left to right are Bob Casey, Bill Lee, John Joyce, Bris Jones, Al Lobre, Moose Zanco, Bob Ice, Nick Gagliardi.

The Susquehanna Band (1924). Left to right, Benny Deichman, Dominick Barocco, Pete Peccopia, Johnny Palisier, Junius Boudreaux, Louis Uhle, Joe Barocco. Deichman and Dominick Barocco are holding each other's instruments. Photo taken up the river at the Godchaux plantation.

Frank Christian's Ragtime Band (1915). On Quarella's Pier at Milneburg. Left to right are Willie Guitar, Manuel Gomez, Harry Nunez, Yellow Nunez, Frank Christian, Charlie Christian, Kid Totts Blaise.

179

The John Robichaux Orchestra, 1896. Seated, left to right are Dee Dee Chandler, Charles McCurdy, John Robichaux, Wendell MacNeil. Standing, left to right, are Baptiste DeLisle, James Wilson, James MacNeil, Oak Gaspard.

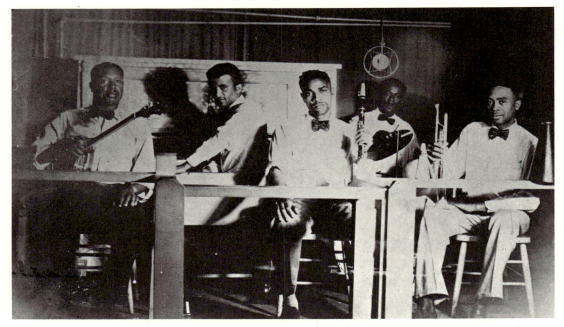

George Parker's Orchestra about 1925. Clarence Tisdale with banjo, Parker at piano, Joseph "Brother Cornbread" Thomas with clarinet, Sidney Jackpierre with cymbal, and Elmer Talbert with trumpet.

THE BRASS BANDS

There's nothing original about the idea of brass bands in Western culture. Every small town has had its firemen, police force, high school, or civic group organize a dozen or so uniformed men with instruments. They usually performed outdoors to help celebrate occasions for which their appearance seemed appropriate. Universally they have specialized in military airs and have been most in evidence on patriotic holidays.

While New Orleans, back to the 1850's, also found use for such groups, the city's exotic cultural pattern developed broader uses for them and involved them more closely in daily life. Only in New Orleans does the brass band figure regularly in funeral plans. Only here do the bands turn out in force mainly on Mother's Day rather than the Fourth of July. Almost every fraternal lodge makes regular provision for the music of the brass band.

Not only is the brass band used unconventionally in the Crescent City, but its music owes little debt to Sousa and Pryor. Peace-loving Orleanians prefer popular tunes, jazz standards, and blues to martial strains, with an occasional solemn dirge or hymn when these are warranted by the circumstances. Our music-loving public relates to its brass bands with affection unparalleled in American culture. It has been known to make folk-heroes of its favorites. The likes of Buddy Bolden, Manuel Perez, and Lawrence Veca were the Mickey Mantles, Willie Mayses, and Babe Ruths of their era. In other climes the brass band on parade has stationary spectators who stand on sidewalks and watch the band go by. The "Second Line"—a mass audience of extroverted enthusiasts—follows along with the musicians, dancing in figures little removed from the Calindas and Bamboulas of the century past. From the ranks of the "Second Line" have been directly recruited the great names of New Orleans jazz. Little Louis Armstrong proudly carried the horns of Bunk Johnson and King Oliver in the street. George Lewis took his turn tagging along as did Pete Fountain and the rest.

The brass bands represent the happiest, most beloved phase of the music of New Orleans.

ALLEN BRASS BAND (1907 to 1940's). Henry Allen, Sr., t, l; Peter Bocage, Joe Howard, Oscar Celestin, t; Jack Carey, Buddy Johnson, Yank Johnson, Harrison Barnes, tb; Lawrence Duhé, cl; Wallace Collins, bh; James A. Palao, ah; Bebe Matthews, sn; Clay Jiles, Red Allen, bd.

BULLS CLUB BRASS BAND (late teens to early 20's). Manuel Calier, t, l; Arthur Stevens, tb. Joe Oliver and George McCullum, Sr., sometimes played with this group.

CAMELIA BRASS BAND (1917–23). Wooden Joe Nicholas, t, l; Buddy Petit, t; Ike Robinson, Joe Petit, Eddie Morris, tb; Alphonse Picou, Johnny Brown, cl; Buddy Luck, sou; Arthur Ogle, sn; Booker T. Glass, bd.

COLUMBIA BRASS BAND (1897–1900). Partial personnel: Punkie Valentin, c; Alcibiades Jeanjacques, t; Bouboul Valentin, tb; Edward Boisseau, bh; Alphonse Picou, cl; Isidore Barbarin, ah; Dee Dee Chandler, bd.

DIAMOND STONE BRASS BAND (1897). An uptown band using mostly non-jazz men, but included Edward Clem, c; and Frank Jackson, bd.

ECLIPSE BRASS BAND (1900–17). "Official" band of the Magnolia plantation, directed by Professor Jim Humphrey. It included Chris Kelly, t; Sunny Henry, Harrison Barnes, tb.

EUREKA BRASS BAND (1920 to present). Partial collective personnel: Willie Wilson, t, organizer and first l; Tom Albert, Alcide Landry, Kid Shots Madison, Percy Humphrey, T-Boy Remy, Willie Pajeaud, Eddie Richardson, Kid Sheik Colar, t; Willie Cornish, Jim Robinson, Earl Humphrey, Albert Warner, Eddie Summers, Big Eye Louis Nelson, Sunny Henry, Chicken Henry, Kid Avery, tb; George Lewis, Albert Burbank, Willie Humphrey (younger), cl; Alphonse Johnson, ah; Johnny Wilson, bh; Red Clark (mgr.), Wilbert Tillman, tu; Alfred Williams, Cié Frazier, Happy Goldston, Fewclothes Lewis, d; Tats Alexander, Manuel Paul, Ruben Roddy, s. T-Boy Remy and Percy Humphrey, in order, succeeded Wilson as leader.

The Tonic Triad Band (1928). Front row, left to right, are unknown, Albert Francis, Albert Francis, Jr., Albert Jones, James Smith, Ace Williams. Middle row includes Isidore Barbarin, unknown, unknown, Albert Warner, Red Clark, ——Lopice; Chicken Henry, John Ever, unknown, J. T. Dalmas. Of those in the back row, the first three are not musicians. The remaining are Gertrude Daily, Ophelia Grigsby, James Harris, Pop Hamilton, Melvin Frank, Geneva Moret, Bea Acheson, Lumas Hamilton, Willie Pajeaud, Alcide Landry, director Professor Henry Pritchard.

The Henry Allen Brass Band (Mardi Gras, 1926). The snare drummer is Ramos Matthews. In the rear is the leader on bass drum. At the right, face hidden by music, is Louis Dumaine.

The WPA Band (1936). Steady employment for a host of jazz greats. At the left stands the leader Pinchback Touro. In the front row, seated left to right, are Willie Humphrey, Albert Mitchell, Israel Gorman, Richard McNeal, Sidney Cates, Leon Saulny, Leo Songier, George McCullum, Jr., Manuel Coustaut. In the second row are Son Johnson (holding saxophone), Howard Davis, John Casimir, Emanuel Paul, Andrew Morgan, Eddie Johnson, Adolphe Alexander, Jr., Raymond Glapion. In the third row are Edward Johnson, Henry Hardin, Manny Gabriel, Sam Lee, Sonny Henry, Chicken Henry, Harrison Barnes. Standing in the back row are Albert Glenny, Sidney Montegue, Cié Frazier, Ernest Trepagnier, Joe Howard, William Brown, Alcide Landry, Kid Shots Madison, Gilbert Young, Ricard Alexis, Henry Russ, Albert Ganier, Louis Dumaine. *Photo, courtesy New Orleans Jazz Society (London)*.

The Reliance Brass Band (1906). Seated are Manuel Belasco and Joe Alexander. Standing are Dave Perkins, Vincent Barocco, Sidney Moore, Pete Pellegrini, Freddie Neuroth, leader Jack Laine.

The Reliance Brass Band (1910). Seated is leader Jack Laine, who sometimes played snare drum. The others are Manuel Mello, Yellow Nunez, Leonce Mello, Baby Laine, Chink Martin, Tim Harris. The "Big Show" is Laine's Greater Majestic Minstrels behind a carbarn at Canal and White streets. A hurricane that year blew down the tent.

EXCELSIOR BRASS BAND (1880–1928). Partial collective personnel: Theogene V. Baquet, c, 1st l; George Moret, Edward Clem, Frank Jackson, Fice Quire, James MacNeil, James Williams, George Hooker, Arnold Metoyer, Nelson Jean, Paul Thomas, Adolphe Alexander, Sr., Peter Bocage, Hippolyte Charles, Sidney Desvigne, George McCullum, Sr., t; Aaron Clark, Anthony Page, Harrison Barnes, Baptiste Delisle, Honore Dutrey, Bernard Raphael, Buddy Johnson, Eddie Vinson, Sunny Henry, tb; George Baquet, Alphonse Picou, Lorenzo Tio, Sr., Lorenzo Tio, Jr., Luis Tio, Charles McCurdy, Sam Dutrey, Sr., Willie Humphrey (younger), cl; Hackett Brothers, Joe Payen (last leader), ah; Edward Boisseau, Vic Gaspard, George Hooker, bh; Isidore Barbarin, Ralph Montegue, ah; Frank Jackson, Frank Robinson, tu; John Robichaux, Clay Jiles, Louis Cottrell, Sr., Dee Dee Chandler, d.

FISCHER'S BRASS BAND (1915). Partial collective personnel: George Barth, Harry Shannon, Richard Brunies, Manuel Mello, t, c; Leonce Mello, Cack Riley, Happy Schilling, Henry Brunies, Merritt Brunies, tb; Johnny Fischer, cl, l; Tony Shannon, bh; Freddy Williams, Charles Hazel, d.

GIBSON BRASS BAND (mid-50's to 1965). Eddie Richardson, Johnny Wimbley, Leon Bajeon, t; Carroll Blunt, F. Thompson, Eddie Morris, tb; George Sterling, David Bailey, d; Louis Keppard, tu; A. B. Spears, Robert Davis, s.

HOLMES BAND OF LUTCHER (1910). Professor Anthony Holmes, c, l; Joe Porter, c; Henry Sawyer, tb; Dennis Harris, cl; Papa John Joseph, s; John Porter, bh; Floyd Jackson, tu; David Jones, sn, mel, s; Nub Jacobs, bd. This band from Lutcher, La. (just south of Baton Rouge) played many carnivals and tent shows, besides parades in N.O.

185

Fischer's Brass Band (1915). Left to right are Freddie Williams, George Barth, Happy Schilling, Harry Shannon, Tony Shannon, Johnny Fischer.

Siegfried Christensen's New Orleans Brass Band (1912). This picture was taken in Chattanooga. Among the identifiable are George Peterson, seated on the white mule. Standing on the wagon behind the mule and holding cornet is leader Christensen. Third from the right is Joe Alexander. On the ground, holding trombone, is Angelo Castigliola; holding the euphonium is the legendary Dave Perkins. *Photo, courtesy Salvadore Castigliola and the New Orleans* Times-Picayune.

The Reliance Brass Band (1912). Firemen's Day parade, Biloxi, Mississippi. Kneeling in front are Vincent De Corda, Manuel Mello, and Jack Laine at far right. Standing, left to right, are Ragbaby Stephens, Chink Martin, Hans———, Henry Brunies, Leonce Mello, Emile Christian, Merrit Brunies, Johnny Palisier, Alfred Laine. The men wearing the white-topped uniforms belong to another group.

St. Francis De Sales Military Band (1910). Seated, left to right, Jimmy Kendall, Father Heffernan, pastor and instructor, unknown. Small boy with snare drum is Louis Burke. Middle row, left to right, Joe Barocco, Hugh Exerstein, unknown, Clem Camp (with eye patch), Larry Shields, next four unknown. Snare drummer, extreme right, Johnny Frisco. Back row, extreme right, Benny Deichman. Next to him is Dominick Barocco. *Photo, Courtesy Harry Shields.*

187

Fischer's Ragtime Military Jazz Band (1909). The musicians are those kneeling in the front row. They are, left to right, Charles Hazel, Henry Brunies, Manuel Mello, Emmanuel Allesandro, Cack Riley, Johnny Fischer, Happy Schilling, Richie Brunies, Angelo De Corda, and "Sox"——. The group is posed with the Big 50 Carnival Marching Club in front of the then-new courthouse at Royal and Conti streets. The little boy seated in the center of the picture is Monk Hazel. *Photo, courtesy Monk Hazel.*

The Reliance Brass Band (about 1911). Left to right are Ragbaby Stephens, unknown, Chink Martin, Henry Brunies, Emile Christian, Martin Kirsch, unknown, Ray Lopez, Gus Zimmerman, Manuel Mello. *Photo, courtesy Jack Laine.*

188

Camelia Brass Band clarinetist, Israel Gorman poses in 1916.

Gus Zimmerman, left, leader of one of the Reliance Brass Band units, and Martin Kirsch take time for a studio photo in 1911. *Photo, courtesy Jack Laine.*

LIONS BRASS BAND (1928). Pop Hamilton, t, l; Al Landry, Manuel Trapp, t; Maurice French, Tom Steptoe, tb; Willie Parker, cl; Lumas Hamilton, fh; "Sheik-O," bh; Ernest Rogers, sn; Arthur Turner, bd.

MASONIC BRASS BAND (1930's). A Masonic organization kept a stock of band caps. Hired men who were available for parade jobs. Some of the regulars, Red Clark, tb; Mrs. Ophelia Grigsby, s; A. B. Spears, bd.

189

Jefferson City Buzzards (1925). This carnival club always used top bands. Wooden Joe Nicholas' Camelia Brass Band was its choice that year.

Kid Rena's Band (1937). The players are marching through the Storyville district. Visible are Kid Sheik Colar, trumpet; Eddie Summers, trombone; George Lewis, clarinet; Edgar Mosley, bass drum.

Tuxedo Brass Band (1920's). The members are taking a break. Kneeling in front is George Hooker. Standing, left to right, are Yank Johnson, Manuel Perez, Oscar Celestin, Ninesse Trepagnier, Charlie Love.

Eureka Brass Band (1958). Traditional Mother's Day parade in Hahnville, Louisiana. Left to right are, leader Percy Humphrey, trumpet; Alfred Williams, snare drum; Willie Pajeaud and Emanuel Paul, partially hidden; Albert Warner, trombone; Robert Lewis, bass drum; Eddie Summers, trombone; Harold Dejan, saxophone; Red Clark, tuba.

Lafon School Band (about 1932). Thomas Jefferson is the second trumpet player from top of photo on the left. Sport Young is second saxophonist from top on the right. The band is playing a funeral.

The Young Tuxedo Brass Band (1959). Left to right are Clement Tervalon, Wilbert Tillman, Alfred Williams, Edgar Joseph, Oscar Rouzan, Andy Anderson, Emile Knox (almost hidden), Andrew Morgan.

Abby Williams' Happy Pals Brass Band (1949). Left to right are Eddie Pierson, trombone; Noon Johnson, sousaphone; Jim Robinson, trombone; Tats Alexander, Jesse Charles, saxophone; Dee Dee Pierce, cornet; Kid Howard, trumpet; Kid Clayton, trumpet; leader Abby Williams, snare drum; Chester Jones, bass drum. *Photo, courtesy Abby Williams.*

The Onward Brass Band (about 1913). Left to right are Manuel Perez, Andrew Kimball, Peter Bocage, Lorenzo Tio, Jr., Adolphe Alexander, Sr., Bebé Matthews, Dandy Lewis, Isidore Barbarin, Buddy Johnson, Vic Gaspard, Eddie Atkins, Eddie Jackson. *Photo, courtesy George Hoefer.*

George Williams Brass Band (1961). Ernest Cagnolatti is kneeling in front. The rest, left to right, are Showboy Thomas, Buster Moore, Jesse Charles, Ernest Poree, William Brown, Albert Walters, Son White Washington, George Williams, Steve Angrum. *Photo, courtesy of Carey Tate.*

The Gibson Brass Band (1961). Left to right are Louis Keppard, A. B. Spears, David Bailey, Eddie Richardson, Johnny Wimberly, Leon Bajeon, George Sterling, Carroll Blunt, F. Thompson. *Photo, courtesy Carey Tate.*

The Eureka Brass Band (1961). The band is shown with some fans. These are, at upper left, and not in uniform, Kid Thomas, Alec Bigard, Creole George Guesnon, and Emanuel Sayles. Band members are, left to right, Chicken Henry, Willie Humphrey, Emanuel Paul, Albert Warner, Happy Goldston, Robert Lewis, Peter Bocage, Kid Sheik Colar, Percy Humphrey. In front, holding his hat, is the Grand Marshal of the Second Line, Slow Drag Pavageau.

The Algiers Naval Station Band (1942). Recruited in New Orleans. Front row, left to right, are Tats Alexander, —— Davis, John Jones, Henry Russ, Harold Dejan. In the second row are Gilbert Jones, Bertrand Adams, —— Brooks, William Spencer, bandmaster Vernon B. Cooper. In the third row are Booker T. Washington, Paul Barnes, Herbert Trisch, Robert Anthony, Sidney Dufachard. In the back row are Ruben Roddy, Alexander, Leon Harris, William Casimir, Frank Fields. *Photo, courtesy Harold Dejan.*

Mathews Band of Lockport, Louisiana (about 1904). This is a true brass band—no reeds. It is the earliest-known New Orleans brass band photograph showing a slide trombone, along with valve trombones customary at that time.

195

The New Orleans Waifs' Home Band and Louis
Armstrong's traveling band (1931). Alumnus Louis
Armstrong returns to visit his Alma Mater, the New
Orleans Waifs' Home; he is seated in the center, in
front of the bass drum. In the traveling band, other
Orleanians are John Lindsay, extreme left; Tubby
Hall, on Louis' right; Preston Jackson, second from
right. Above Jackson, leaning against pillar, wear-
ing band uniform, is Louis' first music teacher
Peter Davis. *Photo, courtesy John Steiner.*

Marching Band (1900). This early marching group
includes Dave Perkins, trombone.

Happy Schilling's Brass Band. The group was hired to advertise the movie "The Music Goes Round" at the Orpheum theater in New Orleans. Left to right are Happy Schilling, Monk Hazel, Howard Reed, George Schilling, Jr. *Photo, courtesy Howard Reed.*

MELROSE BRASS BAND (1900–10). Regular members: Joe Oliver, c; Bernard Raphael, Honore Dutrey, tb; Paul Beaulieu, cl; Alphonse Vache, tu; Willie Phillips, sd. Sometimes Adam Olivier, Bunk Johnson, c; Sam Dutrey, Sr., cl.

ONWARD BRASS BAND (1889–1930). Collective personnel: Manuel Perez, c; Andrew Kimball, Peter Bocage, Oscar Duconge, James MacNeil, Bellevue Lenair, Sylvester Coustaut, Joseph Oliver, Maurice Durand, c, t; Buddy Johnson, Vic Gaspard, George Filhe, Baptiste Delisle, Steve Johnson, Earl Humphrey, Butler Rapp, tb; Lorenzo Tio, Jr., Luis Tio, George Baquet, cl; Joseph Bruno, Isidore Barbarin, Adolphe Alexander, Sr., Bartholemew Bruno, ah; Eddie Atkins, Aaron Clark, bh; Eddie Jackson, Frank Jackson, Albert Tucker, tu; Bebé Matthews, Dee Dee Chandler, sn; Black Benny Williams, Henry Martin, Dandy Lewis, Mike Gillen, Clay Jiles, Happy Goldston, bd.

Young Olympia Brass Band. Continuing the tradition into the mid-60's under the leadership of saxophonist Harold Dejan. Shown in photo are some of the frequently changing members: Paul Crawford, trombone, Emanuel Paul, saxophone, Andy Anderson, trumpet, Allan Jaffe, tuba, Louis Nelson, trombone. Others sometimes in the band, Kid Sheik, trumpet, Nowell Glass, drum, Donald Minor, clarinet.

PACIFIC BRASS BAND (Algiers, La., 1900–12). Basic personnel: George Hooker, Manuel Manetta, c; Buddy Johnson, Frankie Duson, tb; Dude Gabriel, cl; George Sims, George Hooker, bh; Duke Simpson, sn; George Davis, bd.

PICKWICK BRASS BAND (Algiers, La., 1898–1901). Norman "Deuce" Manetta, c. l; Jules Manetta, c; Edward Love, tb; Levi Bailey, fl; Dennis Williams, Tete Rouchon, tu. Others not known.

RELIANCE BRASS BAND (about 1892–1913). Owned, managed, and booked by Papa Laine. Partial collective personnel: Manuel Mello, Fred Neuroth, Joe Lala, Johnny Lala, Richard Brunies, Gus Zimmerman, Merritt Brunies, Albert Brunies, Nick La Rocca, Pete Pellegrini, Frank Christian, Lawrence Veca, George Barth, Harry Shannon, Pete Dientrans, Ray Lopez, Johnny DeDroit, c; Leonce Mello, Dave Perkins, Eddie Edwards, George Brunies, Emile Christian, Marcus Kahn, Bill Gallaty, Sr., Ricky Toms, Jules Cassard, Henry Brunies, Tom Brown, Happy Schilling, tb; Yellow Nunez, Achille Baquet, Martin Kirsch, Sidney Moore, Clem Camp, Johnny Fischer, Larry Shields, Tony Giardina, Gus Mueller, John Palisier, Red Rowling, Leon Roppolo (elder), cl; Alfred Laine, Vincent Barocco, Merritt Brunies, ah; Manuel Belasco, bh; Joe Alexander, Martin Abraham, Sr., tu; Jack Laine, Tim Harris, Ragbaby Stephens, Johnny Stein, Tony Sbarbaro, Billy Lambert, Diddie Stephens, Emmett Rogers, d.

ST. JOSEPH BRASS BAND (Donaldsonville, La., 1888–95). Frequently played for carnival and parades in N.O. Collective personnel: Claiborne Williams, c. l; William Dailey, Sullivan Sproul, Edward Duffy, Israel Palmer, Lawrence Hall, c; George Williams, Ernest Hime, Harrison Homer, tb; Marble Gibson, Ben Bauddeurs, cl; Jim Williams, tu; Joe Walker, Buddy Curry, "Bow Legs," d. Fred Landry sometimes played trombone and piano for concerts where needed.

SCHILLING'S BRASS BAND (1910–17). Composed substantially of members of Happy Schilling's dance orchestra.

TERMINAL BRASS BAND (early 1900's to 1908). Permanent nucleus: Harrison Barnes (usually a trombonist), c; Joseph Petit, tb, l; Willie Parker, cl; "Sheik-O," bh; Henry Robertson, bd.

TUXEDO BRASS BAND (1910–25). Partial collective personnel: Oscar Celestin, t, l; Manuel Perez, Mutt Carey, Louis Dumaine, Alcide Landry, Charlie Love, Joe Howard, Willie Pajeaud, Louis Armstrong, Peter Bocage, Dee Dee Pierce, Amos White, Maurice Durand, c; Bebé Ridgley, Buddy Johnson, Yank Johnson, Sunny Henry, Hamp Benson, Harrison Barnes, Eddie Atkins, Jim Robinson, Loochie Jackson, tb; Alphonse Picou, Sam Dutrey, Sr., Lorenzo Tio, Jr., Johnny Dodds, Jimmie Noone, cl; Isidore Barbarin, Louis Keppard, ah; George Hooker, Adolphe Alexander, Sr., bh; Joe Howard, tu; Chinee Foster, Zutty Singleton, Louis Cottrell, Sr., sn; Ernest Trepagnier, Black Benny Williams, bd.

ABBY WILLIAMS HAPPY PALS (late 1940's, early 50's). Dee Dee Pierce, c; Kid Howard, Kid Clayton, t; Eddie Pierson, Jim Robinson, tb; Tats Alexander, cl; Noon Johnson, sou; Jesse Charles, s; Chester Jones, bd; Abby Williams, sn, l.

GEORGE WILLIAMS BRASS BAND (from late 40's). Partial collective personnel: Albert Walters, Alvin Alcorn, Theodore Riley, Ernest Cagnolatti, t; Buster Moore, Showboy Thomas, tb; Steve Angrum, cl; Ernest Poree, as; Jesse Charles, ts; William Brown, tu; Edward "Son White" Washington, sn; Cié Frazier, George Williams, bd, l.

YOUNG TUXEDO BRASS BAND (1930's to 1963). Partial collective personnel: Alvin Alcorn, Kid Howard, Thomas Jefferson, Kid Shots Madison, Edgar Joseph, Dee Dee Pierce, Vernon Gilbert, John Brunious, Andy Anderson, t; Sunny Henry, Joe Avery, Loochie Jackson, Albert Warner, Clement Tervalon, Wendell Eugene, tb; John Casimir, cl, mgr; Albert Burbank, cl; Adolphe Alexander, Jr., Andrew Morgan, John Handy, s; Eddie Jackson, Wilbert Tillman, tu; Ernest Rogers, Son White Washington, Emile Knox, Cié Frazier, Paul Barbarin, Alfred Williams, d.

WHERE'S WHERE IN NEW ORLEANS JAZZ

Someday a book will be published which will devote itself entirely to a review of jazz landmarks. It will have to be a thick volume indeed to do justice to a subject of historical importance and architectural fascination. The city seemed to spawn its characteristic sound on every corner, in every house. This section of the present work will not pretend to fill the need for a detailed study of places identified with New Orleans jazz. But we hope it will point the way by outlining, in a broad sense, the relationship between the music and some of our town's real estate.

By now, jazz enthusiasts everywhere know, though they've never visited the city, that we have an "uptown" and a "downtown." Uptown is generally westward from Canal Street. The "canebrake" style generated in this area flowered into the likes of Buddy Bolden and King Oliver. The downtown area, below Canal Street and including both the French Quarter and Storyville, gave rise to the so-called "Creole" style mainly associated with Armand J. Piron, John Robichaux, and Alphonse Picou.

Both of these areas produced neighborhood music for dancing, for weddings, for wakes, for picnics and burials, and just for fun. Innumerable church and lodge halls were available for nightly rental. The style of music played depended largely on the section of town in which it was heard.

All styles blended, though, in the city's celebrated resort areas along the Lake Pontchartrain shore where much of the population betook itself on weekends for fun, fishing, boating, and assorted games. Hallowed now in jazz history are the stretches known as Milneburg, Old Spanish Fort, Little Woods, Bucktown, and West End. Commemorated in such evergreen jazz titles as "Milneburg Joys" and "West End Blues," these festive meccas only remain as nostalgic memories. But the names of such bands as The Bucktown Five sprinkled through our discographies help us to remember.

To a limited and lesser extent Storyville, the legal red-light district that operated from 1898 to 1917, served as a forge in which some of the pure gold of jazz was smelted. It, too, has been celebrated in song. "Mahogany Hall Stomp" recalls its most famous brothel, and "Basin Street Blues" and "Franklin Street Blues" bring to mind its most hectic streets.

The role played by Storyville in jazz development has been much exaggerated and deliberately misrepresented by self-elected "historians." TV producers, even on allegedly educational channels, reviewers in magazines and the motion picture screen, along with other media, have seen fit to perpetuate the myth that jazz was a product of the red-light district. This is not only untrue, but offensive and insulting to the vast majority of New Orleans jazzmen, including some of its brightest stars, who not only never played in Storyville, but, indeed, never even *saw* it. The district never employed more than two score musicians on any given night. That includes Mardi Gras! By the time Storyville came into existence there were hundreds of musicians who had already been playing jazz music for more than a decade.

Surrounding the district was an almost unbroken line of cabarets, dance halls, and honky-tonks (this was referred to as the Tango Belt), where top dixieland stars spent their early careers. Here Armand Hug, Sharkey Bonano, Wingy Manone, and Raymond Burke, to name a few, learned about life as jazzmen.

The downtown hotels, especially the Grunewald (now the Roosevelt) and the Jung, presented bands for dancing. These contained future dixieland stars, as did the pit bands of the leading theaters. Tony Parenti, Johnny Wiggs, Leon Prima, and Santo Pecora are among their best known alumni.

Cafes were scattered all over town, many bearing names that still set melodies singing in many a jazz fan's heart—the Tin Roof, the Red Onion, the Halfway House. Ball parks, fair grounds, boxing arenas, all supplied backdrops against which the stars of New Orleans jazz improvised their music.

And consider the streets and alleys whose names are known to the ends of the earth through the music that was brewed in them! "Canal Street Blues," "South Rampart Street Parade," "Burgundy Street Blues," "Bourbon Street Parade," "Perdido Street Blues"—the list seems endless.

In front of the Municipal Auditorium is a tree-shaded park now called Beauregard Square. In an earlier era it was, informally, Congo Square, recreation area for slaves, where African rhythms and vocalizing were first heard in the New World—and where many assert this music of ours was truly born. Almost everywhere you look, you want to install a bronze plaque.

As for the little places over the river in Algiers, Gretna, Westwego, across the lake in Covington and Mandeville, along the Gulf Coast to Biloxi—not to mention such itinerant sites of jazz importance as the riverboats, the tailgate wagons every fan knows about, Smoky Mary, the train that hauled revellers to the lake—well, it becomes more obvious that the book we mentioned is a critical cultural need.

But in these pages we beg you to settle for a sample. Where the "Big 25" stood there is now a parking lot. Nothing on the blank wall of Krauss's Department Store tells us that here once rose Mahogany Hall in all its vulgar splendor. They only live now in our memories and in these pictures. Insofar as it has been practicable, we've listed a great many locations, many important but obscure. We hope the ones selected to show in photos are the ones the reader would most want to see.

200

Interior of the Haymarket Cabaret. Members of the Original Dixieland Jazz Band went on to fame from here.

Jackson Hall was a regular dance spot at the turn of the century. This is the earliest known photo of an advertising "tailgate" wagon publicizing a dance there. No reliable identification of the personnel in this 1900 photograph has been made.

ABADIE'S (1906–17). Downtown lake corner, Marais and Bienville Sts. Richard M. Jones's Four Hot Hounds sometimes included Joe Oliver, Wooden Joe Nicholas, Sugar Johnny Smith.

ALAMO DANCE HALL (30's). Taxi dance hall. 113 Burgundy St.

ALAMO THEATER. 1027 Canal St.

ALHAMBRA GYM CLUB. 535 Seguin St., Algiers, La.

ALLEY CABARET (1920's). Claiborne & St. Bernard Aves. Big Eye Louis Nelson Delisle.

ALTMYER'S, Corner of Annunciation and Robin sts. Tom Brown's Band From Dixieland rehearsed in this saloon almost nightly before making pioneer journey to Chicago in 1915.

ANDERSON'S ANNEX (1901–25). Basin & Iberville Sts. Early period (to 1905), string trio with Tom Brown, mdl; Bill Johnson, b. Middle period (to 1915) assorted jazz groups. Late period (World War I) Luis Russell band. End (1924–25), Amos White.

ANN'S PLEASURE CLUB. 3436 Magazine St.

ARLINGTON ANNEX (same as Anderson's Annex).

Birthplace of Louis Armstrong.

ARMSTRONG, LOUIS (birthplace). Jane Alley, between Gravier and Perdido Sts. Torn down in 1964.

ARTESAN HALL. 1460 N. Derbigny (1930's). Usually mispronounced "Ar-TEE-sian."

ASTORIA HOTEL AND BALLROOM (1895–1963). S. Rampart St. Peak in late 20's, early 30's with Jones-Collins Astoria Hot Eight.

BEVERLY GARDENS RESTAURANT (Suburban Gardens) (from mid-20's). Jefferson Highway. Duck Ernest Johnson frequently led band.

BIENVILLE ROOF (20's, 30's). Lee Circle. Monk Hazel's orchestra. Sharkey.

"BIG 25" (1902–late 50's). Franklin St. (Crozat) near Iberville (Customhouse). Musicians' hangout.

BLUM'S CAFE (1900–16). 114 Exchange Alley. A meeting hall where musicians formed bands.

BOLDEN, BUDDY. At one time lived at 2527 First St. Torn down.

ASSOCIATED ARTISTS' STUDIO. 732 St. Peter St. Informal jam sessions were begun by Larry Borenstein, art entrepreneur, during the forties. Their continued success enabled him to create Preservation Hall, next door to the old gallery, in which took place the revival of traditional jazz in the sixties.

203

The Big 25. Demolished in 1956.

The Astoria Hotel and Ballroom. South Rampart Street near Gravier. Demolished in January, 1964. *Photo, courtesy Carey Tate.*

Old Dauphine Theater. Sophie Tucker made her debut in New Orleans in 1910. Tom Brown's, Schilling's, and Johnny Fischer's bands were among the many great early bands that played here.

THE BROWN DERBY. Villere and St. Ann Sts. This spot, under various names, Gipsy Tea Room, Japanese Gardens, was a stronghold for Kid Rena's bands through the 20's and 30's.

BROWN'S ICE CREAM PARLOR (20's). Spanish Fort. Steve Lewis, p; New Orleans Willie Jackson, entertainer.

BUCKTOWN. Jefferson Parish, just across 17th St. bridge from West End. A rough, tough resort area on the lakefront inhabited by commercial fishermen. Its Bucktown Tavern was the chief point of jazz interest.

THE BUDWEISER. Musicians always have called the premises at 1017 Iberville by this name because of the beer sign which always hung over the banquette there. See the Pup Cafe, Fern Dance Hall No. 2.

BULLS CLUB. A fraternal group that centered in a series of locations, first at Chippewa and Philip Streets; in 1966 between 7th & 8th & Harmony. Among the many trumpeter-leaders who performed under its sponsorship: Manuel Calier, Chris Kelly, King Oliver, George McCullum, Sr.

Bucktown Tavern, about 1920.

THE BUNGALOW (20's, 30's) (also Chez Paree). Pontchartrain Blvd. near the lakefront. Now Masson's Beach House restaurant. Dixieland bands exclusively.

THE CADILLAC (about 1912–25). 342 N. Rampart St. Before 1917, Willie Hightower was the house leader. From about 1918–23, Luis Russell was usually in charge. Later a dixieland stronghold.

CASINO CABARET (1907–13). 1400 Iberville St. In Storyville.

THE CAVE (1920's). A room in the Grunewald Hotel. Tony Parenti, Johnny Bayersdorffer, Johnny De-Droit frequently on the podium. A bizarre decor featuring stalagmites, stalactites remains as part of the laundry room in the Fairmont Hotel basement.

CHEAPSKATE HALL. See Economy Hall.

CHERRY PICKERS HALL. 3rd & Magazine Sts.

CHEZ PAREE (same as The Bungalow).

CLUB FORREST. A smart supper club of the prohibition era in Jefferson Parish. Featured the top name attractions in larger bands. A. J. Piron, Louis Armstrong, the New Orleans Owls, Papa Celestin, John Robichaux, the Prima-Sharkey Orchestra all had their turns.

COBWEB CLUB (1920's). 815 Iberville.

COLE'S LAWN, BETSY. Josephine & Willow Sts. Early jazz patron who frequently gave lawn parties and hired jazz bands; made historic spot of her front yard.

THE COLISEUM (1920's). Boxing arena. Conti & Derbigny Sts. Dixieland bands on wagons roamed the streets advertising prize fights, later entertained in the arena. Pay? The musicians got to see the match free.

COME CLEAN HALL. Gretna, La. Frequently featured the Buddy Bolden band about the turn of the century.

CONGO SQUARE (now Beauregard Square). N. Rampart & Orleans Sts. Recreation area for the slaves where tribal dancing, African rhythms, and musical instruments were perpetuated. Considered by many to be the real birthplace of jazz. These activities forbidden here by city decree in 1843.

CO-OPERATOR'S HALL. Also called "Hopes Hall" by musicians. 922 N. Liberty St.

CRESCENT DANCE HALL. Washington & Prytania Sts.

CRESCENT THEATER. In the Tulane-Crescent Arcade off Baronne St. Minstrel shows, banjo bands.

CRYSTAL CLUB (1930's). 1000 Tulane Ave.

DANGER BAR (late '20's). Bienville St. Amos Riley.

DESOTO HOTEL. 420 Baronne St. In the 20's, 30's a favorite spot for fraternity and high school dances, using top local jazz bands.

DIXIE PARK. Bienville St., between Murat, Olympia Sts. Outdoor amusement area.

DIXIELAND HALL (opened 1962). Bourbon St. A small concert hall featuring authentic jazz artists, playing in a commercial dixieland style. "Uncle Tom" type dancers are regularly featured.

THE DREAM ROOM (closed 1964). 426 Bourbon St. Mainly rock-and-roll bands with occasional dixieland style group.

DREAM WORLD THEATER (1920's). 632 Canal St. Outstanding ragtime pianists accompanied silent movies. Tom Zimmerman, Irwin Leclere.

DRUIDS HALL. 843 Camp St.

EAGLE EYE HALL (1900's). Algiers, La. The phrase Eagle Eye is a corruption of the hall's true name, *Egalite* (French, meaning "equality"). Torn down to make room for bridge approach.

EAGLE SALOON. S. Rampart & Perdido Sts. Headquarters of the Eagle Band from which the band's name is derived.

The Halfway House (about 1920). Only known photograph of the interior. *Photo, courtesy Charlie Cordilla.*

The Piron-Williams Publishing Company at 1317 Tulane Avenue. Now used by the Frank B. Moore, photographers.

EARLY'S, FRANK (1909–13). Franklin & Bienville Sts. Featured Tony Jackson in 1910, 1911, 1912.

EAST END PARK (1900's). Jefferson Parish at the lakefront. Happy Schilling's band frequently seen at picnics. Also Fischer's Brass Band.

EASTMAN PARK (through early 1900's). Off Metairie Road, past cemetery. Picnic and amusement grounds where Happy Schilling, Johnny Fischer frequently played for dancing in a wooden pavilion.

ECONOMY HALL (1885–1940's). 1422 Ursuline St. Buddy Petit, Earl Humphrey, Pinchback Touro, Joe Oliver, frequent leaders. Among musicians, this place was nicknamed Cheapskate Hall.

ELITE (mid-1920's). Night club. Iberville between Rampart and Burgundy.

THE ELKS CLUB. 1125 Dauphine. Regular dances and frequent parades.

THE ENTERTAINERS (1902–early 30's). Franklin St. near Customhouse. Same premises previously known as 101 Ranch, 102 Ranch, Phillips Cafe. Some of the great jazzmen played here.

EUREKA HALL. Bienville & Pelican Sts.

EXCHANGE ALLEY. Between Chartres and Royal Sts., running from Canal to Conti. At Martin's Saloon, the non-union musicians would hang around waiting for a phone call from Jack Laine. Union headquarters was upstairs over the saloon.

FABACHER'S RATHSKELLAR. 410–418 St. Charles. Music was supplied with the celebrated food in the first decades of the century. Jazzmen were frequently employed here—but the music they played was mainly waltzes.

FAIR GROUNDS. Near City Park. The famed race track hired bands, too. Buddy Bolden's band and John Robichaux both were employed before 1910.

FAIRPLAY HALL. 3053 N. Rampart.

THE FAMOUS DOOR (40's to present). Bourbon & Conti Sts. Favorite tourist spot featuring commercial dixieland style music as demanded by the management. Some of top names that have played long engagements: Sharkey, Santo Pecora, Dukes of Dixieland, George Girard.

FERN DANCE HALL NO. 2. 1017 Iberville St. In mid and late 20's, a popular "jitney dance" palace. Many dixielanders got their early "schooling" here. Among them, Armand Hug, Irving Fazola, Julian Laine.

FERNANDEZ', BUTZIE. 1024 Iberville. Active between 1905 and the 20's. Amos White's orchestra.

FEWCLOTHES CABARET (early 1900's to 1917). Basin St. between Canal and Customhouse. Some of its longer-term leaders: Alcide Frank's Golden Rule Orchestra in 1905; Freddie Keppard, 1913; Walter Decou, 1915; Joe Oliver, 1915–16.

FIREMAN'S HALL (40's & 50's). Westwego, La. For many years a regular Saturday night dance with the Kid Thomas Band.

FIVE HUNDRED (500) CLUB (40's & 50's). Bourbon & St. Louis Sts. Long operated by Leon Prima, featuring his own band.

FRANCS AMIS HALL. 1820 N. Robertson St.

THE FRENCHMAN'S (1900–15). Downtown lake corner, Villere & Bienville Sts. Traditional meeting ground for the "professors" of Storyville. Jelly Roll Morton, Tony Jackson, Buddy Carter, Alfred Wilson, Albert Carroll, Clarence Williams all played here after hours.

THE FROLIC (later Top Hat). St. Ann & Dorgenois Sts. Sharkey's band frequently at this location.

FUNKY BUTT HALL (1900's). Perdido St. between Liberty & Franklin. Buddy Bolden's early base of operations. Its right name was Kenna's Hall, but hardly anyone knew it by that name.

GIPSY TEA ROOM. See Brown Derby.

GLOBE HALL. St. Claude and St. Peter Sts.

GOLDEN PUMPKIN (20's, 30's). Pontchartrain Blvd. Featured dixieland-style bands exclusively.

Altmyer's Saloon.

The Orpheum Theater Lobby (1932). The house band played inside for the show, then played in the lobby to attract customers. Left to right are Jac Assunto, Howard Reed, Alfred Gallodoro, Howard Tift, Henry Raymond, Charles Rittner.

GREENWALD THEATER. Dauphine St.

GROSHELL'S DANCE HALL (1905–13). Downtown lake corner, Customhouse & Liberty St. A district hot spot.

GRUNEWALD HOTEL. Later the Roosevelt, now the Fairmont. Various bands played in the Cave and the Fountain Lounge.

HALFWAY HOUSE (1914–30). City Park Ave. at Pontchartrain Blvd. Abbie Brunies led bands that included Stalebread Lacoume, Leon Roppolo, Leo Adde, Charlie Cordilla, and other dixieland luminaries.

HAPPY LANDING (40's & 50's). On road to Little Woods. Some of the leaders: Lawrence Toca, Kid Clayton, Albert Jiles, Charlie Love, Joe Avery, Louis Keppard, Israel Gorman.

HARMONY INN (1920's–40's). Claiborne & Piety. Emile Barnes, leader through many early years. During World War II, George Lewis usually had a trio on the stand.

HAYMARKET CAFE (to about 1917). Iberville St. between Burgundy & N. Rampart Sts. Downtown spot that spawned the Original Dixieland Jazz Band.

HEINEMAN PARK. Baseball park. Carrollton & Tulane Aves. Happy Schilling's band.

HILL'S, BUTCHY. Protection Levee at Oak St.

HOLY GHOST HALL. Toledano St. near Saratoga.

HOPES HALL (1). Burgundy & Spain Sts. Active with jazz bands from about 1900. Also called Esperance Hall, Jackson Hall.

HOPES HALL (2). 922 N. Liberty. Headquarters of the Society of Friends of Hope. Also known as Co-operator's Hall, and Jackson Hall.

THE HUMMING BIRD LOUNGE. 1501 Bienville St.

IRISH HALL. Gravier & Derbigny Sts.

ITALIAN HALL. Rampart & Esplanade Sts.

JEFFERSON CITY BUZZARDS HALL. Near the carbarn at Magazine & Arabella Sts. Headquarters of this active marching group that made jazz part of its life from the early 1900's to the present.

JUNG HOTEL ROOF (late 20's, early 30's). Ellis Stratakos Orchestra.

PYTHIAN ROOF. S. Saratoga & Gravier Sts. In the post-World War I era, Manuel Perez played here.

KOLB'S RESTAURANT (1900's to present). St. Charles Ave. Johnny DeDroit Orchestra.

LALA'S, PETE (1906–17). Customhouse & Marais Sts. Freddie Keppard, Kid Ory, King Oliver.

LA LOUISIANE RESTAURANT. Iberville St. For many years John Robichaux led an orchestra here.

LAVIDA BALLROOM. St. Charles Ave. & Canal St. Many early jazzmen including Tony Parenti, Stalebread Lacoume played in dance bands here. Most groups led by violinists.

LIBERTY THEATER (20's). 420 St. Charles Ave. Tony Parenti's Liberty Syncopators. Steve Loyacano's orchestra.

LINCOLN PARK (uptown). Carrollton, between Forshey and Oleander. Buddy Bolden was often the standout attraction in support of a regularly performed balloon ascent stunt.

LITTLE CLUB NO. 1. Rampart, near Common St. Featured dixieland.

LITTLE CLUB NO. 2. 205 Dryades. Featured dixieland.

LITTLE WOODS. Resort area on Lake Pontchartrain.

LOEW'S STATE. 1108 Canal St. Dixieland in the pit band.

LONGSHOREMAN'S HALL, 2059 Jackson Ave.

LOVE & CHARITY HALL. Corner of Eagle & Poplar Sts.

LUCIEN PAVILION. At Spanish Fort. Dance pavilion.

The Cave, Grunewald Hotel (about 1912–26). It was below the present Blue Room of the Fairmont Hotel.

Papa Laine's Home (1903–1909), 2405 Chartres Street, New Orleans.

LUTHJEN'S (40's–50's). Marais at Almonaster. Popular weekend dance place. Big Eye Louis Nelson, Billie and Dee Dee Pierce were associated with the place for many years.

LYRIC THEATER (–1927). 201 Burgundy St. The house pit band was led by John Robichaux. Burned in 1927.

MAHOGANY HALL (1903–17). 335 Basin St. Celebrated bordello where famed piano men worked—Jelly Roll Morton, Tony Jackson, Kid Ross, Albert Carroll. Demolished in '49.

MAJESTIC HALL. 7th & Magazine Sts. An uptown spot favored by Tom Brown and his coterie.

MAMA LOU'S (40's–50's). On Lake Pontchartrain toward Little Woods. A pier restaurant-dance hall open on weekends with dancing to bands led by Peter Bocage, Kid Shots, and others.

MANDEVILLE SWELLS SOCIAL CLUB (1903–09). 2403 Chartres St. Jack Laine bands.

MANNY'S TAVERN (40's). Benefit & St. Roch Sts. George Lewis.

MARDI GRAS LOUNGE (40's to current). Bourbon St. Owner-clarinetist Sid Davila frequently sat in with the house bands when jazz was played there. Some of the leaders: George Lewis, Oscar Celestin, Percy Humphrey, Sharkey, Freddie Kohlman. Lizzie Miles was regularly featured.

MARTIN'S CAFE. See Bucktown.

MARTIN'S SALOON. Exchange Alley.

MASONIC HALL. See Oddfellows Hall.

MILNEBURG. Sometimes called Old Lake. Busy lakefront resort area. Each of the hundreds of camps had its own music. All jazz musicians worked at Milneburg frequently. The seawall put in by WPA in the mid-thirties was the end of the camps.

MOULIN ROUGE (from 1918). Bourbon St. Operating since World War I, this is now a strip joint, but in 1919 it offered the Silver Leaf Orchestra, and for many later years was the home base of Sharkey's Kings of Dixieland.

THE MUSIC BOX (1920's). Canal & Prieur Sts. Willie Pajeaud.

NANCY HANK'S SALOON (about 1900). Later, Rice's Cafe.

NATIONAL PARK. Ball park, 3rd & Willow. Customarily bands were employed by sports entrepreneurs.

NEW ORLEANS COUNTRY CLUB. Pontchartrain Blvd. All of the top bands played here, but the A. J. Piron Orchestra was most steadily employed.

NEW ORLEANS JAZZ CLUB MUSEUM (1961–present). 1017 Dumaine St. Museum operated by the N.O. Jazz Club.

NO-NAME THEATER. 1025 Canal St. Minstrels, blues singers, prior to World War I.

NEW SLIPPER NIGHT CLUB (1933). 426 Bourbon St. Merritt Brunies orchestra.

OASIS CABARET (early 1920's). Iberville St.

ODDFELLOWS HALL (also Masonic Hall). 1116 Perdido St. Scene of the notorious French Balls given by "The Two Well-Known Gentlemen" every carnival for the madams and girls of Storyville.

OLYMPIA HALL. Carrollton Ave. & Oak St.

THE ORCHARD. 942 Conti. Later, Pete Herman's Ringside Cafe.

ORPHEUM THEATER. 125 University Place. Emile Tosso was leader of pit band, but some jazzmen were frequently employed.

PADDOCK LOUNGE (1940's, 50's, 60's). Bourbon St. Papa Celestin, Alphonse Picou, Lee Collins, Albert Burbank, Octave Crosby, Paul Barbarin among leaders. Management has always demanded a commercial product.

PALACE THEATER. 201 Dauphine St.

St. Katherine's Hall.

Preservation Hall. Allan and Sandra Jaffe welcome jazz fans of the 60's.

Mama Lou's. *Photo, courtesy Carey Tate.*

Luthjen's. Destroyed by fire, January 30, 1960.

Economy Hall.

Associated Artists' Studio (1950's). Performers are the Noon Johnson Trio. Left to right are Noon Johnson, Sam Rankin, Harrison Verret.

The Halfway House, New Basin. New Orleans.

Washington Artillery Hall. St. Charles Avenue.

Heineman Park (1936). Here the Pelicans played baseball and Happy Schilling's band played dixieland. This photograph shows Happy Schilling, guitar; Henry Knecht, trumpet; Bob Aquilera, trombone.

Fern Cafe and Dance Hall, No. 2. *Photo, courtesy "Scoop" Kennedy.*

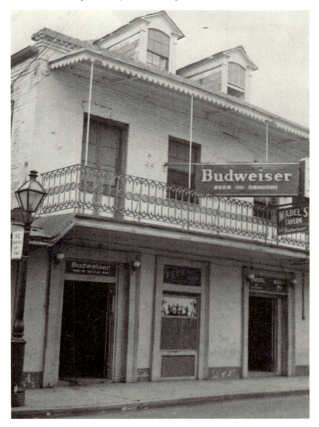

PALM GARDENS. Algiers, La.

THE PARISIAN ROOM (late 40's, 50's). 112 Royal St. Tony Almerico's base from which his frequent coast-to-coast broadcasts emanated and where the N.O. Jazz Club had its first session.

PATTERSON HOTEL. Rampart near Julia St. George Lewis, Kid Punch Miller were frequent performers.

PELICAN HALL. Royal and Bienville Sts.

PELICAN STADIUM (formerly Heineman Park). Tulane Ave. & Carrollton Ave. Baseball park. Happy Schilling, Tom Brown, Johnny Fischer, Punch Miller.

PENNY-WONDERLAND (about 1915). Canal St. J. Russell Robinson, piano, and his brother, drums, made a regular vaudeville act out of accompanying Original Dixieland Jazz Band records.

PERFECT UNION HALL. Also called French Union Hall. N. Rampart & Dumaine Sts.

217

PERSEVERANCE HALL. 1642 N. Villere St.

PIG ANKLE CABARET (early 1900's). Iberville and Franklin Sts.

THE PIG PEN (also The Kingfish). Decatur & Ursuline Sts. Dee Dee and Billie Pierce.

PRESERVATION HALL (1961–current). 726 St. Peter St. Bastion of traditional New Orleans jazz. Surviving maestros include Peter Bocage, Kid Thomas, Sweet Emma Barrett, Percy Humphrey, George Lewis, Punch Miller, Jim Robinson, Johnny Wiggs.

PRINCESS THEATER (20's). 1828 Felicity St.

POODLE DOG CABARET (about 1908–17). Liberty & Bienville Sts.

PUP CAFE. 1017 Iberville St. Until prohibition this was a leading jazz cabaret. The premises became a taxi dance hall in 1920, Fern Cafe No. 2.

QUARELLA'S. At Milneburg. This popular lakefront spot was a stronghold for early dixieland stars. The Christian brothers, the Brunies family and most of Jack Laine's gang here on week-ends. Sharkey, a nephew of the owner, got his start here as a teen-ager playing clarinet.

THE RED ONION. Julia & S. Rampart Sts. Louis Armstrong, Johnny Dodds.

RICE'S CAFE (1904–13). Marais & Iberville Sts. Earlier, Nancy Hank's saloon. Manuel Perez.

RINGSIDE CAFE (Pete Herman's since 30's). Dauphine & Bienville Sts. Broadcasts of Melon Pickers band emanated from here, with Raymond Burke. Later George Hartman led a group for many years.

ROOSEVELT HOTEL (30's to 70's). Now Fairmont. University Pl. Originally the Grunewald Hotel. Many rooms where bands play—Blue Room, Fountain Lounge.

SAENGER THEATER (30's). Canal & N. Rampart Sts. Louis Prima frequently featured here. Famed pit band with many dixieland stars.

ST. CERE HALL. N. Claiborne between Columbus & Kerlerec Sts. Early Stomping ground for N.O. Rhythm Kings.

ST. CHARLES HOTEL MEZZANINE. A. J. Piron.

ST. KATHERINE'S HALL. 1509 Tulane Ave. A major dance hall where Kid Ory, Bunk Johnson, Joe Oliver, John Robichaux, and the Crescent band frequently appeared.

SAN JACINTO HALL (to 1966). 1422 Dumaine St., between Villere & Robertson Sts. Historic spot where Bunk Johnson's band made celebrated American Music discs. Top traditional stars worked here. Used as late as 1965 for recording.

SANS SOUCI HALL. 2832 Howard St. Bunk Johnson played here.

SHIM SHAM CLUB. 229 Bourbon St. The mid-30's.

SHOTO CABARET (early 1900's). Iberville & Franklin Sts.

THE SILVER SLIPPER. 426 Bourbon St. Premises became Dream Room. Tony Parenti, Jules Bauduc led groups here in the 20's.

SIXTH WARD ATHLETIC CLUB. Boxing arena. Tom Brown, Happy Schilling, Johnny Fischer.

SOCIETE DES JEUNES AMIS. 1321 N. Robertson St. Also known as Thomy Lafon Hall.

SPANO'S (about 1900). Franklin & Perdido Sts. Bunk Johnson, Jelly Roll Morton.

SPEC'S MOULIN ROUGE (40's, 50's). Marrero, La. Kid Thomas.

SPORTSMAN'S PARK. Gretna, La.

STAND-BY HALL (about 1910). Frenchmen & Decatur Sts. Frequently featured Frank Christian's Ragtime Band.

STORYVILLE (1898–1917). Bounded by N. Basin St., Robertson St., St. Louis St., Iberville St. The only

Congo Square.

219

legally constituted red-light district in the history of the Western Hemisphere. Some jazzmen worked in its cabarets, and many pianists in its brothels.

STRAND THEATER (20's). Baronne & Gravier Sts. Music frequently supplied by the N.O. Owls.

SUBURBAN GARDENS (Beverly Gardens, Embassy Club, 1936) (about 1915–mid-20's). Jefferson Parish, La. Oscar Celestin held this job down in early years. During the 20's the N.O. Owls were often the house band; and in early depression years, Louis Armstrong opened here, on his triumphal return to his hometown. Joe Capraro's orchestra in the 30's.

TAMMANY SOCIAL AND ATHLETIC CLUB (early 1900's). 334 S. Liberty St.

THOM'S ROADHOUSE (1918–38). Pontchartrain Blvd., almost to West End.

THREE OAKS PLAYGROUND. Little Woods. Popular picnic spot with open dance pavilion where many dixieland musicians performed.

TIN ROOF CAFE. Washington St. & Claiborne Ave. Immortalized in song, the Tin Roof became a vinegar factory before 1910.

TIP TOP CLUB (–50's). West Bank. Stomping grounds for Kid Thomas band.

TOKYO GARDENS (20's). Spanish Fort. Long-time stronghold of Johnny Bayersdorffer's orchestra.

TONTI SOCIAL CLUB (20's). 823 N. Tonti St.

TRANCHINA'S RESTAURANT (1920's). Spanish Fort. Long-time post of the A. J. Piron Orchestra.

TRIANGLE THEATER (1918 through 20's). 814 Canal St. Irwin Leclere accompanied silent movies on the piano.

TULANE ATHLETIC CLUB (boxing arena). Howard St. between Canal and Gasquet Sts. Tom Brown, Happy Schilling.

TUXEDO DANCE HALL (1909–13). Franklin St. near Bienville St. This is where the Original Tuxedo Orchestra began. Oscar Celestin, Peter Bocage were leaders here. A shooting brawl shuttered it.

THE TWENTY-EIGHT (1895–1902). Franklin St. between Canal and Iberville Sts. Buddy Bolden's orchestra.

TYLER'S BEER GARDEN (30's, 40's). 119 Walnut St. Tillman-Avery Band in 40's.

VENICE INN (same as Bucktown Tavern).

VIEUX CARRE INN (Pete Fountain's) (current). Bourbon & St. Ann Sts. Usually the Pete Fountain group.

VILLA CABARET (1906–17). Franklin St. between Bienville and Iberville Sts.

WAIF'S HOME. Canal Blvd. & City Park Ave. Careers of Louis Armstrong, Kid Shots Madison, Kid Rena began here.

WASHINGTON ARTILLERY HALL. 729–737 St. Charles Ave.

WEST END. At the end of Pontchartrain Blvd. on the lake. Northwest corner of the city. Resort area.

WEST END ROOF GARDEN (1920's). West End. Some of the leaders: Kid Ory, Oscar Celestin. Also the Owls, the Silver Leaf Orchestra, many others.

WHITE CITY (1900's). Carrollton & Tulane Aves. An amusement park where many bands played for concerts and dancing. Later became N.O. ball park.

WINTER GARDEN (to 1915). Boxing arena. Baronne St., near Poydras St. Tom Brown's band, Fischer's band, Happy Schilling's band, Jack Laine.

WOW HALL. 2501 Urquhart St. Frequently hired for dances. The famed Johnny Wiggs record session that produced "King Zulu Parade" and "If Ever I Cease To Love" was made here in 1954.

Y.M.G.C. ROWING CLUB. Bayou St. John. The Invincibles. Six and 7/8 String Band.

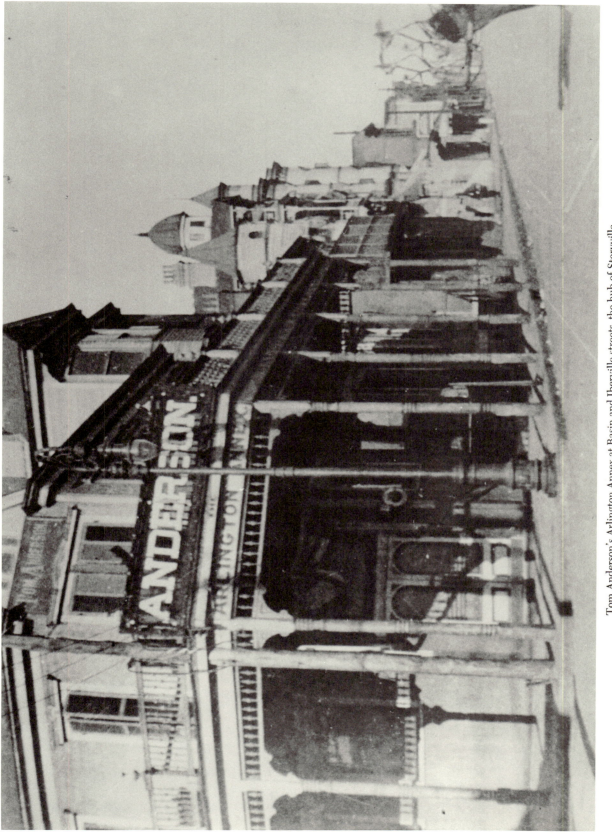

Tom Anderson's Arlington Annex at Basin and Iberville streets, the hub of Storyville.

The Happy Landing.
Photo, courtesy Carey Tate.

Frank Early's Saloon.

Mahogany Hall.

Old Spanish Fort.

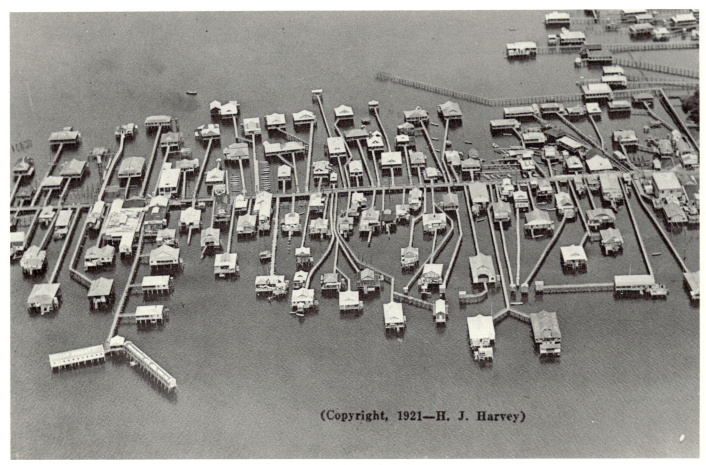

(Copyright, 1921—H. J. Harvey)

Milneburg, 1921.

Pete Lala's.

The bandstand at Tom Anderson's Rampart St. (1923). At work are, left to right, Paul Barbarin, Arnold Metoyer, Luis Russell, Willie Santiago, Albert Nicholas.

Artesan Hall. The high bandstand is designed to protect the musicians from unruly celebrants.

The Champagne Room (1937), later the Paddock. The Willie Joseph Trio. Left to right, Joseph, Alton Purnell, Alvin Woods.

226

West End's Bandstand. Free seats at sides and at tables, where refreshments could be ordered. The white-painted seats in the center were reserved. Note Mannessier's Ice Cream Parlor and the entrance to the scenic railway.

Buddy Bolden's home.

Storyville, 1906.

Magnolia Plantation.

At the Lavida Dance Hall in the Vieux Carré (about 1922). Left to right are Eddie Faye, Harold Peterson, Buzzy Williams, Charlie Fishbein, Florenzo Ramos, Joe Kinneman, Stalebread Lacoume. *Photo, courtesy of Mrs. Lacoume.*

Thom's Roadhouse.

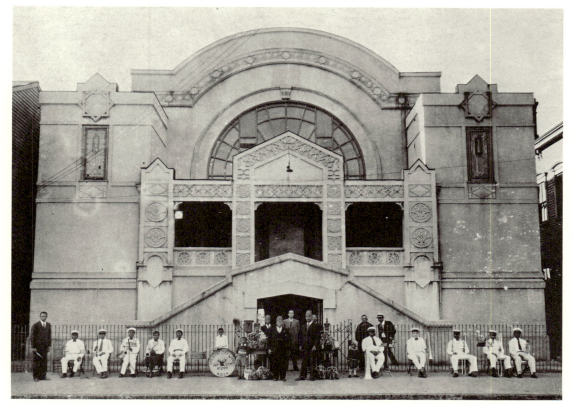

The Elk's Club was the scene of much musical activity in the 30's. The Masonic Brass Band has been hired for a function. Some of the musicians are Albert Jones, leader, clarinet; Ophelia Grigsby, saxophone. Next to her right is A. B. Spears. Fourth from right is Red Clark, trombone.

The Shim Sham Club, 229 Bourbon Street, in the mid-30's. The band featured was led by saxman Harold Jordy and consists, from left to right, of Emile Guerin, Dave Winstein, Von Gammon, Bob Wiley, Martin Abraham, Tony Almerico.

Druids Hall (1922). Lodge official Dominick Barocco used his own band. Left to right are Ferdinand Knecht, Gus Zimmerman, Martin Kirsch, Joe Barocco, Dominick Barocco, Leonce Mello.

Ringside Cafe (1927). The New Orleans Harmony Kings on the bandstand. Left to right, Martin Abraham, Freddie Neumann, Joe Capraro, Sidney Arodin, Sharkey, Augie Schellang.

NEW ORLEANS JAZZ
AFLOAT

Part of the legend of New Orleans jazz is the role that steamboats played in its history. Some of these side and stern wheelers plied Lake Pontchartrain as excursion boats. Others, more famous, carried passengers and musicians up the river to such exotic ports of call as Chicago and St. Louis. The roster of jazzmen who served their time supplying music for these cruises reads like a *Who's Who* of early jazz.

More affluent members of the community who owned yachts and other seaborne equipment felt that homegrown jazz was just the thing to enliven a nautical party. Such personalities as Blaise D'Antoni frequently cruised his friends to Central America on the boats belonging to his family's Standard Fruit Company, and carried a complement of dixielanders. One of his favorites, Sharkey, still uses the $500

French Selmer trumpet D'Antoni gave him as a token of esteem. Rear Admiral Ernest Lee Jahncke owned various boats and often threw musical parties on them.

Surrounded by Lake Pontchartrain and the Mississippi as the city is, it's no wonder that jazz found its way to the water, too. Many of the older jazzmen cherish recollections of playing on these boats among their fondest memories.

S.S. CAPITOL (demolished by 1942). Fate Marable orchestra. Walter Pichon, A. J. Piron, Sidney Desvigne.

S.S. DIXIE (20's–30's). Jazz by N.O. bands on an ocean run between N.O. and N.Y.

S.S. GREATER NEW ORLEANS. A river steamer. Desvigne orchestra.

S.S. ISLAND QUEEN. Sidney Desvigne orchestra.

S.S. "J.S." Fate Marable.

S.S. MADISON. A Lake Pontchartrain steamer.

S.S. NEW CAMELIA. A lake excursion steamer of the 20's.

S.S. OLD CAMELIA. An excursion boat on Lake Pontchartrain in the pre-World War I years.

S.S. PRESIDENT (to 1966). Saturday night dance cruises with Dutch Andrus band in late 50's; Crawford-Ferguson Night Owls thereafter.

S.S. ST. PAUL. Streckfus Line riverboat and one of the first to offer jazz on the river.

S.S. SUSQUEHANNA. A lake steamer which, in 1923–25, featured the music of the Barocco brothers.

The S.S. *Dixie* was a riverboat of the 30's. Here on deck are Harold Dejan, seated; Lester Santiago standing behind the life preserver; and Casimir Paul.

During the 30's Fats Pichon brought his band aboard the *Capitol*. Here he is standing fourth from left. The others, wearing four-in-hands, are trombonist Irving Douroux, banjoist Sam Casimir; Al ———; Clarence "Perch" Thornton and Jack Lamont, trumpet; Harry Lang, saxophone; Manuel Crusto and Willie Casimir, tuba; Ray Brown, trumpet.

In 1958 the NOJC celebrated its tenth anniversary on the Streckfus liner *President*. The function was telecast on the NBC network as part of Dave Garroway's Wide, Wide World. On deck for a breath of fresh air are Bill Russell, whose contributions to the preservation of New Orleans jazz and its history are well known, and Mr. and Mrs. Raymond Burke. The group is standing next to the *President*'s calliope.

The S.S. *Capitol,* largest of the Streckfus line boats, always offered superb music. Leader Fate Marable, here at the piano, probably was the best known bandmaster on the river. His group includes Henry Kimball, Boyd Atkins, Johnny St. Cyr, David Jones, Norman Mason, Louis Armstrong, George Brahear, and Baby Dodds. Early 20's.

236

The S.S. *J.S., photo, courtesy Frederick Way, Jr.*

Somewhere on the Mississippi, aboard the Streckfus steamer "*J.S.*", reedman Meyer Weinberg (Gene Meyer), leader and Emile Guerin, piano, try the calliope. (1931).

The S.S. *Madison* plied the lake during the 30's usually with a quorum of jazzmen aboard. Among them, left to right, are Louis Barbarin, Emanuel Sayles, Eddie Pierson.

The Six and 7/8 String Band aboard the *Aunt Dinah*, a houseboat belonging to Admiral Ernest Lee Jahncke, about 1921. Left to right, kneeling, are Howard McCaleb, Charlie Hardy, Hilton "Midget" Harrison, Edmond Souchon, Bill Gibbens. Standing are Bob Reynolds, Admiral Jahncke, Shields O'Reardon.

Another great Fate Marable band. On the S.S. *Sidney*, another Streckfus boat, in 1918. Left to right are Baby Dodds, Bebé Ridgley, Joe Howard, Louis Armstrong, leader Marable, David Jones, Johnny Dodds, Johnny St. Cyr, Pops Foster.

The S.S. *Capitol* Band in the early 20's included many future jazz stars. Left to right: Harvey Lankford, trombone; Floyd Casey, drums; Sidney Desvigne, trumpet; Ed Allen, cornet, leader; Johnny St. Cyr, banjo; Ike Jefferson, piano; Walter Thomas, Norman Mason, Gene Sedric, reeds; Pops Foster, tuba.

The Tuxedo Jazz Band and the Young Tuxedo Jazz Band. Members of both bands were aboard Admiral Jahncke's yacht for a party in 1923. The musicians of the two bands posed together here are, left to right, seated, Henry Julian, Bush Hall, Willard Thoumy, Lawrence Marrero, John Marrero. Standing, Chinee Foster, Milford Dolliole, Bebé Ridgley, Bob Thomas, Duck Ernest Johnson, Eddie Marrero. *Photo, courtesy of Milford Dolliole.*

The old lake steamer, *Mandeville*, made excursions from West End to Mandeville. It carried horses and buggies—later small cars—so that passengers could use them on the other side of the lake. It then proceeded up the Tchefuncte River and docked near "Three Rivers," making the return trip the same evening. And jazz music all the way.

S.S. *Susquehanna* about 1915–25. Lake Pontchartrain.

NO BUSINESS LIKE
SHOW BUSINESS

References to Louis Armstrong as America's Number One Good-Will Ambassador are now commonplace. New Orleans jazz as an international language is, at last, a fact of twentieth-century life. As these lines are typed, Satch is booked for a visit behind the "iron curtain." Meanwhile, George Lewis' band has toured Japan, and more New Orleans jazz records are sold in Copenhagen than in the entire United States. There is a color feature on Preservation Hall in an Italian magazine, and German TV viewers can enjoy the Eureka Brass Band on superbly produced film. The faces of Pete Fountain and Al Hirt grin at British shoppers from album displays, and we look forward soon to worldwide Telstar programs featuring the stalwart sons of New Orleans.

Since the beginning of the century, the jazz gospel

has been exported via tent shows, medicine shows, revivals, minstrel shows and carnivals, later via vaudeville, radio, motion pictures and now, TV. What was virtually a neighborhood music, essentially functional in character, has, alas, often had to warp its form and style to meet the superficial tastes of an ever growing audience. Indeed, in its earliest touring days, the jazzman faced his audience as a clown or buffoon, his true art finding no listeners. Applauded for his novelty and the eccentricity of his musical conduct, he learned to wear funny hats, rube outfits, striped blazers, convict suits. He performed while standing on his head. He learned to toot two horns at once. He learned to take his instrument apart as he blew, finally coaxing a blues out of his mouthpiece alone.

Later more "sophisticated" audiences permitted themselves to be awed by the musician's ability to sustain a single note through three whole choruses and to marvel at the alacrity with which he managed to play a couple of octaves above the intended range of the horn. Our pioneer cultivated these freak talents assiduously because they put meat on his table and coins in his pocket. More people would pay to hear animal imitations than ingenious polyphony.

Unhappily, as a result, out-of-town audiences of the twenties and thirties never got the chance to hear the true sound of New Orleans jazz. Entrepreneurs applied the pressures to pander to a public to whom music was not a part of daily living, but an occasional exotic thrill. The musician never thought of himself as an artist, but as an entertainer. As long as the pay was attractive he permitted himself to be exhibited rather than presented. But among musicians, it became a cliché that you couldn't work out of town unless you were prepared to play, in their words, "loud, fast and wrong."

Mainly through the issuance of phonograph records, a hard-core serious listening audience developed which eventually provided concert platforms for serious New Orleans jazzmen. Now it is possible for a jazzman to appear before his public wearing street clothes, and, without benefit of mugging or burlesque routines, hold a rapt audience for hours. New Orleans jazz is now performed with dignity once or twice a year in most large cities and on some college campuses. It is even to be seen on television, although rarely.

In these photographs you can see how the New Orleans jazzman looked in the strange environments supplied by show business. Some are superficially funny until you realize the circumstances that forced these great artists into such dress and settings. The situation was equivalent to a Toscanini, because of straitened economic circumstances, having to lead a pit band for a flea circus.

This sometimes depressing portfolio of the jazzman away from home was hard to accumulate and is mainly unpublished. Most of the boys don't look as happy as they do in hometown photos—and we don't wonder.

The Tulanians (1925). During the Roaring Twenties playing jazz was not limited to the lower economic levels. On stage at the Strand theater are, left to right, insurance broker Harry S. Kaufman, Jr.; investment broker Herman S. Kohlmeyer; attorney John M. "Buddy" Gehl; architect William Follansbee; sugar and rice tycoon Alfred Broussard; Gerald "Skinny" Andrus (King Rex of 1963), head of N.O. Public Service and later president of Middle South Services, Inc.; dentist Fred Fridge. Another Tulanian, not shown, is Isidore Newman II, now national president of City Stores, Inc., and owner of Maison Blanche department store.

"Rhapsody in Black and Blue" a Paramount short subject (1931). The film starred Louis Armstrong and his orchestra. *Photo, courtesy of Ernest Smith Collection, John Steiner.*

Jules Bauduc Orchestra (1928). At the Silver Slipper are, left to right, Mike Lala, Luther Lamar, Roland Leach, Monk Hazel, Paul Peque, Jules Bauduc, Horace Diaz, Eddie Powers, Oscar Marcour. *Photo, courtesy Monk Hazel.*

Welcome to Disneyland (1960). Two resident bands greet arriving New Orleans All-stars. On the left, Johnny St. Cyr's Hot Five. St. Cyr is almost hidden, second from left. Clarinetist Paul Barnes and trumpeter Mike Delay are native Orleanians. On the plane steps, arriving from the Crescent City are Thomas Jefferson, trumpet; Paul Barbarin, drums; Frog Joseph, trombone; Raymond Burke, clarinet. Next to Burke is Stanley Mendelson, piano. The uniformed dixieland band on the right is the Straw Hat Six.

Connie Boswell (1955). This member of the famed Crescent City singing trio was a guest on the Tony Almerico Show. *Photo, courtesy Mrs. John Menville.*

The Original New Orleans Owls (1924). At the Old Sazerac Ballroom. Left to right are Dick Mackie, Monk Smith, Red Mackie, Benjy White, Eblen Rau, standing; Rene Gelpi, seated; leader Earl Crumb. *Photo, courtesy Rene Gelpi.*

Sharkey auditions Mickey Rooney (1940's) following the Hadacol medicine show fiasco of the 40's.

The Bobcats (1939). Four of Bob Crosby's eight finest were Orleanians—Ray Bauduc, drums; Nappy Lamare, guitar; Eddie Miller, saxophone; Irving Fazola, clarinet. Bob Crosby is seated, studying the live cat. The others are Bob Haggart, string bass; Jess Stacy, piano; Billy Butterfield, trumpet; Warren Smith, trombone. *Photo, courtesy Ray Bauduc.*

Remnant of fame (1962). Johnny Bayersdorffer stands in front of his old band banner which hangs in the NOJC Museum.

Louis Prima (early 1930's). Left to right are Gene Meyer, Godfrey Hirsch, Louis Prima, Frank Pinero, Frank Federico, Louis Masinter. *Photo, courtesy Duncan P. Schiedt.*

Sharkey tours the Orient (1940's). On the right runningboard is pianist Roy Zimmerman. Joe Rotis is the trombone man. Sharkey is wearing a derby. This photograph was taken in Tokyo.

Manuel Manetta played piano and any other string, brass, or wind instrument. In 1965 he was still teaching music at his home in Algiers, Louisiana.

Crescent City Cutie (1940). Dorothy Lamour takes a paradiddle lesson from maestro Ray Bauduc in Hollywood, as Eddie Miller stands by. *Photo, courtesy Ray Bauduc.*

Henry Saparo, New Orleans, banjoist, and Sidney Bechet, far right, go oriental with Benny Payton's orchestra in Paris. *Photo, courtesy Duncan P. Scheidt.*

Original Dixieland Jazz Band (1938). At the Texas Centennial. Sharkey has replaced Nick La Rocca as trumpet man in the revived group. Larry Shields is on clarinet. Eddie Edwards plays trombone and Tony Spargo holds the drumsticks. The other standing musicians are an unidentified piano player and Harry Barth, string bass.

Sharkey in New York (1930's). The Sharks of Rhythm. The group includes Orleanians Bill Bourgeois, clarinet; and Johnny Castaign, drums. *Photo, courtesy Sharkey.*

Buckley's New Orleans Serenaders (1850's). A minstrel show of the 1850's. This assembly was not from the Crescent City, but its use of this name indicates the prestige already attained by New Orleans music in pre-Civil War days.

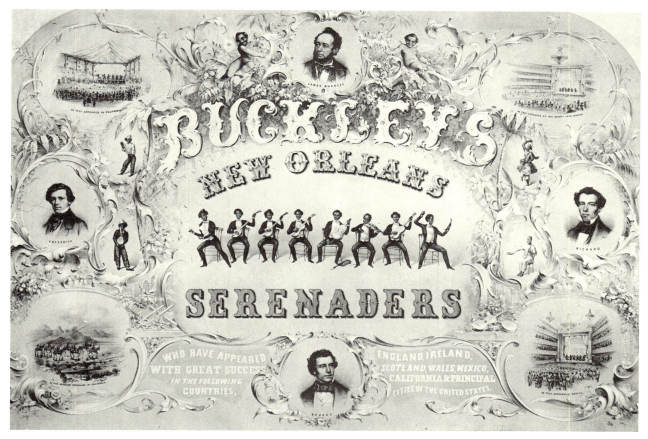

A royal welcome, Chicago style (1915). The king of vaudeville comics Joe Frisco greets Tom Brown's Band From Dixieland at the station. Billy Lambert is the drummer behind Frisco's right hand. Brown, in straw hat, can be seen over Frisco's left shoulder. Next, left to right, wearing caps are Ray Lopez, Larry Shields, and Deacon Loyacano. At the left, leaning on Brown's trombone case is future monarch of the underworld Al Capone. Directly above him, with white handkerchief in breast pocket, is musical comedy star Joe Cook. *Photo, courtesy Mrs. Agnes Brown.*

The legendary Tony Jackson (about 1918). On stage with a trio of "Pretty Babies," including the celebrated Florence Mills. *Photo, courtesy Duncan P. Schiedt.*

The Five Rubes (Tom Brown's Band From Dixieland) on tour in vaudeville. Accompanying dancer Joe Frisco are, left to right, Al Williams, Tom Brown, Ray Lopez, Larry Shields, Deacon Loyacano.

Papa Mutt Carey led this group in Los Angeles in 1924. Included are Leo Davis, sax; Bud Scott, guitar; Ram Hall, drums; L. S. Cooper, piano. Seated right front is trumpeter-leader Carey.

Opera versus jazz (1925). This "duel" took place at the Metropolitan (Paramount) theater in Los Angeles. Representing jazz are "Bayersdorffer's Red Devils."

Clint Brush's Band (1919). Chicago. Two Orleanians, Tom Brown, trombone, and Tony Giardina, clarinet, made this into a jazz band far from home. Leader is on banjo.

Zue Robertson (pre-1920). Zue brought a Crescent City sound to the Kit Carson Wild West Show. He stands second from left. *Photo, courtesy Dave Stuart.*

PROF. TONEY JACKSON

The above cut is a good likeness of Prof. Toney Jackson, Pianist at Russell and Dago.

Mr. Jackson is one of the best entertainers in the city, and is well liked. He is a good card.

Professor Tony Jackson (1912). Featured in an advertising throwaway from a Chicago cabaret.

Barnum and Bailey's Circus (1909). Shows were livened by George McCullum's horn. *Photo, courtesy Mrs. Charlotte Boutney.*

The Blair-Saenger Harmony Hoboes (1933). Taken near the railroad tracks on Basin Street, across from the Saenger theater. In the front row, left to right, are Ellis Stratakos, Jake Gensburger, Johnny Miller, George Brunies, George Schilling, Jr., Joe Capraro. In the back row, Jimmy Rush, Mike Ryan, two unidentified members, Luther Lamar, Marion Suter. *Photo, courtesy Mrs. Ellis Stratakos.*

Making the vaudeville circuit (1917). Left to right are Roy Palmer, Sugar Johnny Smith, Lawrence Duhé, Mamie Lane, Herb Lindsay, Louis Keppard, Montudie Garland. *Photo, courtesy Louis Keppard.*

François and his Louisianians. Francis Mosley, a New Orleans drummer, led this little group in Chicago. The only other Louisianians present are Kid Punch Miller, center, and guitarist Charles Ducasting, right. *Photo, courtesy Punch Miller.*

The band that never was (1914). In rehearsal for an Orpheum Circuit vaudeville tour that didn't materialize, this band of superstars includes: standing, left to right, Clarence Williams, John Lindsay, Jimmie Noone, Bebé Ridgley; seated, left to right, Oscar Celestin, Tom Benton, Johnny St. Cyr. The snare drummer, left front, is Ernest Trepagnier. The violinist, center front, is Armand J. Piron.

The New Orleans Rhythm Masters (1926). This group never played in New Orleans, but appeared at least once in Shreveport. The distinguished lineup includes, front row, left to right, Jack Teagarden, Red Bolman, Sidney Arodin, Charlie Cordilla, drummer Amos Ayala. The others, not "from home" are Terry Shand, piano; George Shaw, vocalist, and, standing, banjoist Jerry Fresno.

The Oliver band in vaudeville (1922). California. Left to right are Ram Hall, Honore Dutrey, King Oliver, Lil Hardin, David Jones, Johnny Dodds, James A. Palao, Montudie Garland. *Photo, courtesy W. C. Allen.*

In the California bay area (1921–22). Here, for a while, the Kid Ory Original Creole Jazz Band held forth. Left to right are Baby Dodds, Kid Ory, Mutt Carey, Ed Garland, Wade Whaley.

Richard M. Jones's Jazz Wizards entertained in the 20's. Left to right are Jones, Johnny St. Cyr, Albert Nicholas.

Brass section of Joe Robichaux's Big Swing Band (late 30's). Seated are Kildee Holloway, John "Turk" Girard, Gene Ware. Standing are Frog Joseph, Clement Tervalon.

The Argentine Dons (1930's). These were all Orleanians under the direction of Slim Lamar. Left to right are Tony Almerico, Irwin Kurz, unidentified, Jimmy Rush, unidentified, Slim Lamar, unidentified, Von Gammon, George Schilling, Jr., Steve Messico, Ellis Stratakos. The central figure below the stairs is the master of ceremonies. This picture was made at the Peabody Hotel, Memphis.

King Zulu (1949). The king was Louis Armstrong, who also brought his All-Stars for a concert.

New Orleans Police Department Minstrels (1920). Seated, front, left, Major Fenerty, Dominick Barocco. Standing, left to right, Freddie Williams, Joe Vitari, Manny Blessing, Yellow Nunez, Alex Coulon.

On the Road (1930). Posed on running board of this 1925 Studebaker is Charlie Cordilla in fashion-approved plus fours and argyle sox. Right behind him is trumpeter Bill Gillen. Opposite, in dark coat is Joe Capraro, behind him, Leo Adde.

Catskills or Bust (1930). This jalopy carried a whole band from New Orleans. Charlie Cordilla, Martin Abraham, Bill Gillen, Leo Adde, Sidney Arodin, Red Jessup were all aboard, besides the driver, Joe Capraro, seen seated on the front fender.

Sal Margiotta (cl) with Governor Jimmy Davis at the police convention in Shreveport, 1960.

Gene Austin's accompanists, 1934. Center, Monk Hazel; right, Coco Himel. On the left is the second "Candy" who replaced the original Candy Candido.

A NEW ORLEANS JAZZ
FAMILY ALBUM

New Orleans jazzmen "at home" are far different from the kind of individuals jazz musicians are considered to be by most of the public. The marijuana-smoking, gin-guzzling, hip-talking "cat" who turns night into day belongs to a different place, a different time, a different music.

Your Crescent City jazzman is usually a family man. In most cases he has more children than the average parent. Usually he has a full-time occupation outside the music business. Alcoholics, narcotic addicts, homosexuals are rare in this fraternity. Few have ever been in serious trouble with the law.

So, when you consider the size of our "family," it's obvious that there is reason for some pride as we introduce them to you at home and at play in these informal photographs.

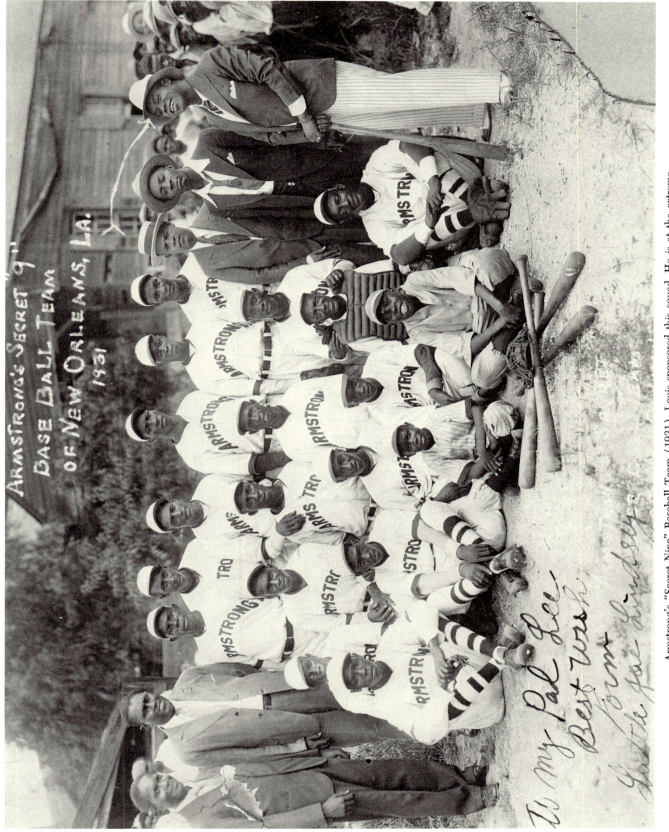

Armstrong's "Secret Nine" Baseball Team (1931). Louis sponsored this squad. He is at the extreme right. Next to him are Sherman Cook, a radio announcer, and Little Joe Lindsey in the straw skimmer.

Mardi Gras (1946). Bunk Johnson, trumpet; Jim Robinson, trombone; George Lewis, clarinet, help celebrate.

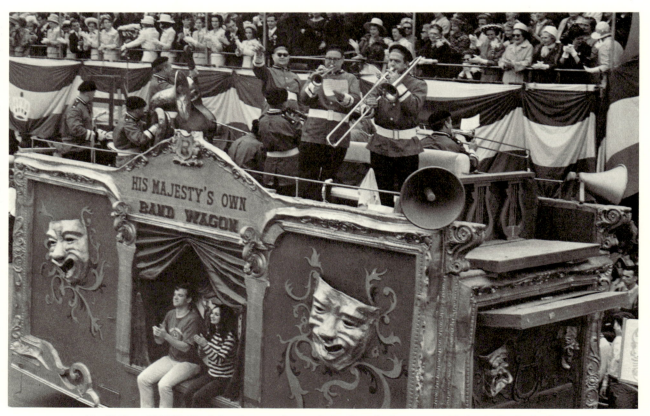

Mardi Gras (1966). Rex's bandwagon featured the Crawford-Ferguson Night Owls. Co-leader Crawford is facing trombone; Jack Bachman, trumpet; Al Rose (dark glasses) is "bandmaster."

Emergency Relief Administration Band (Jan. 15, 1935). Jackson Square. Front row, left to right: First five unknown, Wilfred Ledet, Happy Goldston, Cié Frazier, Louis Dumaine, Dave Ogden, Abby Williams, Judge Riley, Raymond ——, —— Ridgley, Alphonse Johnson. Second row: Paul Moliere, Jimmy Clayton, unknown, Richard McLean, Raymond Glapion, Son Thomas, Lionel Tapo, Ernest Trepagnier, Peter Raphael, Emile Knox, Sam Morgan, unknown, Douglas Hood, Eddie Morgan, Leo Songier, Ernest Penn, Alcide Landry, Kid Shots Madison. Third row: unknown, unknown, Bob Antler, Kid Harrison, Gilbert Young, unknown (almost hidden), unknown, Ricard Alexis, Charlie Peterson, unknown, Burke Stevenson, next three unknown, Henry Russ, unknown, Sonny Williams, Wilbert Tillman, George McCullum, Jr., unknown, William Brown, unknown. Fourth row: Albert Ganier, unknown, Frankie Duson, Oscar Henry, Sunny Henry, Joe Harris, Isaiah Robinson, Israel Gorman, Melvin Frank, next four unknown, Albert Jones, —— Green, unknown, Arthur ——, Joe Morris. Fifth Row: Pinchback Touro, unknown, Tom Steptoe, unknown, John Anchor, unknown, —— Taylor, Eddie Morris, unknown, unknown, Andrew Morgan, Manuel Paul, unknown, Alan "Hunter" Gordet, unknown, unknown, Eddie Edward, Harold Davis, unknown, unknown, Ernest Poree, Frank Crump, Tats Alexander.

Jazz Little Leaguers of 1910. All three little boys went to the big league of jazz. Buck Rogers, snare drum; Abbie Brunies, cornet; George Brunies, alto horn. The youngsters played for tips on street cars. The picture was taken at the carbarn, Arabella and Magazine streets.

City Slickers (about 1918). Chicago. Freddie Keppard, seated, and Sidney Bechet.

Some of the Founding Fathers of Jazz (1944). Left to right are Big Eye Louis Nelson Delisle, Pops Foster, Willie Santiago, Sidney Bechet, Albert Glenny, Alphonse Picou. The picture was taken in front of the office of Dr. Leonard Bechet.

Bunk Johnson (1949). On the steps of Mahogany Hall. *Photo, courtesy Mrs. John Menville.*

Frankie Duson, right (about 1922). At home. *Photo, courtesy Dave Stuart.*

Concert in the Parisian Room (1948). Left to right are Roy Zimmerman, Joe Loyacano, Frank Federico, Sharkey, Monk Hazel, Irving Fazola, Julian Laine, Buglin' Sam Dekemel. *Photo, courtesy Lee Tilton.*

Clarinet Trust (1955). Left to right are Raymond Burke, Tony Parenti, Harry Shields. Photo taken at wedding reception for Mr. & Mrs. "Little Abbie" Brunies in Joe Mares' patio

Alphonse Picou, left, and Oscar Celestin, right, with Mrs. John Menville at the NOJC Congo Square festival in 1951. Mrs. Menville was for many years secretary of the organization.

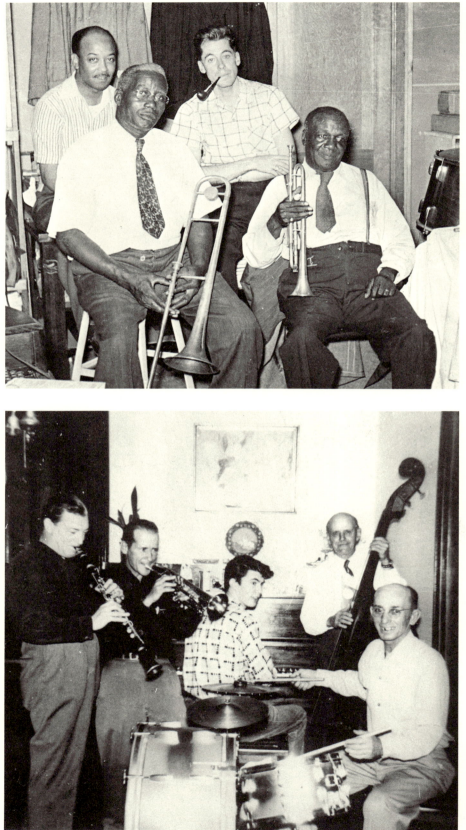

Record Session (1949). The meeting featured rarely photographed Kid Avery and Wooden Joe Nicholas. In the rear, left, Danny Barker looks on.

Fun in the Parlor (1950's). The parlor belongs to trumpet man Albert Artigues. Others are Raymond Burke, clarinet; Johnny McGee, piano; Bill Walde, string bass; Katz Maestri, drums.

Dr. Leonard V. Bechet (1946).
Photo, courtesy Mrs. John Menville.

Milneburg Joys (1920's). Raymond Burke, left, and his uncle, Leo "Dookey" Cassard disport themselves at the lakefront.

Future Jazz Greats (1912). Rehearsal in front of a brewery at Jackson Avenue and Tchopitoulas Street. Holding instruments are, left to right, Happy Schilling, trombone; ten-year-old George Brunies, Abbie Brunies, Harry Shannon, Richie Brunies, cornet; Bud Loyacano, drums.

Storyville Alumni (1944). In front, left to right, are Big Eye Louis Nelson Delisle and Sidney Bechet. At the back are Alphonse Picou, Manuel Perez, Willie Santiago.

Watchin' All the Girls Go By (1956). Left to right are Eddie Pierson, Jim Robinson, Kid Howard, Chester Jones, Louis Gallaud, Jim Little.

Desvigne's Bandsmen Take a Break on the S.S. *Island Queen* (about 1929). Left to right are Louis Nelson, Percy Servier, Fats Pichon, Henry Julian, Gene Ware, Ransom Knowling.

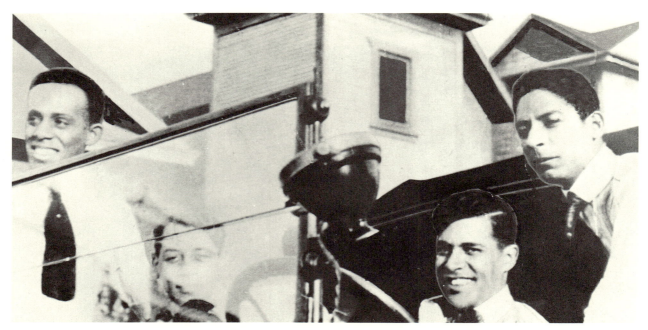

Jelly Roll Morton, right (1917). Los Angeles. Taken while he was doing a "single" in vaudeville. *Photo, courtesy Duncan Schiedt.*

Burnell Santiago (1930's). The New Orleans piano man is shown here with Sidney Pflueger, guitar, and Ollie Papa, string bass. *Photo, courtesy George Hoefer.*

284

Professor Manuel Manetta (top), Oscar "Sonny" Celestin (bottom). In later years he was called "Papa," but in 1924, when this photograph was taken, he was still called "Sonny."

Ready to March (about 1912). Left to right are Honore Dutrey, Louis Warnick, George McCullum, Sr. *Photo, courtesy Mrs. Charlotte McCullum Boutney.*

Kid Rena (about 1931). The gang from the Gypsy Tea Room. The men in the front row are Harold Dejan, Kid Rena, Burke Stevenson. Behind Rena is his brother, Joe Rena. Third from right is Clarence Tisdale. Behind Dejan is Pleasant "Smilin' Joe" Joseph.

The New Orleans Jazz Club is Born (1948). Kneeling, front row, left, Frank Federico; right, Don Perry. Standing, Boojie Centobie, Armand Hug, Freddie King, Al Diket, Gilbert Erskine, Julian Laine, Johnny Wiggs, Chink Martin.

Manuel Perez (1944). Shown in his last days. *Photo, courtesy "Scoop" Kennedy.*

Jelly Roll Morton (about 1938). This picture was taken by Danny Barker. *Photo, courtesy Duncan P. Schiedt.*

Holmes Band of Lutcher in 1910. Left to right are David Jones, Floyd Jackson, Nub Jacobs, Henry Sawyer (said to be the first jazz band slide trombonist), leader Professor Anthony Holmes, Dennis Harris, John Porter, Joe Porter.

Don Juans of the High Seas (1919). These 20th-century versions, Tony Spargo, left, and suave Emile Christian find a pair of fair damsels on shipboard as they sail for England. With other ODJB men Nick La Rocca and Larry Shields, they were about to introduce dixieland to the British Isles.

Lakefront Loungers (about 1920). Abbie Brunies, Charlie Cordilla, Stalebread Lacoume at West End.

A Pair of "Cake-Eaters" (1915). Tom Brown, left, and Larry Shields. *Photo, courtesy Harry Shields.*

Alfred "Pantsy" Laine in His Western Union uniform.

Long's Blacksmith Shop (1898). Left to right are Frank Christian, Jack Laine at the anvil, John Cazzeaux. The others are unidentified. Laine was already organizing and training men for his bands.

Two Sheiks from New Orleans (1918). Eddie Shields, left, and Emile Christian pose for their fans. *Photo, courtesy Harry Shields.*

Louis Prima's First Band (about 1922). Left to right are Louis Prima, Ewell Lamar, unknown, Irving Fazola, Johnny Viviano, and unknown.

Smoky Mary. This train carried merry-makers to Milneburg via Elysian Fields Avenue for fifteen cents.

Members of Tom Brown's Band From Dixieland (1915). Members sent this shot home from Lamb's Cafe in Chicago. Billy Lambert is seated. Standing are Deacon Loyacano, Ray Lopez, Gussie Mueller.

Jack Laine (1919). Laine brings his band to an open-air theater in Alexandria, Louisiana. Here, he's seen playing drums. The piano man is Jules Reiner, with Herman Ragas on the bass. Seated on the piano, left to right, are Baby Laine, George Brunies, Charlie Cordilla. *Photo, courtesy Jack Laine.*

King of the Zulus (1949). For that year's Mardi Gras, Louis Armstrong came home to accept the crown.

Four New Orleans Kids (1930's). On a Victor record session. Soprano saxman on left is Sidney Bechet; drummer in rear center is Zutty Singleton; Albert Nicholas plays clarinet, center; and Jelly Roll Morton grins at the piano. The outlander on the trumpet is Sidney De Paris.

Kid Moliere (about 1937). Moliere heads the band for this party at an uptown bistro. Dave Bailey plays the drums.

294

Buglin' Sam's Waffle Wagon. Buglin' Sam really used his valveless horn in 1921 to sell waffles (four for five cents) from this wagon. The senior Dekemel is the chef. The little lady in black is Sam's mother.

Chester Zardis and tuba. Chester began thinking like a bass player when he was only fifteen.

Norman Brownlee was one of the first amateur pilots. Here, in 1925, with his plane for a back-drop, he shakes hands with Joe Loyacano.

Jelly Roll Morton was in vaudeville in 1917. Jelly is third from left, and the lady in front of him is "Bricktop" who, years later, became a celebrated cafe owner in Paris. This photo was taken in Los Angeles. *Courtesy, Floyd Levin.*

TILL THE BUTCHER
CUT HIM DOWN

To pretend that New Orleans jazz as we have known it will go on forever is whistling in the dark. The jazz form cannot die, it's true, but very soon there won't be anybody around to play it. The music of the century is in its final, though exuberant, years. Even as this volume was in preparation, literally dozens of the titans of jazz departed from the scene, none replaced by stars of a rising generation. In the course of our work we have regretfully penned in the death dates of such as Tom Brown, Alphonse Picou, Nick La Rocca, Papa John Joseph, Joe Robichaux, Lester Santiago, Happy Schilling, Kid Howard, Papa Jack Laine, and Johnny St. Cyr—the list is longer than we like to think about.

We have selected the photos in this section because they do illustrate some social and historical facts about New Orleans jazz that no words can. The fierce pride in their art that has led some to claim for themselves the paternity of jazz even unto having it chiseled on their headstones is at first amusing, then dramatic. The unmarked grave of Bunk Johnson near his home in New Iberia, Louisiana, clearly demonstrates how little conscious the local folk are of the cultural importance of the great music; while Sidney Bechet's black marble crypt gleams in oriental splendor near Paris as a testimonial to the idolatry in which the jazz pioneers are held elsewhere in the world.

Funerals of fellow musicians seem a little sadder, the dirges a trace more lugubrious than other funerals. The faces of the survivors in these pictures seem to convey this. We see them here as pall-bearers and mourners. And, alas, we shall see them with increasing frequency in this role.

But don't for a minute think they're not going out in a blaze of glory. There's more great jazz being played in New Orleans today than since the heyday of Milneburg—and if you hurry on down you can still hear it in superb form. While he lives, the Crescent City jazzman continues to blow up an unabating storm.

Too soon, the butcher will cut him down—but until that unfortunate day, he'll ramble and he'll ramble.

"World's First Man in Jazz"
is inscribed on Nick La Rocca's tomb.

Leon Roppolo's tomb.

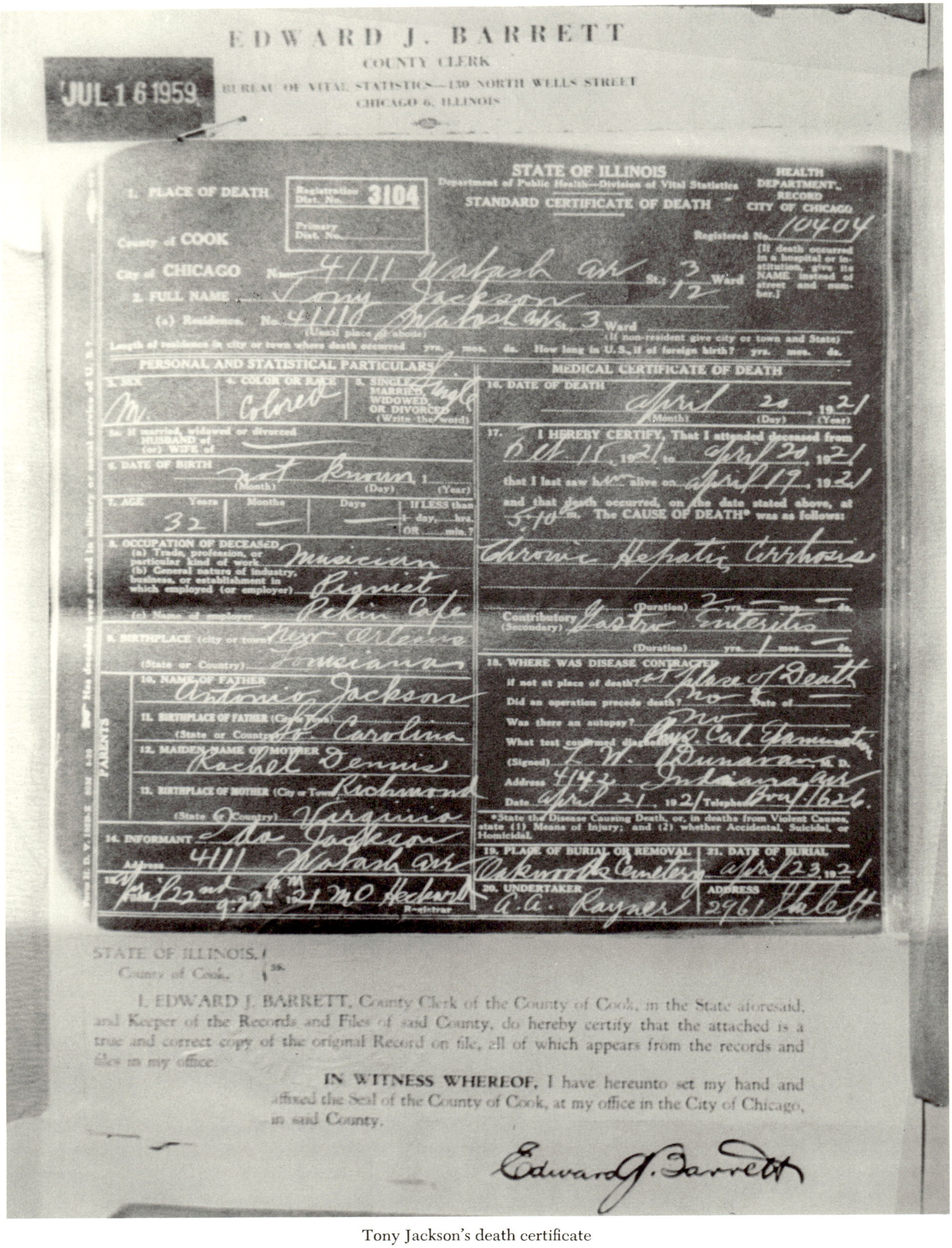

EDWARD J. BARRETT
COUNTY CLERK
BUREAU OF VITAL STATISTICS—130 NORTH WELLS STREET
CHICAGO 6, ILLINOIS

JUL 16 1959

STATE OF ILLINOIS
Department of Public Health—Division of Vital Statistics
STANDARD CERTIFICATE OF DEATH
HEALTH DEPARTMENT, RECORD CITY OF CHICAGO

1. PLACE OF DEATH
Registration Dist. No. 3104
Primary Dist. No.
County of COOK
Registered No. 10404
City of CHICAGO No. 4111 Wabash av St.; 3 12 Ward
(If death occurred in a hospital or institution, give its NAME instead of street and number.)
2. FULL NAME Tony Jackson
(a) Residence. No. 4111 Wabash av St. 3 Ward
(Usual place of abode) (If non-resident give city or town and State)
Length of residence in city or town where death occurred yrs. mos. ds. How long in U.S., if of foreign birth? yrs. mos. ds.

PERSONAL AND STATISTICAL PARTICULARS
3. SEX M.
4. COLOR OR RACE Colored
5. SINGLE, MARRIED, WIDOWED OR DIVORCED (Write the word) Single
5a. If married, widowed or divorced HUSBAND of (or) WIFE of
6. DATE OF BIRTH not known (Month) (Day) (Year)
7. AGE 32 Years — Months — Days If LESS than 1 day, hrs. OR min.
8. OCCUPATION OF DECEASED (a) Trade, profession, or particular kind of work Musician
(b) General nature of industry, business, or establishment in which employed (or employer) Pianist
(c) Name of employer Pekin Cafe
9. BIRTHPLACE (city or town) New Orleans
(State or Country) Louisiana
PARENTS
10. NAME OF FATHER Antonio Jackson
11. BIRTHPLACE OF FATHER (City or Town) (State or Country) So. Carolina
12. MAIDEN NAME OF MOTHER Rachel Dennis
13. BIRTHPLACE OF MOTHER (City or Town) Richmond
(State or Country) Virginia
14. INFORMANT Ida Jackson
Address 4111 Wabash av
15. Filed April 22nd 1921 M.O. Heckard Registrar

MEDICAL CERTIFICATE OF DEATH
16. DATE OF DEATH April 20 1921 (Month) (Day) (Year)
17. I HEREBY CERTIFY, That I attended deceased from Feb 15, 1921, to April 20, 1921
that I last saw him alive on April 19, 1921
and that death occurred, on the date stated above, at 5.40 a.m. The CAUSE OF DEATH* was as follows:
Chronic Hepatic Cirrhosis
(Duration) 2 yrs. mos. ds.
Contributory (Secondary) Gastro Enteritis
(Duration) yrs. 1 mos. ds.
18. WHERE WAS DISEASE CONTRACTED if not at place of death? at Place of Death
Did an operation precede death? No Date of
Was there an autopsy? No
What test confirmed diagnosis? Phys. Cal. Examination
(Signed) L. W. Dunavan M.D.
Address 4142 Indiana av
Date April 21, 1921 Telephone Dou. 1626
*State the Disease Causing Death, or, in deaths from Violent Causes, state (1) Means of Injury; and (2) whether Accidental, Suicidal, or Homicidal.
19. PLACE OF BURIAL OR REMOVAL Oakwoods Cemetery
21. DATE OF BURIAL April 23, 1921
20. UNDERTAKER G.A. Rayner
ADDRESS 2961 State St

STATE OF ILLINOIS, County of Cook, } ss.

I, EDWARD J. BARRETT, County Clerk of the County of Cook, in the State aforesaid, and Keeper of the Records and Files of said County, do hereby certify that the attached is a true and correct copy of the original Record on file, all of which appears from the records and files in my office.

IN WITNESS WHEREOF, I have hereunto set my hand and affixed the Seal of the County of Cook, at my office in the City of Chicago, in said County.

Edward J. Barrett

Tony Jackson's death certificate

Alphonse Picou's funeral. New Orleans, Louisiana, February 9, 1961. The Eureka Brass Band at graveside.

Funeral of John Casimir.

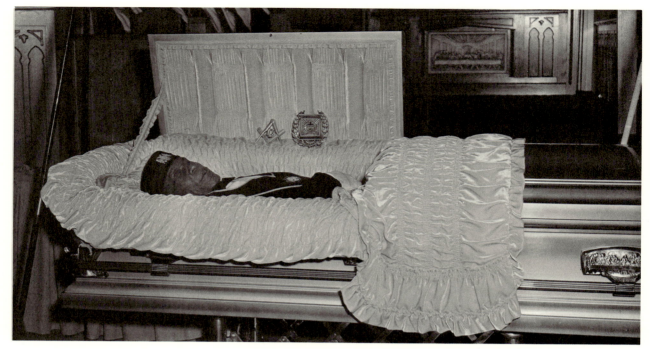

Oscar "Papa" Celestin lies in state, 1954.

Jelly Roll Morton's grave, Los Angeles, California. *Photo, courtesy Floyd Levin.*

Bunk Johnson's unmarked grave, New Iberia, Louisiana. In the
Negro Catholic cemetery.

Kid Rena is laid to rest (1949). Eddie Summers and Alec Bigard,
left and right, are pall bearers. *Photo, courtesy "Scoop" Kennedy.*

"Originator of Jazz Music" is the claim on the headstone of
Stalebread Lacoume.

Sidney Bechet reposes in marble splendor, Paris, France. *Photo,
courtesy Charles Delauney.*

SUPPLEMENT

WHO'S WHO IN NEW ORLEANS JAZZ

BABIN, AL (d). b. N.O., Sept. 10, 1927. Leading dixieland drummer has had top assignments. Santo Pecora, Sharkey, *et al.*

BAZOON, OTIS (cl). b. N.O., Feb. 19, 1947. French Market Jazz Band, Dukes of Dixieland.

BAPTISTE, MILTON (t). b. N.O. Young Olympia Brass Band, Preservation Hall with Harold Dejan.

BERGEN, STUART "RED HOTT" (t). b. N.O., July 8, 1911. Career spans fifty years in jazz. With Tom Brown, Irving Fazola, Larry Shields, other major stars.

CALLISTE, LESTER A., JR. (tb) b. N.O., Aug. 13, 1947. Grandnephew of Buddy Petit. Olympia Brass Band, Young Tuxedo Brass Band.

CAMPO, MURPHY (t). b. Delacroix, Island, La., Dec. 30, 1935. House bandleader at Famous Door since 1968. Long time on road with Big Tiny Little.

CHAFFE, JOHN (bjo, tu, mdl). b. N.O., March 29, 1938. Banjo virtuoso, cofounder of "The Last Straws." Is recorded with Doc Souchon as "The Banjo Bums."

CHRISTENSEN, SIEGFRIED (p). b. N.O., Oct. 27, 1907. Outstanding dixieland pianist of the 20's. Retired from music to practice law.

STUART BERGEN ("RED HOTT")

LARS EDEGRAN

ORANGE KELLIN

JOE MARES

CRUSTO, MANUEL (cl, s, t). b. N.O., May 2, 1918. With Fats Pichon on the S.S. *Capitol* in the 30's and 40's. Often heard through 1977 at Heritage Hall, Preservation Hall.

DEMOND, FRANK (tb, bjo). b. Los Angeles, April 3, 1933. Preservation Hall Jazz Band. One of few younger musicians able to play correctly in the Kid Ory-Jim Robinson tradition.

EDEGRAN, LARS IVAR (p, g, cl, s, l). b. Stockholm, 1944. Moved to New Orleans 1966. Leader, New Orleans Ragtime Orchestra; International Jazz Band. Played with Sharkey, Alvin Alcorn, New Orleans Joymakers. Recorded with Kid Thomas, George Lewis, Jim Robinson, "Dee Dee" Pierce.

EDWARDS, JOHNNY (d). b. N.O., 1922; d. Lorman, Miss., Dec. 21, 1973. Basin St. Six, Dukes of Dixieland, Al Hirt, Pete Fountain.

FERBOS, LIONEL (t). b. N.O., July 17, 1911. New Orleans Ragtime Orchestra.

FINOLA, GEORGE (t). b. Chicago, Oct. 5, 1945. Student of Johnny Wiggs. Regular on Bourbon St. 1970–75.

GUTIERREZ, SAL (d). b. N.O., 1905; d. Aug. 10, 1974. Dixielander played with top N.O. names.

HALL, ANDREW (d). b. Chesterfield, Eng., Oct. 5, 1944. Played in Society Jazz Band with Tony Fougerat, and with Mike Casimir's band in England.

HARDY, CHARLES J. (uk). b. N.O., 1895; d. Sept. 22, 1966. Original member of the "Six & 7/8 Band."

HILL, SCOTT (tb). b. N.O., Oct. 7, 1947. Leader of French Market Jazz Band.

JONES, JOHN L. (g). b. N.O., Dec. 12, 1910.

KELLIN, ORANGE (cl). b. Sweden, 1944. Moved to New Orleans, 1966. Associated with Lars Edegran. Leader, New Orleans Joymakers on European tours. New Orleans Ragtime Orchestra. Frequently at Famous Door, Maison Bourbon.

LEWIS, "FATHER AL" (bjo, g, vo) b. N.O., Aug. 8, 1903. Preservation Hall; With N.O. Joymakers.

LEWIS, WALTER (p, b). b. N.O., Sept. 2, 1918. With Louis Cottrell, Alvin Alcorn.

LESLIE MUSCUTT

WILLIAM RUSSELL

MARES, JOSEPH P. (cl). b. N.O., Aug. 20, 1908. Made great contributions to jazz, mainly as founder of Southland Records and by promoting great New New Orleans jazzmen. Younger brother of famed New Orleans Rhythm Kings leader Paul Mares, Joe had opportunity to play with those stars in his youth.

MASSICOT, PERCY "BUTZ" (d). b. N.O., May 11, 1910. Dixieland drummer very popular with musicians. Spent many years in Roosevelt Hotel (now Fairmont) dance orchestra.

MINOR, ANDERSON (tu). b. N.O., Sept. 20, 1901; d. N.O., Nov. 22, 1973. Young Tuxedo Brass Band, Young Olympia Brass Band. A familiar figure as a grand marshal in street parades.

MINYARD, FRANK (t). b. N.O., Aug. 30, 1930. Coroner of the City of New Orleans. Played with Pete Fountain, sometimes with French Market Jazz Band.

MIX, WES (t). b. N.O., Oct. 9, 1946. French Market Jazz Band.

MOLIERE, FRANK "LI'L PAPA" (p). b. N.O., Oct. 4, 1914. Reactivated as a jazzman in the late 60's. Often heard at the kitty halls and Maison Bourbon.

MORAND, MORRIS (d). b. N.O., *ca.* 1903. Brother of Herb Morand. Played with Tommy Ladnier, Sidney Bechet.

MUSCUTT, LESLIE (bjo, g). b. Barrows-In-Furness, Eng., Jan. 30, 1941. Outstanding jazzman made himself a place among top jazzmen during 70's. French Market Jazz Band.

NAUNDORF, FRANK (tb). b. Dresden, Ger. 1940. Society Jazz Band.

PAULIN, ERNEST "DOC" (t). b. N.O., *ca.* 1902. A non-union leader of small dance and street parade bands.

PISTORIUS, STEVE (p). b. Port Sulphur, La., Nov. 16, 1954. New Orleans' only specialist in classic piano rags. Worked at Gateway Lounge on Bourbon St., 1974–75. On the *Admiral* and *Robert E. Lee* riverboats in St. Louis in 1976. Had a long run at the Levee in Ft. Myers, Fla.

PRESTON, WALTER (bjo). b. N.O., *ca.* 1880. With Punch Miller in 1915.

PREVOST, JAMES (b). b. Houma, La., Feb. 7, 1919. Polished musician who became active in the jazz scene in 1961 at the Paddock with Octave Crosby. Regular performer at Preservation Hall.

RAPHAEL, PETER (d). b. N.O., 1905; d. N.O., May 5, 1963. Rhythm man of the Eureka Brass Band.

ROUZON, OSCAR (s). b. N.O., Jan. 10, 1912. With Young Tuxedo Brass Band, many dance bands.

RUSSELL, WILLIAM (v). b. Canton, Mo., Aug. 26, 1905. Distinguished jazz archivist, writer, composer, and musician. Regular member of the New Orleans Ragtime Orchestra.

HERMAN SHERMAN

BLANCHE THOMAS

JOE TERREGANO

CLIVE WILSON

SCHREINER, TONY (d). b. N.O., *ca.* 1912. Dixieland drummer often seen under leadership of Tony Fougerat.

SHERMAN, HERMAN E. (as, ts), b. N.O., 1923. With George Williams, Eureka Brass Bands. Leader of Young Tuxedo Brass Band since 1972.

SIMPSON, RON (g, bjo). b. London, Jan. 17, 1935. Society Jazz Band.

STEWART, ALONZO (d). b. N.O., Apr. 13, 1919. Regularly seen in Preservation Hall especially with Kid Thomas, Harold Dejan.

SUTER, MARION (p). b. N.O., *ca.* 1903; d. N.O., Aug. 3, 1974. Dixieland pianist with most of the popular bands of the 30's, 40's, 50's.

THOMAS, BLANCHE (vo). b. N.O.; d. N.O., April 20, 1977. Blues singer. Veteran entertainer on Bourbon St. since the 40's. Dixieland Hall in the 60's Heritage Hall in the 70's.

TORREGANO, JOSEPH C. (cl) b. New Orleans, Feb. 28, 1952. With Doc Paulin's Dixieland Band 1970–71), Fairview Brass Band (1971–72). Also, Gibson Brass Band, Young Tuxedo, Onward, Olympia Brass Bands.

TOYAMA, YOSHIO (t). b. Tokyo, March 5, 1944. Came to New Orleans with wife, Keiko (bjo) and made sensational impression among cognoscenti. Returned to Japan Oct., 1969, and organized a New Orleans jazz band. Since then he has toured the United States and Europe with Barry Martyn's International Jazz Band and has been on the road with Alton Purnell and Louis Nelson.

WILSON, CLIVE (t). b. London, Aug. 19, 1942. Arrived 1964 became one of most authentic lead horns in town. Studied with Johnny Wiggs.

YANCY, MELVIN (b). b. N.O., June 9, 1922. Veteran musician, playing in 1977 with the Society Jazz Band.

The French Market Jazz Band. Left to right: Otis Bazoon, clarinet; Dr. Frank Minyard, trumpet; Art Langston, tuba; Scott Hill, leader, trombone; Walter Lastie, drums; Les Muscutt, banjo; David Lastie, saxophone. *Photo Johnny Donnels*

A JAZZ BAND BALL

FRENCH MARKET JAZZ BAND. Street band playing for tips in French Quarter in ancient tradition. Wes Mix, Dr. Frank Minyard, t; Scott Hill, tb, l; Otis Bazoon, cl; David Lastie, s; Les Muscutt, bjo, g; Pete Vriondes, tu; Walter Lastie, d.

NEW LEVIATHAN ORIENTAL FOX-TROT ORCHESTRA. A large orchestra playing tunes of the period 1890–1920, including classic rags and Jelly Roll Morton numbers. Plays numerous sellout concerts in New Orleans area. Talented comic vocalist, George Schmidt.

NEW ORLEANS JOYMAKERS. Sensationally successful on European tours. Percy Humphrey, t; Louis Nelson, tb; Orange Kellin, cl; Lars Edegran, p; "Father Al" Lewis, g, bjo; Chester Zardis, b; Louis Barbarin, d.

NEW ORLEANS RAGTIME ORCHESTRA. Organized 1967. Plays classic rags, cakewalks, other material of era 1890–1915. Performs over United States and Europe. William Russell, v; Lionel Ferbos, t; Paul Crawford, tb; Orange Kellin, cl; Lars Edegran, p, l; Walter Payton, Jr., b; John Robichaux, d, vo.

SOCIETY JAZZ BAND. An "international" band with Tony Fougerat, t; Ernest Poree, s; and Melvin Yancy, b, of New Orleans; Ron Simpson, g, bjo; Andrew Hall, d, of England; and Frank Naundorf, tb, of Germany. This band has been playing regularly (1974–75) at the Maple Leaf Club in the Carrollton section of New Orleans.

The New Leviathan Oriental Fox-trot Orchestra.

The New Orleans Joymakers, London, 1972. Front, left to right: Louis Nelson, Father Al Lewis. Rear: Percy Humphrey, Orange Kellin, Chester Zardis, Louis Barbarin, Lars Edegran.

WHERE'S WHERE IN NEW ORLEANS JAZZ

BOUDIO'S GARDEN was a Milneburg resort at the end of the main street, before the piers. White jazzmen were always featured here, notably Harry Shields.

BRUNING'S PAVILION, on Shell Road in West End featured gambling and great music in the 20's and 30's. Merritt Brunies favored the place, but all the dixielanders played there.

COLUMBIA PARK on the Bayou St. John opposite Southern Park had a few poorly kept rides, but mainly it was a picnic ground. Families came there for recreation and sometimes brought their own bands with them.

CRESCENT PARK in Algiers sometimes had ball games, but otherwise it was for general recreational use. Henry Allen, Sr., often played there with his band.

CRESCENT PARK in Gretna frequently had Emmett Hardy and Sidney Arodin playing for picnics.

ELMIRA PLEASURE GROUNDS, Belleville and Evalina Sts., Algiers, was kept up by several lodges and burial societies. Brass bands like Henry Allen's rehearsed there.

LAKEVIEW PARK. Terminal, West End, on the Electric Railroad. Private clubs maintained headquarters around here during the Gay Nineties, mainly featuring traveling attractions. Ben Harney, the "Creator of Ragtime" played here at the Magenta Club in 1897.

NEW DIXIE PARK, Bienville and Olympia Sts. The big feature was a wading pool, but there were picnics with music, too.

PECAN GROVE, near Harvey's Canal, Gretna. Beer and dancing under the stars to the music of Elton Theodore or even Chris Kelly.

PERSEVERANCE HALL #4, Dumaine and St. Claude. Once the site of Masonic dances with music by the likes of Kid Rena, or even the Tonic Triad Band. It still stands in the middle of the Louis Armstrong Park jazz complex and is soon to become a jazz theater, featuring films of N.O. jazzmen.

PYTHIAN HALL, Bermuda St., Algiers. Favorite spot for weddings and dances. Manuel Perez, Bunk Johnson, Edouard Clem played here.

RIVERSIDE PARK, Dauphine and Andry Sts. Tent shows, traveling carnivals, midway gambling games. Local jazzmen hired to play "pit" jobs for minstrel shows. Eli Green shows played here.

SOUTHERN PARK. Bayou St. John via Esplanade cars. Known in pre-Civil War days as Tivoli Gardens. Built on the old Allard Plantation.

SOUTHERN RIFLE CLUB HALL, Claiborne Ave. near Marigny St. A dirty old saloon of the barrelhouse variety where some good piano players could be heard, notably, in the 30's, Burnell Santiago.

STOLTZ'S UNION HALL, 132–34 Exchange Place. This was an old fashioned barroom where idle white musicians would gather and drink.

THOMAN'S HALL, Dauphine near Elmira St. Some dancing, but also boxing matches. Pre-World I.

WASHINGTON GARDEN, Milneburg. Not on the piers. Much like a German beer garden. Dixieland jazz and barbershop quartets.

The Reliance Brass Band, 1914, in the first film ever made of Mardi Gras. From a French (Gaumont) newsreel.

Old Spanish Fort showing the "Frolic," lower left, 1924. *Photo courtesy Joe Mares*

ILLUSTRATIONS

Louis Armstrong, left, when he joined King Oliver
in Chicago.

An army of New Orleans stars turned out for "Little Abbie" Brunies' wedding reception on
May 24, 1954. Standing, left to right: Sharkey, Paul Edwards, Jack Delaney, Harry Shields,
Stanley Mendelson, Raymond Burke, Tony Parenti, Sherwood Mangiapane, Santo Pecora.
Kneeling: Joe Mares, Chink Martin. Behind Martin is Bill Huntington. At the drums is the
guest of honor. Photo made in Mares' patio.

Louis and Lil Armstrong right after their marriage in the mid-20's. *Photo courtesy Joe Mares.*

The Waifs' Home and its administrator, Captain Joseph Jones, during the period of Louis Armstrong's residency.

Part of Wingy Manone's band in 1930. Left to right: Sidney
Arodin, Wingy, George Brunies, Bobby Laine.

Henry Brunies.

Martin Abraham welcomed to Chicago, May 24, 1923.

The Arcadian Serenaders.

Paul Mares, top, and George Brunies arrive in Chicago in 1922.

Naylor's Seven Aces, 1924. Back row: Bill Creger, clarinet; Charles Hartmann, trombone; Jules Bauduc, banjo; Oliver Naylor, piano, leader. Front: Louis Darrough, drums; Newton Richardson, tenor sax; Pinky Gerbrecht, cornet.

Wingy Manone organized a different Arcadian Serenaders band for this 1924 Okeh date. They cut eight sides in eight hours. Wingy is the only "New Orleans kid" in this group.

The Young Tuxedo Orchestra (*ca.* 1925). Left to right: Josiah "Cie" Frazier, drums; Paul Ben, trombone; Sam "Bush" Hall, trumpet; Dwight Newman, piano; Lawrence Marrero, banjo; Simon Marrero, bass; Louis Cottrell, Jr., clarinet, sax; Pop Hamilton, bass.

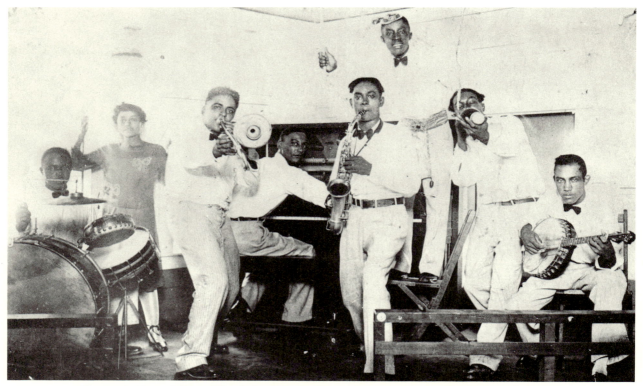

On tour in Texas, left to right: Arthur Joseph; Annie ————, vocal; Freddie "Boo Boo" Miller; Octave Crosby; Henry Julian; Sherman Cook, master of ceremonies; Lee Collins; Percy Darensburg.

Wendell Eugene.

"Pee Wee" Spitlera and Al Hirt.

320

Henry Campo and the Jazz Saints. Left to right: Johnny Sansone, piano; Lucien Jourdan, bass; Campo, trumpet, leader, vocal; Oscar Davis, clarinet, sax; Joseph Morton, drums, vibraphone.

Young Tuxedo Brass Band, 1974. Left to right: Frank Naundorf, trombone; Jerry Green, tuba; Lawrence Trotter, snare drum; Daniel Farrow, tenor sax; Emile Knox, bass drum; Herman Sherman, leader, alto sax; John Simmons, trumpet; Reginald Koeller, trumpet; Gregory Stafford, trumpet; Joseph Torregano, clarinet; Darrell Johnson, grand marshal.

Eddie Miller and Al Rose recording for the state of Louisiana, 1974.

INDEX

Boldface numerals indicate main listing of subject.

Italicized numerals indicate subject is represented in photograph.